MAX REINHARDT
AND HIS THEATRE

MAX REINHARDT TODAY

MAX REINHARDT AND HIS THEATRE

EDITED BY

OLIVER M. SAYLER

Translations from the German

BY MARIELE S. GUDERNATSCH
and Others

*With 57 Illustrations in full Colors
and 164 in black-and-white*

NEW YORK
BRENTANO'S
PUBLISHERS

TO

SALZBURG

GEM OF THE AUSTRIAN ALPS
HOME OF MAX REINHARDT
CRADLE AND CAPSTONE
OF HIS ART

PREFACE

Max Reinhardt has made his entry into the American theatre at the psychological moment. The strange fate which drove him from his native Austria to a career in Berlin more brilliant than any other metropolis could have provided for him and which sent him back home to Salzburg and Vienna three years ago to reap the riper fruits of a career and reputation already won, has brought him to our shores at a time when he can do more for our theatre than on any previous occasion. If he had come ten years ago, when the first proposal to bring him here was thwarted by the war, he would have received credit for many of the superficial ideas and innovations which others in the meantime have snatched, imitated, and usually misapplied. Coming today, he avoids all the false furore over non-essentials and stands for us as the personal embodiment of a living theatre.

On our part, he finds us safely through the adolescent period of obsession with trick scenic effects and ready to have our own native impulses toward a more vivid theatre crystallized by mature precept and example from abroad. As I have said in a previous work: "Something has happened to our American theatre. Not so long ago, it was a luxury, a pastime, an industry. Today, it is the most provocative of the arts. The art of the theatre in the midst of life, drawing new life therefrom. Something has

[vii]

happened. Not only to the theatre itself, but to the whole public attitude toward the theatre. Many things have happened. Working together, they have given the theatre a vitality, an importance, a significance, it has never known before on our continent."

Reinhardt himself, in the second place, is readier than ever before to answer the challenge of this situation, to give it inspiration and guidance. His doubts have been resolved—if pioneer experiments along apparently paradoxical lines can legitimately be called doubts. His inner force, more dynamic, more relentless, more driving than that possessed by anyone else on the contemporary stage, still has the virility of early youth, but it has been brought under a rigid economy and control which permit none of its potential influence upon others to be dissipated. In addition, this inner force has the cognate quality of youth: receptivity and enthusiasm for new ideas, to which is added a mature knowledge of how to apply them.

In reality, the seeming paradoxes are a measure to Reinhardt's inner force and stature. Others have pursued single paths more intensively, but none has charted for himself so many or such diverse paths. A strange duality may be detected in the annals of Reinhardt the producer—duality within duality, thus making for unprecedented multiformity. His all-embracing attention has welcomed simultaneous activity in the large theatre and in the small; with masses and with intimate groups; in the theatre of illusion and in the theatre for the theatre's sake; with the super-civilized dramas of Strindberg and Wedekind, and with naïve Miracle and Morality plays like "Everyman"; on his own stages as well as on those of London, Paris,

PREFACE

Stockholm, Copenhagen, Munich, Dresden, Stuttgart, Vienna, Salzburg, Budapest, Bucharest and New York.

For instance, America and Austria today share his attention at the same time, without either losing by the division. Within this duality, he sets and controls the pace for mass productions in Salzburg, side by side with experiments with the *commedia dell'arte* in Vienna. Duality becomes protean in the dramatic literatures he taps. As Heinz Herald has said: "Everywhere, beyond the borders of every country, Reinhardt the producer follows his poet —into all fairylands, however remote, however incredible they may seem." Poets from classic and contemporary Germany and Austria, from Russia, from England, from Ireland, from Scandinavia, from France, from Belgium, from Italy, from America.

The advent of an artist of this achievement, this stature, naturally arouses public demand in America for a comprehensive record of the man and his work. No such record exists, either in English or in German. In the latter tongue there is a whole shelf of books on Reinhardt, but each one views him through the prism of a single critical personality. Obviously, however, no one man can tell the story of Reinhardt. No matter how broad his sympathies, the subject slips beyond the critic's range at one point or another. To obviate this limitation, therefore, I conceived the project of calling upon experts and specialists in their several professions, to paint a picture of Reinhardt as each of them had seen him through years of intimate collaboration with him, or of observation of him and his work. Such pictures might be limited in their scope, but in their totality they could be made more in-

[ix]

PREFACE

clusive than any single portrait, no matter how able. And finally, in order to mold these portraits into a unity and an entity, I put myself into as close contact with Reinhardt, the man and the artist, as if I were going to paint the portrait myself. The result, I hope, proves to be, from the standpoint of expert opinion, a kind of Domesday Book, focusing the probable verdict of fifty years hence for use today. The result, too, I am confident, is a kind of text-book on the modern theatre, on the living theatre, on its annals and esthetics, by virtue of the catholicity of Reinhardt's achievements. I like to think that the making of such a record is a typically American task. Reinhardt's understanding of the America he has finally discovered is keen enough to reveal to him that one of our greatest gifts is our eclectic talent. And, for this reason, and this alone, he has consented to break a lifelong rule and to cooperate to the extent of contributing his own views on certain subjects which are too intimate for any observer to record. Needless to say, he has refrained from further contact with the work.

I have had able and generous assistance, however, from other hands, notably from Rudolf Kommer, Austrian playwright and critic; from Heinz Herald, author of two excellent books on Reinhardt; and from Auguste Adler, Reinhardt's secretary.

To Morris Gest, whose ambition and vision enabled Reinhardt to come to America at this time, I am indebted for permission to use the *Regie* Book of "The Miracle," and to him and to Norman-Bel Geddes, for permission to use the color plates of costumes and scenes from "The Miracle." I also give credit to Kenneth Mac-

[x]

PREFACE

gowan and Robert Edmond Jones, and their publishers, Harcourt, Brace and Company, for permission to use the color engraving of the Redoutensaal and the chapter "Reinhardt and the Formal Stage," from "Continental Stagecraft," thoroughly revised and rewritten for present purposes; to *Hearst's International* for right to reprint von Hofmannsthal's "Reinhardt as an International Force"; to the *International Studio* for Frank E. Washburn-Freund's "The Evolution of Reinhardt"; to the *Freeman* for von Hofmannsthal's "Reinhardt as an Actor"; and the *Theatre Arts Monthly* for the engraving of "Hamlet" at the Grosses Schauspielhaus, and for brief portions of Chapters IX and XVI.

OLIVER M. SAYLER

New York City,
January, 1924

CONTENTS

[xiii]

CONTENTS

[xiv]

CONTENTS

LIST OF ILLUSTRATIONS

IN COLOR

[xvii]

LIST OF ILLUSTRATIONS

[xviii]

LIST OF ILLUSTRATIONS

IN BLACK-AND-WHITE

[xix]

LIST OF ILLUSTRATIONS

[xx]

LIST OF ILLUSTRATIONS

LIST OF ILLUSTRATIONS

LIST OF ILLUSTRATIONS

[xxiii]

MAX REINHARDT
AND HIS THEATRE

CHAPTER I

THE MAGICIAN OF LEOPOLDSKRON

BY RUDOLF KOMMER

[In this age of specialists, of feats physical and scientific, of records made and broken between dawn and dawn, the terms wizard and magician are bandied about like a juggler's balls. To be called magician and to be one are two very different things. If anyone in the realm of the stage deserves this title, however, it is Max Reinhardt of Baden, Vienna, Salzburg, Berlin and the world at large. Others have seen a vision of a new theatre, others have brought a portion of that vision to pass; but it is safe to say that no one on the contemporary stage has been so fecund as this dynamic, determined little man, who in the course of thirty years upon the stage and, in particular, within the two decades since he became a producer on his own account, has been responsible for upwards of five hundred productions, each of them contributing more or less vivid stimulus to the contemporary world-wide rebirth of the theatre as an art. Where the theatre was a realm of careful routine in central Europe, he made it a source of expectancy and emotional excitement. Where the theatre elsewhere was a complacent pastime in a deep rut, he stirred it to emulation of his achievements. In short, under the wand

[1]

of his will and imagination, he has caused to grow a tree of many branches, just like the magician of some fairy-tale.

To present the phases of this process of phenomenal growth as a matter of impersonal theories and forces, would be to ignore the intensely human element of the driving power behind the process. For that reason, this survey of Max Reinhardt and his theatre is prefaced by a full length portrait of Reinhardt the man, in action in his chosen sphere, by Rudolf Kommer, Austrian playwright and critic, whose service in arranging for Reinhardt's coming to America has brought him into intimate relations, the last few years, with the master of Leopoldskron.—THE EDITOR.]

THE Municipal Theatre of Salzburg, the little capital of the little duchy of Salzburg, was opened in 1894. Its first season was also the first theatrical season of a young boy from Vienna whose talent for the stage had been discovered in an evening school for acting. It must have been remarkable indeed, for while still at school the boy was pointed out to Otto Brahm, the greatest German producer of the time, and the "little giant Brahm" engaged him at once for the two seasons following his first one in Salzburg.

Proceeding from the narrowness of his bourgeois home in Vienna, the young actor, called Max Reinhardt, became enamored with the lovely city on the Salzach. It was a year of young love, of young ambition and of young freedom. The very idea of leaving that quaint paradise for the cold north of Berlin became a threatening nightmare. With the charming unreasonableness of youth, the nineteen-year-old specialist in elderly character rôles sat down and wrote a long letter to Otto Brahm, begging to be released from the Berlin contract.

THE MAGICIAN OF LEOPOLDSKRON

It was undiluted madness. To give up an engagement at the foremost theatre of Central Europe in order to remain in an insignificant provincial town was so absurd that any other theatrical manager would have resented the mere request and would have left the young nobody to oblivion. But Otto Brahm was adamant. He insisted on the execution of the agreement and Max Reinhardt had to honor his signature.

Broken-hearted, he left the home of his heart. His fellow-actors gave him a farewell party at a small country inn under the shadow of the big walls of the Castle Leopoldskron, where a cranky German hermit resided. Young wine and old songs and leave-taking. With wet eyes Max Reinhardt started toward an "uncertain future."

* * *

For many years it has been Max Reinhardt's desire to see the land of the almighty jazz. The syncopated rhythms that displaced the waltzes of his beloved Vienna and subdued the whole world were to him the symbols of a new and strange vitality, which he wished to observe at its place of origin. When at last, flushed with expectation and curiosity, he did come to the country of the victor, the sensing of the rhythm of America became a wonderful event in his life.

There is a story of a war-meeting in the house of Maximilian Harden in the Grunewald, at which the great German publicist was explaining to his guests the ideas contained in his famous article, "If I Were Wilson." In a passionate outburst, Harden expressed his admiration for Woodrow Wilson and his adherence to the open diplomacy of the Fourteen Points. A profound silence followed this impressive oration, and then the awed voice of Max Reinhardt was heard to mutter in a dreamy way: "Syncopated diplomacy."

I don't know whether this story is true and I wonder whether Max Reinhardt has found New York as syncopated and syncopating as he expected. No book, be it English, French or German, has ever succeeded in conveying the atmosphere of America, and every foreign visitor has to be a new Columbus for himself. Whatever disappointments and surprises may have been in store for Max Reinhardt, it seems certain at least that he has found the traffic syncopated enough.

A great number of books and innumerable essays, articles and reviews have been written on the theatrical art of Max Reinhardt. Like all theorizing on matters of art, they have been dominated by the eternal tendency to reduce the complex of an artist's personality to a convenient formula. Accordingly he was labeled a neo-romanticist, an impressionist, a neo-impressionist, a symbolist, an expressionist, an eclectic par excellence, and even an "Austrian hedonist." It has also been said of him that he "barnumized the classics," although it would prove impossible to find the slightest foundation for this catchy phrase. Nothing easier than to replace all this formula by coining a new one in putting him down as an everlastingly adventurous experimentalist—if it were not for the fact that this glorious errant knight of the theatre abhors the experiment for the experiment's sake and indulges in experimenting only when confronted with an artistic problem. Leaving all attempts at labeling behind,

[4]

REINHARDT AT THE TIME OF THE WORLD
PREMIERE OF "THE MIRACLE" IN LONDON, 1911-12

REINHARDT AT THE TIME HE ASSUMED CONTROL
OF THE DEUTSCHES THEATE, 1905

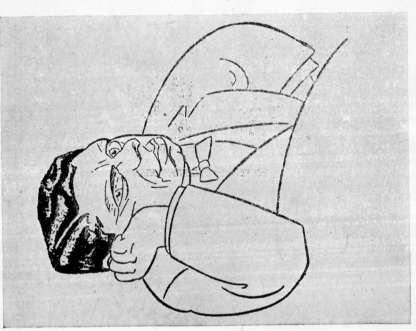

it may prove more advantageous to review the artistic career of Max Reinhardt.

That he was born and brought up in Baden near Vienna is not merely a biographical detail. His Austrian origin accounts for a good deal in his art; and some of his implacable critical adversaries in Berlin have been reminding their readers for years that, after all, he is only an Austrian and that one can not expect depth from an Austrian. The conspicuous absence of any dullness from his productions of the classics made him extremely suspicious in the eyes of those pundits who grow painfully uneasy at any show of brilliancy. His Austrian blood endowed him with an unconquerable passion for light, color, music, with a lightness of touch unknown in Northern Germany, with a peculiar gracefulness and taste. It was only natural, therefore, that some of the cerebral dignitaries of Berlin denounced the young newcomer as a hedonist, if not a sensualist. In spite of all such misgivings his success was instantaneous and phenomenal. After a short time he had made Berlin the theatrical centre of Europe, and when he abandoned his work there three years ago it was only to return to Vienna, his spiritual home, and to settle down in Salzburg, where Mozart was born, and where he himself had started on his career as an actor nearly thirty years ago. There, in the decorous solitude of his castle, Leopoldskron, he is working on the plans for his dramatic "Bayreuth" at Salzburg, and thence he set out for the riotous rialto of New York.

As a producer, or rather *regisseur*, he began his work in Berlin by assuming the leadership of the neo-romantic movement, which was directed against the dominating

[5]

school of naturalism as well as against all official art approved by the court and by that self-appointed arbiter, Wilhelm II. The "naturalism" of those days was a sordid outgrowth of realism and was faithfully accepted as the irrevocable final phase in the evolution of the drama. Mechanical photographers of the seamy side of life were the leading dramatists, and the dreariness and dullness of these perverted materialists were considered as sincerity and truthfulness. Alas, all the shining lights of those days have faded away; the very titles of their innumerable plays are forgotten; the only survivor, Gerhart Hauptmann, has dropped, long ago, all the dogmas of naturalism, and it seems that of his early plays only "The Weavers" will stand the test of time.

All this was accomplished on one evening in 1905 at Max Reinhardt's Neues Theater. Reinhardt fought the royal battle against drab naturalism under the star of Shakespeare. It was not a German play that won the fight for romanticism of a new brand; it was the fanciful comedy, "A Midsummer Night's Dream." Nothing could have suited Reinhardt's imaginative temperament better; no other play could have been more programmatic.

To understand fully the portent of that theatrical event, one must visualize the general currents in the intellectual life of the time. Apart from naturalism, there were Henrik Ibsen and Shakespeare ruling supreme over the German stage. Ibsen may have been overrated then as he is now underrated, but he was certainly misinterpreted. His Norwegian grayness spread like a heavy fog over the European theatre, and his symbolism only intensified the inclination to mistake the delivery of his dia-

[6]

logue for the celebration of a mass. As for Shakespeare, he was a most venerable classic. His plays belonged to the repertory of all German theatres, a hundred times more so than in any other country, but they were really much more an element of general education than of the theatre. Even Goethe, one of the humblest devotees of the Bard of Stratford, remarked a hundred years ago, in his capacity as director of the theatre in Weimar, that the "modern stage" had outgrown the primitive technique of the Elizabethan drama, that Shakespeare's plays could and should be performed only in cautious but thorough-going adaptations, if they were not to disappear entirely from the theatre, and that it would be altogether best to read or recite instead of perform them. Goethe's strange advice was never followed. But the German theatre developed a ponderous style for its Shakespearean productions that was rather dead, though decorous. And "A Midsummer Night's Dream," in particular, deteriorated into a sort of fairy play for the theatregoing youth of the country.

Upon this state of things burst Reinhardt's first Shakespearean production. It was a revelation. Berlin was jubilant. He had not added a word, he had not cut a line. And yet, it seemed a new play entirely. Full of life, color, music and joy, it had a message that did away in one evening with all the voluptuous pessimism and sordidness of the preceding fifteen or twenty years of naturalism. Through the whole season, the Neues Theater was besieged by multitudes clamoring for seats, and there was no French bedroom farce, no Viennese musical comedy, no Hungarian melodrama, that could

[7]

compete with this or the following Shakespearean productions in their popular appeal. "A Midsummer Night's Dream" made Reinhardt famous; it inaugurated a new period in German literature; it opened the way for the neo-romanticists, von Hofmannsthal, Vollmoeller, Eulenberg, Schmidtbonn, Ernst Hardt, Stucken, Beer-Hofmann and so on. Even a realist like Arthur Schnitzler was inspired to write the poetic drama "Der Schleier der Beatrice" ("The Veil of Beatrice"), and the historical romance, "Der junge Medardus" ("The Young Medardus").

Having dislodged naturalism and established his new art and himself so quickly, he fought his second adversary in that three-cornered fight by ignoring him. Although recognized as Germany's foremost producer, he did not pay the slightest attention to the predilections of Kaiser Wilhelm and the court, which had caused what may be described as officious Potsdamnation in art and literature. The rather amusing aspect of Reinhardt's relations or lack of relations with Wilhelm II showed itself best in the famous "Minna von Barnhelm" incident.

Reinhardt's Deutsches Theater was one of the centres of intellectual opposition against what is now called the "Wilhelmian spirit" in art and literature. It was the time when Kaiser Wilhelm tried his hand at regulating the emanations of the German mind. Wilhelm perorated at every opportunity against modernism, and he was equally annoyed by Max Liebermann, the painter; Gerhart Hauptmann, the poet; Richard Strauss, the musician; and Max Reinhardt, the producer. But he did not have his will, and in utter disgust and exasperation, he turned to the

OFFENBACH'S "ORPHEUS IN THE UNDERWORLD"

COPENHAGEN, 1921

The Gate of Heaven, Designed by Max Rée

Italian Leoncavallo (whose moustache had always been an affinity of the imperial decoration), and commissioned him to write the ill-fated opera, "Der Roland von Berlin" ("The Roland of Berlin").

Apart from this intellectual antagonism, Max Reinhardt happened to become the Emperor's particular *bête noire*. It came to the knowledge of Kaiser Wilhelm that, although the Reinhardt theatres were strictly boycotted by the Prussian court, several Hohenzollern princes, and particularly—*horribile dictu*—the Crown Prince, had been secretly attending Reinhardt's dress rehearsals. The apologies made and explanations given by these royal and imperial heretics to their lord and master are unfortunately not known; but for once the Emperor desired to show his open-mindedness, and so he ordered a special performance of a classical comedy, Lessing's "Minna von Barnhelm," from the repertory of the Reinhardt theatres, to be given at the castle in Potsdam. Everything might have gone well, if Wilhelm had not been told that Max Reinhardt was an actor. He was deeply hurt when he discovered that the cast did not contain the name of Max Reinhardt. He considered this a personal affront and left his box. No conciliation was possible thereafter and the state of war continued. The boycott of the Reinhardt theatres was upheld, Wilhelm continued to pay homage to "Charley's Aunt," and the princely heretics continued to break the boycott. Even during that other war, the World War, they were seen furtively appearing in the background of boxes at the Reinhardt theatres during dress rehearsals.

Years after that first encounter, in 1913, came a more

serious clash.   Germany was celebrating the centenary
of the war of liberation (1813); Gerhart Hauptmann had
written a sort of festival masque; and Max Reinhardt produced it at Breslau.   Not being a poet-laureate but a man
and a poet, Hauptmann had also dealt in his play with
the shameful aftermath of the war of liberation, when the
kings and princes of Germany broke the solemn pledges
given to their subjects at the outset of the campaign
against Napoleon, and re-established a most sinister re-
actionary regime instead of the constitutional order they
had promised.   Wilhelm II was furious.   He did not wish
Germany to be reminded of the infamy of his ancestor,
and he did his best to stop the performances.   He did
not succeed in this, and his anger against Hauptmann and
Reinhardt was so much the greater.   It seems that he for-
gave Hauptmann during the World War, for he bestowed
some decoration upon him, but it was a decoration of the
lowest order, and, besides, Hauptmann refused to accept
it.   He did not find, however, any occasion to forgive
Reinhardt.   The war did not cause any change in Reinhardt's attitude toward the plays of Ernst von Wildenbruch, Joseph von Lauff, and their insignificant brethren,
and the sadly heroic times even failed to induce him to
open his theatres to the plays of the war favorite of Wilhelm II, the dramatist-patrioteer, Hans Müller.   The only
heroic plays he did produce all through the war were the
plays of Shakespeare.

    There are three things characteristic of the personality
of a producer: his relation to the author, to the actor, and
to the mechanics of his stage.   Considering Reinhardt's
European reputation, one might mistake him for a super-

[10]

"A MIDSUMMER NIGHT'S DREAM"

At the Neues Theater, January, 1905

The Artisans Rehearse Their Rôles for the Play to be Given before the Court of Theseus

A Scene in the Fairy Wood

The Artisans Give Their Play Before the Court of Theseus

"A MIDSUMMER NIGHT'S DREAM"

At the Neues Theater, June, 1905

man of the theatre. He may or may not be a superman among *regisseurs,* but he certainly does not behave like a superman at his theatre. The play is the thing and the stage belongs primarily to the actor, who is the executive organ of the author. Reinhardt never considers a play or an actor as the raw material for the use of the producer. The author is always supreme in his theatres. The *regisseur* is the butler in the household of the poet, as it were. His duty toward the actors consists in obtaining adequate freedom of action for them. Reinhardt never permits his scenic effects to interfere with the acting. The unsophisticated playgoer may not come to contemplate that there is a producer behind the performance, but even the connoisseur is never led to forget the play for the actor, or the actor for the producer. *Le théâtre c'est moi* is not Reinhardt's dictum. His theatre is a complex of author, actor, designer and musician—all relying on his creative imagination, his judgment in selection, his sense of proportions and his ability in co-ordination. Accordingly, he is not a star surrounded by minor stellar lights, for it is the fate of the *regisseur,* whatever his light may be, to remain invisible.

Nearly all the great actors of Germany belonged to his repertory theatres; most of them had been discovered and trained by him. He supported Alexander Moissi for years against the violent onslaughts of the Berlin critics, who objected to his insufferable Italian accent (Moissi is an Austrian of Italian-Albanian parentage) and to his conspicuous lack of talent, until he became the greatest actor of the German stage. Max Pallenberg was a musical comedy favorite of Vienna; a few years after he joined

[11]

the Reinhardt ensemble, he was enthusiastically recognized as the demoniac tragedian of the German stage, and, at the same time, as its greatest comic actor. Tilla Durieux, Else Heims, Gertrud Eysoldt, Helene Thimig, Leopoldine Konstantin, Rosa Bertens, Albert Bassermann, Paul Wegener, Emil Jannings, Werner Krauss, and many others of international reputation, are what they call in Germany, Reinhardt actors. A number of actors and artists who were associated with him at one time or another are to be found now in these United States of America. Foremost of all is Rudolf Schildkraut, who is still unforgotten in Germany as the greatest Shylock of its contemporary stage. Joseph Schildkraut received his training at the Reinhardt school of acting. Lillebil Ibsen played the nun in "The Miracle" and danced in several pantomimes at the Deutsches Theater. Asta Fleming played the Madonna in "The Miracle." Richard Ordynski started his career with Reinhardt and was one of his stage assistants. Ernst Lubitsch began acting as one of the two thousand supers in the London production of "The Miracle." Max Rée, the gifted Danish artist, designed "A Midsummer Night's Dream," "Orpheus in the Underworld," and other productions.

Equally instructive is Reinhardt's relation to the mechanics of the stage. He has introduced innumerable stage devices and lighting appliances, but they always remained strictly subordinated to the organic necessities of the play, and were never permitted to deteriorate into tricks and stunts. A mechanical monstrosity like the "Kreisler stage," exterminating the play and paralyzing the actor, is the best negative illustration of Reinhardt's sense of

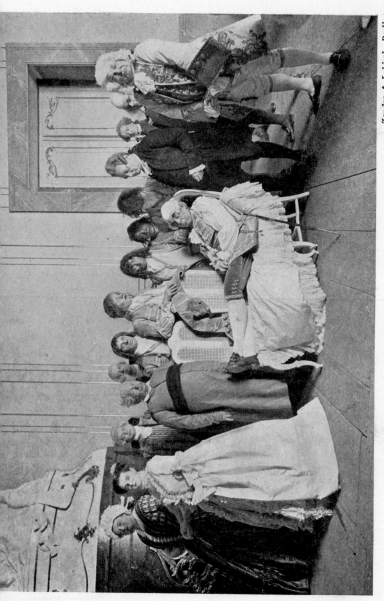

A REHEARSAL GROUP FOR "DER ROSENKAVALIER"

AT ITS WORLD PREMIERE IN DRESDEN, JANUARY, 1911

Zander & Labisch, Berlin

THE WORLD PREMIERE OF "DER ROSENKAVALIER"

Two Settings from Designs by Alfred Roller for Reinhardt's Production of the
Opera by Strauss and von Hofmannsthal in Dresden, January, 1911

proportion, which would never have tolerated such a perversion of the functions of the theatre. In "Sumurûn" he introduced the runway with striking effect. Not being a specialist, nor a maniac, it so happened that he never used the runway again, although he was imitated all the world over until the runway was run to death. In some of the comedies of Molière and Shakespeare he used curved bridges, gangways, passages, stairs, to accentuate movements, utilizing all three dimensions of the space at his disposal. Nobody who has seen his production of "Julius Caesar" at the Grosses Schauspielhaus will ever forget the thirty or forty steps in the centre of the arena leading up to Caesar's throne. When stabbed from behind, the great Julius tumbles down from step to step, being stabbed again and again by the conspirators against whom he is reeling on both sides of the steps. The "vertical dimension" has never been used to greater advantage, and yet Reinhardt, who never theorizes, did not elaborate his steps into a *Weltanschauung*, as one of his followers did, who is using steps on every possible and impossible occasion, reducing them to a mystical abstraction and leading them thus *ad absurdum*. Reinhardt's vision is not obscured by his own mechanical devices, by his runways, steps, bridges, revolving stages, aprons, spotlights and the like. He is the past master of stage mechanics, but he never permits his tools to master him.

The scope of his activities seems unlimited. He was the first German producer who was ever invited to produce plays in foreign countries. He has done so in Paris, at the invitation of Antoine; in London, sponsored by Cochran; in Stockholm, Copenhagen, Zurich, Berne,

Budapest, Vienna, Prague, Bucharest, and so on. Practically all the plays of Shakespeare, Molière, Goethe, Strindberg, Wedekind, Ibsen, Shaw, Tolstoy, Gorky, Verhaeren, Maeterlinck, von Hofmannsthal, Vollmoeller and Eulenberg belong to his repertory. He produced "The Yellow Jacket," by Benrimo and Hazelton; Zoe Akins' "Papa" is to be produced at the Deutsches Theater. Of Russian dramatists living in New York he presented Sholom Ash's "The God of Vengeance," Ossip Dymow's "Nju," and David Pinski's "The Treasure."

The classical musical comedies of Jacques Offenbach are among his most striking successes. He also produced Richard Strauss's greatest opera, "Der Rosenkavalier"; and "Ariadne auf Naxos," at the request of Strauss and von Hofmannsthal, who dedicated their work to him.

Among his "resuscitative productions" are not only Shakespeare and Molière, but also Euripides, Sophocles, Calderon, Goldoni, moralities, pantomimes and masques. He has been criticized for the catholicity of his taste and interests, which was mistaken for indiscrimination. But one has only to consider the classics which he did not try to revive—thus Corneille, Racine, the ancient Hindus, and so on—to discover that, wide as the range of his interests may be, his catholicity is that of a subtly differentiating personality.

He has been called inconsistent because he originated the Little Theatre as well as the Arena Theatre of the Five Thousand, because he produced his plays in the open air as well as in churches, because he staged pantomimic spectacles like "The Miracle" with two thousand performers as well as little fragile psychic plays with a

[14]

BORKMAN'S STUDY

WINTER NIGHT

IBSEN'S "JOHN GABRIEL BORKMAN"

AT THE DEUTSCHES THEATER, MARCH, 1917

Two Settings Designed by Ernst Stern

cast of four or five. If the theatre has anything in common with life, it is its richness in forms. This may justify him or not—yet he has always been consistent in one thing: among the hundreds of plays he has produced there is not a single one of which he need feel ashamed.

* * *

Such is the man who grew out of the boy "specializing in elderly character roles," who dreaded to start from graceful Salzburg into "an uncertain future." Berlin has given him all the opportunities required by his talent, and that uncertain future has become a glorious past.

But he did return to Salzburg. Not as an actor at the Municipal Theatre, not even as its director. He came back as the new master of Schloss Leopoldskron, that "pearl of the Austrian baroque," built by Archbishop Leopold Firmian two hundred years ago. The little country inn, where his farewell party had taken place some thirty years back, is one of the outlying properties of the castle.

How strange the lines of fate are! Would Max Reinhardt have returned to Salzburg if he had not left it?

Chapter II

REINHARDT AS AN INTERNATIONAL FORCE

BY HUGO VON HOFMANNSTHAL

(English Translation by Sidney Howard)

[Safe in his hillside garden off a side street in the little village of Rodaun, a suburb of Vienna, three trolley rides distant from the Austrian capital, Hugo von Hofmannsthal would seem to be the last person to write of Reinhardt as an international force, but although "Der Rosenkavalier," "Elektra," "Ariadne auf Naxos," and a dozen other operas and plays were written in this garden on a rough table with stray stones for paper weights, the soul of their author roamed the far places of the earth. And in personal collaboration with the producer, he has shared with Reinhardt intimate experiences in nearly every continental capital. Consultation with him in regard to a translator for his latest work, "The Great World-Theatre," brought out an amazingly acute critical valuation of the entire field of contemporary American letters.

Von Hofmannsthal's kinship with Reinhardt is spiritual as well as material, and no one understands better than he the dynamic possibilities of Reinhardt's imagination, a fact which I recognize by frequent resort to his testimony throughout this book. If anyone can do justice, therefore, to the subject of Reinhardt as a power transcending national borders, it is this genial poet and critic with a world vision and a world reputation of his own.—THE EDITOR.]

REINHARDT'S genius goes to the very heart of the theatre. Meeting the elements which press about a worker in

[16]

IBSEN'S "GHOSTS"

At the Kammerspiele, November, 1906

Two Sketches for Settings Made by the Norwegian Artist, Edvard Munch

ARISTOPHANES' "LYSISTRATA"

At the Grosses Schauspielhaus

the theatre—poetry, mimicry, rhythm, stage mechanics
and administration—Reinhardt emerges such a universally theatric master as has not appeared in a century.

I believe that the breadth of his international reputation and influence is rooted in the fact that he springs
from the Austro-German theatre. For that theatre has
its being in internationalism, in a catholic sensitiveness
which is a direct heritage of the general European spirit
of three centuries, the sixteenth, seventeenth and eighteenth. The repertory of the German legitimate theatre
—as well as of the theatre of opera and spectacle—includes the whole of the world's dramatic literature. The
opera of Gluck and Mozart is established as a living and
permanent treasure beside the opera of Wagner, Verdi or
Berlioz. Just so, on the dramatic stage, Sophocles, Calderon or Molière—not to mention Shakespeare—stand
together, in the regular repertory, with Goethe and Schiller, with Bernard Shaw, Hauptmann, Ibsen and Tolstoy.

I say, not to mention Shakespeare. The statistics of
the yearbook of the German Shakespeare Society often
show as many as three thousand performances of Shakespeare yearly. And this showing does not mean that some
theatre in Berlin or Vienna produces some one of Shakespeare's plays for a long run. The performances are distributed over the entire German-speaking area. The theatre of Basle or Innsbruck is no less ambitious than that of
Cassel or Königsberg or Wiesbaden.

And anyone traveling a year on business or pleasure
through the German land will find, if he troubles to examine the theatrical billboards, that, with the possible exception of "Cymbeline" or "Two Gentlemen of Verona"

and some of the historical plays—perhaps "Henry VI," he may see performed all of Shakespeare's plays, not alone those that he commonly regards as the important ones, but even such plays as "Troilus and Cressida," "King John" or "Henry VIII."

This repertory which embraces the dramatic output of all times and of every country, is the strength and pride of the German theatre; it has now been maintained for more than a century. It is the legacy of our great poets of the end of the eighteenth century, particularly of Goethe, and not even the violent nationalism of the present day has succeeded in destroying this universal spirit of the German stage. Every stratum of society concurs in supporting the international and timeless character of the "great repertory"—the small German sovereigns, who maintained their court theatres often at great sacrifice; the universities and societies of learning; the middle classes, which, taken by and large, attain a high level of culture and have constituted the theatrical public for one hundred and fifty years; journalists of widely opposed political and social views. It would require a serious upheaval of the entire thinking public—to which not only the middle classes but the organized laboring classes belong in Germany today—to bring about any change of heart.

The pride of the German stage is grounded in these spiritual tendencies which, in the course of six generations, have become part of the nation's flesh and blood. Grounded, too, therein, is the claim (to which not all will agree) of the German stage to be considered, in certain respects, the first in Europe.

[18]

A SCENE IN THE GARDEN

THE BANQUET HALL

"MUCH ADO ABOUT NOTHING"

DEUTSCHES THEATER, JANUARY, 1912

Two Settings Designed by Ernst Stern

REINHARDT AS AN INTERNATIONAL FORCE

Germany's dramatic talent can not be valued so high. In the field of acting the Russians are without doubt stronger than the Germans, and next to the Russians I should place the Italians. I know very well how the genius of acting has been embodied, generation after generation, in a Rossi or a Salvini, a Ristori or a Duse. The French theatre, or, more properly speaking, the Parisian theatre, is unsurpassed in the society play, in the revue and in the farce. In its theatre Paris sees itself reflected as in a mirror of a thousand prisms. But its repertory is limited and bears upon the spirit of this single city and of a single time—the immediate present. This is its strength and its weakness.

The English theatre has a glorious past. How wonderful to think that England produced the greatest dramatic poet of all time, Shakespeare, and, almost two hundred years later, the man who appears to have been the greatest actor of all time, David Garrick. Today it is a patient at whose sickbed such wise and experienced physicians as Bernard Shaw, Granville Barker and Galsworthy labor in vain. Everything fine that is attempted on the English stage—and much that is lofty and beautiful *is* attempted—is as if it were written in water. We see the skilful directing of Granville Barker, or a brilliant phenomenon like Gordon Craig, genius both as painter and director, but the broad current flows on and the writing disappears. Everything fine that is attempted is the affair of only a small minority. A few authors, a few artists, a few rich men, a Madame Maecenas like Lady Cunard, join forces and organize a production of high quality and much individuality. The event creates a certain sensation. The

[19]

sensation is not felt beyond the circle of the minority. The great public, the nation, remains dependent for its theatrical needs upon producers who have the purely commercial point of view and who permit the public to sink deeper and deeper into the bog of its own bad taste.

In twenty years since he has been director of one or more theatres, Reinhardt has never for a moment ceased to impress his taste on the public, and it is to this circumstance that he owes the enormous prestige that he enjoys not only among the artists and esthetes of Europe but among the masses. In those twenty years he has produced plays by writers of every country, but I venture to assert that in the selection of none of these did anything influence him but his own taste and his own desire to produce that particular play at that particular time.

It is this quality in him that has guarded him so astonishingly from repetition and routine. He attacks each fresh piece of work as a child attacks a new toy, with the absolute unconcern of a visionary who, before he enchants his audience, wishes first of all to enchant himself. And the double meaning of the word "to play"—as it relates to the art of the theatre—retains its inmost significance for him as for no one else I have ever known.

But his fancy is exacting, far more exacting than that of other people. In order to realize it, he demands, as the foundation for his play, the creation of a great dramatist, or, at the least, of a notable writer who presents in an unusual manner some phase of modern life. And in order to give this creation its fullest dramatic expression (and nothing less than the fullest expression will satisfy

[20]

Goldoni's "The Servant of Two Masters"
At the Kammerspiele, October, 1907

"Revolution in Krähwinkel" by Johann Nestroy
At the Deutsches Theater, November, 1908

TWO SCENIC AND COSTUME SKETCHES BY ERNST STERN
FOR OLD COMEDIES

"ANDROCLES AND THE LION"

A Scene from the Production of Bernard Shaw's Comedy at the Kammerspiele, November, 1913, with Victor Arnold as Androcles and Ernst Matray as the Lion

"THE YELLOW JACKET"

A Scene from the Production of the Chinese Play by Benrimo and Hazelton at the Kammerspiele, March, 1914

him) he employs a host of individuals quite as a great painter uses on his palette a varied wealth of colors.

He uses painter, musician, skilled mechanic, lighting expert, and ballet master—uses and squanders them in a manner totally different from that of any other theatrical director, glorifies them far beyond the limits of their own abilities—uses and squanders, in short, every person, every device, every talent, every idea, every nerve, every intelligence that appears above his horizon (and his horizon is broad) that seems capable of serving the theatre or that can be pressed into the theatre's service.

He squanders all this material as unconcernedly as he squanders his own existence, so that his theatre may live, a theatre to meet the requirements of his vision—requirements that change every moment and always demand the utmost of brilliance, of harmony and intensity. For he is not the entrepreneur, not the founder, not the dramaturgist, not even the pioneer or forerunner; not avid of money or power, not concerned with ideas or system; he is the visionary—the visionary who seeks to realize his vision; and in its pursuit he displays extraordinary powers of organization.

No one ever has felt less constrained than he by national and spiritual boundaries. In this he follows altogether the great tradition of the Austro-German theatre. He is so full of vitality himself that he sees everything, however remote in time or space, only as a slice of life. He sees everything with his own immediate sight and not at all from the historical point of view. And he sees everything through the eyes of the theatre. The foreign artist, the foreign civilization, the foreign era—such restrictions

[21]

do not exist for him. Lady Diana Manners, Maria Carmi of Florence, or Rosamond Pinchot of New York—he sees only a beautiful woman, a body with the possibilities of gracious movement, a lovely face that may command a certain range of expression. These are the things he uses. He has learned much from Gordon Craig, that lonely pioneer, whose dream was to control the scene by means of changing light, and to create "an ever shifting maze of color, form and motion." He learned much from him, but only in order to create out of what he learned something newer, more powerful, better suited to the practical theatre. Always when he took he gave more. He took certain things from the Japanese theatre and from the theatre of antiquity; he owes much to the ceremonies and pageantry of the Catholic church. Venice, that dream city, its architecture and history more theatrical than anything else in the world, has always fired his imagination. No national procession that he watches in a mountain village, no picture that he sees in a museum fails to enrich him, but what he makes of it all is something peculiar to himself, and something apparently inexhaustible.

I remember his advent clearly, and the years which developed him from an "interesting young director" to the leading figure in the German theatre. At the beginning of his career he was twenty-six years old. Three milestones marked, first his capture of a secure position in his own theatre, then the first place in Berlin and finally in Germany.

The first milestone was the production of Gorky's "The Lower Depths" ("Nachtasyl"), a realistic drama. Reinhardt's production gained its unusual quality chiefly

[22]

from the casting. The parts (they are many and no one of them stands out, in the usual sense) were filled in every case by distinguished actors, two-thirds of whom had been recently discovered by him. The interplay was remarkable, and particularly one felt—for the first time what one was to feel so often afterward—a harmonious rhythm behind the whole which gave to the separate scenes their extraordinary tempo, from fast to slow, from pianissimo to fortissimo. On the whole, it was a production that resembled in quality the productions that Stanislavsky was making then and later on.

The next milestone was "A Midsummer Night's Dream." There a complete new world was revealed. Whereas in "The Lower Depths" each perfect dramatic nuance was related to every other, here the acting seemed almost a secondary consideration, so artfully was everything related to the music. The third milestone was Sophocles' "Œdipus Rex," and here again was a new world, a new manner of direction which made so prodigious an impression that this play, first presented in an enormous hall in Munich, later toured for two years through the cities of Germany, Scandinavia, Holland, Poland and Russia.

It is impossible to make any hard and fast statement about a Reinhardt genre based on these three productions of wholly dissimilar plays, of different epochs and civilizations. It consists perhaps in his remarkable ability to give to each of these presentations its peculiar rhythm and by means of this rhythm to mold each one into a living breathing organism—a thing made possible, of course, by the author, but which only a director of genius could transfer to the stage with such unimpaired vigor.

For him the process of a theatrical performance goes on not on the stage but in the imagination of the audience. He looks upon the place in which he is playing as the important factor in capturing that imagination. Hence his constant moving about from place to place, of which so much has been written in ten thousand newspapers and which has been explained by so many uncomprehending people as a hankering after sensation. Only a restless search for conditions in which a certain vision may be realized, and not concern for a superficial impression, influences his actions.

He considers place in the highest degree important. For months and sometimes for years he has dreamed of how a room will shut an audience in, whether with solemnity of height as in a church, or with solemnity of breadth as in the ancient theatre, or mysteriously, as in some grotto, or agreeably and socially, as in a pleasant, peopled salon. And his dreams are all realized in the end.

In Berlin he had first a theatre of ordinary size and played comedies and tragedies there, modern plays and costume plays. Two years later he had instead of one theatre three; quite a large one besides the one in which he had begun and a third small one with neither loges nor gallery, simple and elegant as a Pullman car, with leather armchairs for three hundred spectators and the walls entirely unadorned except for their handsome woodwork.

What he dreamed of was a house resembling as closely as possible the body of a violin and, like the violin, at-

"ŒDIPUS REX" BY SOPHOCLES

Costume Sketch by Ernst Stern. Used as a poster

tuned to receive and respond to the slightest vibration. That was the famous Kammerspiele, in which he later produced all plays which depended for effect on intimacy, and spiritual delicacy, on wit or smartness of dialogue: Bernard Shaw and Wilde, Maeterlinck too, and Knut Hamsun, much of Goethe, and particularly the supernatural plays of Strindberg's last phase.

When Reinhardt produced "The Miracle" for the first time in Olympia Hall in London—in a building that had been constructed for the accommodation of automobile shows and athletic meets—he was bold enough not to treat the twenty or thirty thousand spectators as a mass in front of which to build the structure of his medieval church. He took his audience, as part of the production, into the church—a church whose walls had been built inside the hall, partly of actual building materials, partly of monstrous masses of shadow. The whole room which so held the tens of thousands of spectators and the thousands of performers was lighted dimly by a Gothic window at an immense height, a window, if I am not mistaken, of thrice the diameter of the famous rose window of Notre Dame in Paris.

Three years ago, when he produced my new version of the ancient "Everyman" theme on the square in front of the Salzburg cathedral, the cries uttered by invisible spirits to warn Everyman of his approaching death sounded not only from the church before whose façade the stage had been built, but from all the church-towers of the city, as twilight deepened about the five thousand spectators. One of these criers had been placed in the highest tower of a medieval castle, built far above the city, and his voice sounded, weird and ghostly, about five seconds after the others, just as the first rays of the rising moon fell cold and strange from the high heavens on the hearts of the audience.

But he is certainly not limited to working in gigantic dimensions nor with enormous crowds. What fascinates him is the solution of any given problem. He is always setting himself new problems that always require new methods for their execution. He never permits his successful methods to master him. When the materials of a creator become stronger than the creator himself, routine, which is the ghost of achievement, is sure to follow. He avoids any system. He has never decided in favor of any scenic formula.

I remember, for example, the scenery for Ibsen's "Ghosts," which he designed with the help of the famous Norwegian painter, Edvard Munch, who came to Berlin and stayed weeks expressly for that purpose. The room was of medium size, a sort of salon in the style of 1850; but the combinations of colors and the shape of the furniture breathed a spirit of oppressiveness, of grief and of the sense of destiny which broods over this tragedy, as a tragic overture breathes the motif of an opera. At times he has used a tall flight of steps leading to a palace or a temple as the principal part of his set, as in "Œdipus Rex," but he has never made its use monotonous, as other directors have.

He played "A Midsummer Night's Dream" in a set in which the trees of the wood were plastic and so more nearly approximated reality. The forest floor was made of a firm carpet of tall grass, in which the pairs of lovers, or

[26]

Titania and her enchanted ass, lay as naturally as young people do in a field that they have found on a day in the country. But less than a year ago he told me that he was thinking of presenting "A Midsummer Night's Dream" soon again in Vienna, without scenery, on a bare stage in front of a green curtain representing a forest. This may be taken to prove that he has the rare creative faculty of freeing himself from his own ideas, even the most successful of them.

Indeed I see no limit to his ability to draw fresh theatrical possibilities from every new situation. If by chance he had been imprisoned during the war and, like so many artists, had been compelled to spend years in a prison camp in Siberia, for example, I have no doubt that he would not only have organized excellent theatrical productions there, but, what is more, would have found in the very conditions and limitations of the place, in such a strange and unhappy situation, unexpected spurs to his imagination. It is not unlikely that on the edge of Manchuria or on the banks of the Amur, looking out over a military barracks and with his actors drawn from the captured Europeans, Siberians and Chinese, he would have presented an unforgettable performance of "King Lear."

Chapter III

THE SPIRITUAL SOURCES OF REINHARDT

BY HERMANN BAHR

(English Translation by Mrs. Frank E. Washburn-Freund)

[Back of every personal force, whether national or international, lies a fund of spiritual vitality on which drafts may be made in emergencies and which serves constantly as subconscious guide and preceptor. It may be literary or artistic ancestry, the formative influence of another great personality in youth, or the potent atmosphere of an old, established but still vigorous community.

It is the latter stimulus which has served in the case of Reinhardt—the urbane, dignified, exacting and ever-alert civilization which belongs peculiarly to the Vienna in which Reinhardt spent his early years. But if Vienna was the spiritual parent of Reinhardt, giving him poise, tradition, taste, an appreciation of the joy of life, Berlin was his foster-parent, a spiritual force no less potent but coarser-grained and more vigorous, instilling in him the ambition and the technique of putting to practical and concrete use the finer impulses of his earlier inheritance. No one is better fitted than the genial, conversational, shaggy-headed Hermann Bahr to analyse and trace to their fountain-heads these two impacts on Reinhardt. Viennese himself by habitat, but also citizen of a world which includes not only the German capital but our own metropolis through production of such plays as "The Concert," and gifted with the knack of summoning a startlingly truthful picture,

THE OLD BURG THEATER, VIENNA

In the Gallery of This Venerable Old Playhouse, Nestled in a Niche of the Rambling Hofburg until Its Demolition in December, 1888, to Make Room for an Imposing Gateway, the Youthful Reinhardt Obtained His First Inspiration for His Dramatic Career

THE JOSEFSTÄDTER THEATER, VIENNA

An Interior View of Reinhardt's Latest Theatrical Home, from an Old Print. With a Coöperative
Company of His Best Actors, He Plans a Revival Here of the
Formal Theatre of the Commedia dell'Arte

THE SPIRITUAL SOURCES OF REINHARDT

whether by fact or by fanciful anecdote, he is well equipped to depict the background which formed and molded the youthful Reinhardt and started him on his career.—THE EDITOR.]

I HAVE known Max Reinhardt ever since he began his career in Berlin. For twenty years I have watched him with the curiosity of the psychologist who closely observes every single trait in a man, in order to try to draw his innermost secrets from him. I have been with him in various and changing relationships, so that I have always been able to see him from different sides and in different lights. I was already well-known and he just beginning to be known when we first met. I was a dramatic critic at that time, and his attitude toward me was that of reverential distrust which the actor always assumes before the critic. Afterwards, he produced some of my plays and I watched him staging them. Later on, he engaged me for a time to stage a few productions. And once we even worked together in Venice. We lay for hours on the hot sand of the Lido, and while the waves surged on the shore beside us, he staged for me the whole play of "Julius Caesar" with little balls of sand.

From all these experiences, I know that he is a man of tremendous unity of purpose. At the first glance he seems to be a born impressionist, receptive of every sensation, absorbing everything greedily, inhaling every stimulating breath, but also assimilating it with every fibre of his being, till the fleeting impression is transformed into his own expression. He listens to everyone. No one could be a better listener. But he himself is a silent man. He hardly ever contradicts because he has

[29]

no need to be on the defensive, so firm and strong are his
inward convictions as to the message he has to deliver.
He can go into any venture calmly because he knows
that he will always find his way back to himself with
new courage. He winds his way upwards in a great
spiral, as it were, as sure and confident of himself as a
somnambulist. The first theatre he had when he began
his career, sometimes resembled a cabaret. Later it was
a circus. Then he played in the open in a great public
square before masses of people. And finally it was in a
Roman Catholic church, one of the most beautiful
baroque churches in the world. But in cabaret or circus,
in public square or church, he is always the same: the
kindly nature with the magic gift of being able to see
the hidden meaning behind appearances. As Theseus
says in "A Midsummer Night's Dream," he has

> "Such shaping phantasies, that apprehend
> "More than cool reason ever comprehends."

Vienna, the spiritual cradle of this impressionist, is a
true theatre city. The delight in dancing and mirth is
bred and born in the Austrian. For generations the Austrian peasant has been accustomed to some form of acting.
Even their native dance, the "schuhplattler," and their
doggerel verse, the "schnadahüpfl," already contain a
kernel of the drama. The church soon took advantage
of this inborn love for the theatre and the result was the
Church Plays, mimic representations of religious stories:
as, for example, "The Birth of Christ," "The Three
Kings," "Lazarus and the Rich Man," and so on. Even
today, in the secluded little valleys of the Austrian moun-

tains, these same religious plays can be seen, performed with all the simple touching reverence of the old days, mixed with the same rough horse-play and coarse wit. The Benedictine monks made use of this old custom in the schools; and, on feast days and holidays, tragedies by Seneca were performed in Latin by the pupils before the assembled teachers and the proud and happy parents. Strange, how history repeats itself!

The Jesuits pushed this tradition still farther and developed it into something really imposing. The result was the baroque theatre, which had in no sense a private character. It was actually a state affair, a public dramatic festival in honor of the Emperor, given by the highest clergy and nobility. On this occasion, everyone—author, architect, painter, actor, lighting mechanic, master of fireworks, dancer, singer, clown—competed in friendly rivalry to show their arts to the best advantage. The performances took place out-of-doors on a stage erected in the largest square of the city. And the whole population, young and old, rich and poor, men and women, were invited to be present.

. In the seventeenth century, these performances became more and more important, to the grief and vexation of the Minister of Finance, because they cost enormous sums of money. For instance, a single performance for the Emperor Carl VI ran to the stately figure of 60,000 gulden. Three Hapsburg emperors—Ferdinand III, Joseph I, and Carl VI, all three passionate musicians also —were so fervently devoted to the theatre that they sometimes seemed to forget the less diverting duties of governing. These were the great times of the theatre, the times when it was not merely an amusement house but held almost the same proud position as the theatre in Athens at the time of Pericles. In other words, it was a state affair. In any case, it was something that the whole people—the finest courtier as well as the merest vagabond—considered of greater interest than anything else. And these great times, although long since departed, are still alive today, deep down in the secret heart of every Viennese man and woman.

Theatre-going is, for the Viennese, not merely an amusement, a way of passing the time. It is the centre around which their intellectual life revolves. And even to the most frivolous Viennese, who is never serious about anything, the theatre is holy ground. Thus it happens that even now, in Vienna, every question concerning the theatre receives the greatest attention and is discussed with passion, devotion, or bitterness, according to the merits of the case and the temperament of the debaters. To the outsider, this is as hard to understand as is the importance of the Burg Theater to the Viennese, for only the Viennese themselves or someone who has lived for long years in Vienna—better still in old Vienna—can truly appreciate its significance.

What Olympia was to Greece, what the Circus was to Imperial Rome, what the court life was to the France of Louis XIV, that was what the Burg Theater meant to Vienna until about thirty years ago. To obtain a seat at a performance, the young people would betake themselves to the theatre at four o'clock every afternoon, where they would wait, packed like sardines, until the doors to their paradise were at last opened. The stairs were disposed

TWO SCENES FROM "ŒDIPUS REX"
At the Zirkus Schumann, November, 1910
From Original Lithographs by Emil Orlik

"THE ORESTEIA" BY ÆSCHYLUS

In the Zirkus Schumann, Berlin, October, 1911

of breathlessly, three steps at a time, in order to get a "good" place in the gallery, i. e., a little corner where, in a precarious position, hanging forward rather than standing, they could snatch a slanting view of the performance. They knew the plays almost by heart, and when one of the lesser parts was given to a newcomer, excitement was at fever heat for days before. For every spectator had the exact intonation in his ear with which each single word had always been spoken, and woe to the new impersonator if the smallest point missed its expected effect! Bloody and bitter battles were often fought in the Olympus of the Burg Theater. Friends or enemies sealed life-long compacts. And if a marriage had "been arranged" up there, it was safe to assume that Fate would pour blessings on the happy couple with a lavish hand.

Things remained like this until well into the nineties of the last century. In the meantime, Vienna had grown, had begun to have new interests, had even gradually taken to politics. A new generation had arrived who were unable to understand how anyone could, as it were, live and die only in the Burg Theater. But just at this time of threatening murmurs against the reign of the Burg Theater, changing Vienna, startled, gathered together for the last time all the tenderness it had inherited for the Burg Theater from its fathers, realizing that it was now slowly saying farewell to the old place forever. And just that feeling added a gentle sorrow to the traditional admiration, for all knew that they were watching the twilight of the Burg Theater, and this knowledge lent a brilliancy to these performances which could never be forgotten. Among the "gods" in the gallery of the Burg Theater at

[33]

that time, was a poor Austrian who had just come to Vienna in search of luck. His name was Max Reinhardt.

Soon after, Reinhardt made his first appearance on the stage. At that time, Vienna was, in fact, still so much of a theatre city that, among others, it had a theatre that did not live on the kind patrons who went to the theatre to *see*, but on the actors who wished to be *seen*. This theatre was in one of the suburbs, and its manager not only gave his actors no salaries but let them pay *him* for graciously permitting them to play. Each rôle had its own price. And in this theatre Max Reinhardt played his first part. Schiller's "Die Räuber" ("The Robbers") was the play. He would probably have given his life to have been able to appear as Carl or at least Franz Moor, but his life would not have satisfied the manager who demanded cash down, and all the ready cash the young Austrian could command was just enough to buy him the rôle of Spiegelberg. From that evening, he gave himself up to the theatre body and soul.

At first he had no luck. Then he got an engagement in Salzburg for small rôles. Salzburg at that time was a quiet little provincial town that went to sleep for the winter and only wakened up for summer and tourists. With the latter, by chance, came Otto Brahm, on his journey to Gastein. Brahm at that time was at the height of his fame. Fifteen years before, he had started in Berlin as a journalist and had fought bravely for Ibsen. In 1889, following the example of Antoine in Paris, he had founded the *Freie Bühne* and was the first to fight for Gerhart Hauptmann. Then in 1895, he had taken over the management of the Deutsches Theater in Berlin.

THE SPIRITUAL SOURCES OF REINHARDT

So here was Brahm in Salzburg, and since it was raining, as it generally does in Salzburg, he let himself be persuaded by some friends, out of pure boredom, to go to the theatre to see a much-lauded "star" hero about whom the whole town was raving. He would most likely engage the star on the spot, his Salzburg friends assured him, for such great talent had not been seen on the German stage for decades. He went. But after the first scene he had already had enough of the star, for he found him impossible and was on the point of getting up to leave the theatre when something in the bearing of one of the young actors, cast for a very small rôle, caught his attention. The young man was awkward and embarrassed and seemed not yet to be able either to walk or stand on the stage. Yet there was something characteristic and individual about him that pleased Brahm. He sent for the young actor the next day, and engaged him on the spot for the Deutsches Theater in Berlin, never suspecting that the young man would soon be his most dangerous rival and, in fact, would be his successor in the management of the Deutsches Theater. For this awkward young actor of small unimportant parts was none other than Max Reinhardt, now director of the Salzburg Festival Theatre and master of the Castle of Leopoldskron. In such queer ways does Fate wind her threads.

With Reinhardt's arrival in Berlin, we might almost say that his life only really began. Looking backward from today, there was something providential in the move. For Reinhardt brought with him to Berlin, at that time a new theatre city, something that it lacked, something that it needed; while in Berlin Reinhardt found what he lacked

and what he needed.   If in those years, he had not gone
with Brahm to Berlin but had obtained an engagement in
Vienna instead, his talent would certainly have been recognized there, too, and quickly enough, for the Viennese can
pick out talent at first sight.   The trouble is, it takes them
years to acknowledge it.   They have too much of the spoilt,
blasé *"grand seigneur"* in them to let a man notice that
they need him.   In Vienna it is not so much talent as
such that counts, but the particular talent of being able
to wait.   And much as Reinhardt can do, it is just exactly
"wait" that he can not do.   In his youth especially, he
was possessed by a consuming impatience which did not
make for rest, either for himself or for those about him.
And just this quality seemed to have made Fate predestine
him for Berlin.   For the Berlin to which he came was no
longer the Berlin that Bismarck knew, that felt itself content and secure in its old Prussian traditions and its past.
Still less was it the romantic Berlin of E. T. A. Hoffmann.
No.   It was an entirely new Berlin, a city that had shot up
over night and was being impelled forward, ever forward,
with a consuming impatience something like Reinhardt's
own.

In those days when, of an evening, a few Berliners
foregathered to have a good time together, they were
hardly seated before they were asking: "Well, what shall
we do now?"   It actually seemed as if the entertainment
of the evening consisted in dropping into a different café
every half hour on an average, to discuss the vital question: "Where shall we go now?"   Evidently a real thrill
was induced by every change of café.   And it was the same
way in intellectual matters. Danger as well as strength lay

· P U K ·

"A MIDSUMMER NIGHT'S DREAM"

AT THE GROSSES SCHAUSPIELHAUS, APRIL, 1921

A Costume Plate for Puck by Max Rée

in the haste with which Wilhelmian Berlin unceasingly
"changed the café," whether the "café" were philosophy,
art, or even religion. If you had seated a Berliner of those
days at the altar of any new art, after five minutes he
would say: "Well, what shall we do? Where shall we go
now? "And during the twenty years of his sojourn in
Berlin, Reinhardt was always ready with a prompt answer
to this perpetual question.

To begin with, Reinhardt made Berlin into a theatre
city again. Not that it had never been so before: it had
been, in the time of Iffland. Those were the days when
the Hamburg Theatre, the Berlin Schauspielhaus, and
the Vienna Burg Theater, vied with each other in importance, in giving the stamp of style, and in influence that
reached beyond the merely artistic to the moral fibre of
the nation. Then came fifty years during which all the
talent and all the interest of Berlin became more and
more absorbed by politics, and only after the German Empire was completed in the form Bismarck had shaped for it,
did the Germans gradually remember the duties they owed
to art. It was to a moment of such artistic introspection
that the Deutsches Theater in Berlin owed its existence.
/ The Deutsches Theater was founded in 1883, for
national reasons, with perhaps a somewhat jealous glance
at the Comédie Française and the Burg Theater. Berlin
wished to show that what Paris and Vienna could do, she
could do also. And by founding the Deutsches Theater,
she wished to give herself the stamp of legitimacy, so to
speak, as the cultural capital of Germany. / She forgot,
however, that theatres can not be raised at the word of
command; that they must grow gradually; that they need

[37]

a fine tradition. In Vienna, thanks to the old church plays and the baroque period, influenced by the Benedictines, the Jesuits, and the Hapsburg emperors, a great tradition already existed in the air, as it were, for every child to absorb. It could be detected in their marionette theatres and Punch and Judy shows. Even in bad times, when the work of the theatres in Vienna was on the downward path, the tradition remained as strong as ever, because it was still alive in the heart of the public, although the stage seemed, for a time, to have lost it. In Berlin, not only did the theatre lack such a deeply-rooted tradition, but, above all, it was lacking in a public. In fact, it can be said quite truly that "Berlin lacked a public." A heterogeneous mass of people gathered together in a theatre by chance is not a public. For the actors of the Deutsches Theater of those days, the task was made doubly hard, for they had to create for themselves a new public every night. A real public can come into being only when the mass of strangers begins to feel that it is not a company but one entity in which one heart beats; when each person ceases to be himself, gives up his own feelings, and becomes one with all the others.

On the whole, it might be true to say that Reinhardt's greatest achievement did not consist so much in what he accomplished on the stage as in his success in creating a Berlin public. Through that, the theatre in the highest sense of the word was made possible again in Berlin. His most beautiful stage settings would not have made half the impression they did if he had not, first of all, "staged" a real audience. All truly creative men of the theatre have always held that the theatre does not consist exclu-

[38]

OBERON

"A MIDSUMMER NIGHT'S DREAM"

AT THE GROSSES SCHAUSPIELHAUS, APRIL, 1921

A Costume Plate for Oberon by Max Rée

sively of authors and actors, but that it can do its work only if and when the audience plays, too. Schröder in Hamburg, Goethe in Weimar, Iffland in Berlin, Schreyvogel, Laube, Dingelstedt, and finally Burckhard and Mahler in Vienna, were not only trainers of their actors; they were also the greatest trainers of their audiences. They created the audience they needed, made of it an instrument so sensitive that they knew they could use it, as well as their actors, to give full expression to their art. Therein lies the secret of Reinhardt's phenomenal influence in Berlin, his almost magic power over a city otherwise mockingly superior and with little talent for enthusiasm.

As a matter of fact, Reinhardt was really predestined by Fate for the Burg Theater. But it was so arranged in the Austria of Franz Joseph, that a man could become anything except what Fate had ordained him to be. The great ambition of Austria was not to let itself be talked into anything by Fate. In that country a state official was more than Fate. In fact, state officials made Austria, and Fate had to be content to take a back seat. So there was nothing for Reinhardt to do but to make his foreordained Burg Theater in Berlin, instead of in his own country.

Reinhardt brought with him to Berlin what Berlin needed: an old and firmly-rooted tradition, while Berlin gave him in exchange the confidence, the quick pulse, the eager daring, the impatience and love of adventure of a young, selfish city, willing to take any risks. Only in Berlin could it have been possible to do the work of half a century in about fifteen years.

Reinhardt began in the Kleines Theater on Unter den

Linden. There never was a smaller theatre: it could hardly even be called a hall. Nevertheless, the whole of Berlin was forthwith declaring that the only right place for plays was a room. A decade later, the same Berlin was declaring that real plays were possible only in a circus. Thus perfectly did Reinhardt and Berlin understand each other. It seemed almost as if the one had been waiting for the other. And just because they were, and, as a matter of fact, still are, strangers to each other at heart, they supplement each other so happily. /On his arrival in Berlin, Reinhardt found a style of acting which had developed since the eighties of the last century, as the result of the war waged by naturalistic Young Germany, under the influence of Antoine and his *Théâtre Libre* in Paris, against the empty, declamatory Court-Theatre manner. This development was hastened through playing Ibsen, Arno Holz and Gerhart Hauptmann's first pieces. The main characteristics of the new style were great objectivity, complete subordination of the actor to the author, and a drab, colorless honesty that went so far as to avoid all dramatic effects. Nevertheless, as a cure for the bad tricks of "virtuosity" and for weaning the actors from meaningless posing, this style turned out to be a blessing for the German stage. And if, at bottom, the result was only negative, still, it can not be denied that it rendered service by sweeping away abuses and thus making a real art of playing possible again. This style, however, had not, in itself, the strength to create a new art of the theatre in response to the continuous and impetuous demand of the public. In naturalistic plays it was able to cover up its weakness, but when it ventured

[40]

"TURANDOT" BY GOZZI-VOLLMOELLER

Deutsches Theater, October, 1911

Two Designs by Ernst Stern for Silk Drop Curtains

into the province of the classical drama, its impotence at once became apparent. Brahm himself knew this very well and tried to find a style beyond the naturalistic which could be used for the classics also. But he did not succeed./ It remained for Reinhardt to achieve that feat.

In the first years of his career, Reinhardt had been entirely a naturalistic actor, but he had too clear an eye, too much imagination, too much inborn longing for movement, change, surprise, to tolerate for any length of time the monotony and drabness of naturalism. Then unexpected help came to him from quite a different quarter: from the young painters. Everywhere in the Germany of that . time, secessions from the academies were taking place, led by the impressionists. But the latter were soon pushed aside by the impetuous demand for a decorative style. In Munich the "Jugend style" and in Vienna the "Wiener Werkstätte" came into being. A riot of youthful brightness took possession of the homes, and this new colorful scheme of interior decoration was, one might say, the prelude to Reinhardt's stage settings, for, with his ever-receptive eye, he was quick to perceive the great and fundamental change this kind of decorative art could work in the theatre.

This knowledge is the secret of Reinhardt's fame. His work may be summed up in these words: Taking over from Brahm the new naturalistic style of the young modern painters, he gained, by this union of the two arts, a wealth, breadth, and depth of expression that equipped him equally well for the Greek drama and for the classical and naturalistic plays. Not only that: He could stage wordless plays, operas, and operettas by the same methods. Thus he had arrived at the same point as the long-forgotten baroque producers of two hundred years ago. If his work gives the impression of being so startling and new, we must not forget that it is, in reality, the grand old baroque tradition of two centuries ago come back to life in him, a tradition that sums up in itself the whole art of the Middle Ages. Even in his first decisive Berlin success—the production of "A Midsummer Night's Dream" —he had used, as if in a dream, the baroque tradition, having pressed *all* the arts into the service of the stage and once more freed the theatre from the tyranny of the spoken word, whose slave it had been for at least a hundred years. For the actor had become, more and more, a mere speaker of words, and blank verse ruled the German stage. One might almost say that the theatre was no longer a theatre, that it was not there for seeing but only for hearing words, for listening to the recitation of verses apportioned among different rôles. For this, the actor had to thank the so-called "regular play," which appeared soon after the demise of the baroque theatre. Contrary to the baroque play, this "regular play" was not one which grew organically out of *all* the arts and their friendly rivalry. It was, rather, the work of the author alone, the outcome of his poetic conception, entrusted solely to the vehicle of the writer: the spoken word. Briefly, a spoken work. The healthy instinct of the people had always secretly rebelled against the sway of blank verse and the spoken word. And, for that reason, the people were hardly ever to be seen in the bourgeois theatres, which gradually became more and more exclusive and finally

[42]

were considered the special property of the "intellectuals" and "high-brows."

It was Reinhardt who first ended the sway of this literary play. He made the theatre, which, for a time, had become the exclusive domain of the art of speaking, once more the common property of *all* the arts. In this he is a direct follower of Richard Wagner, because each one of his productions is a *"Gesammtkunstwerk"* (the joint work of *all* the arts). That explains his unequalled importance for the German stage. He has fought the tyranny of the mere word, and prevailed. The theatre is no longer simply the intellectual enjoyment of the "elect"; it appeals to all the senses because it calls into action *all* the powers inherent in man.

Chapter IV

THE EVOLUTION OF REINHARDT

BY FRANK E. WASHBURN-FREUND

[An artist of fifty who is not something different from what he was at twenty-five, is not likely to have a book written about him. Few artists in the course of an entire lifetime, however, evolve through as wide a range as has Reinhardt, who is still in his prime. Whither the arc of his development will ultimately lead, probably he doesn't bother to think himself, in his profound engrossment with the task in hand. And yet, in view of the calm assurance with which he has taken every step, no matter how apparently revolutionary, throughout his career, he may know whither he is tending better than anyone suspects.

From the naturalism of the nineties to the neo-romanticism of the new century; from the constricted intimacy of the Kammerspiele to the broadly sweeping intimacy of the Arena and the Grosses Schauspielhaus; from the theatre of illusion to the theatre of make-believe; from the theatre as theatre to the theatre as life, in his recent productions in Salzburg; from the theatre as life to the theatre as a consciously formal art, such as he proposes in the Theater in der Josefstadt in Vienna— these are steps which, on their face, seem revolutionary. But a critic with the experience and powers of observation of Washburn-Freund is able to relate these apparently paradoxical tendencies and to show how they develop as the logical unfolding of a tireless imagination.—THE EDITOR.]

[44]

THE EVOLUTION OF REINHARDT

LYING in front of me on my desk is an illustrated book of the year 1911 titled "On the Art of the Theatre." Its author is Edward Gordon Craig. No one who wants to write about any phase or personality of the modern theatre movement can neglect it or its author if he wishes to be fair and give honor where honor is due. The same book explains why, from the seed sown by its author, no tree has grown to shelter under its mighty branches and leaves a great living theatre of the English speaking countries, modern in the best sense of the word. On the jacket of this book a writer expresses the pious wish that "someone would give the author a free hand, for as many years as he might choose, to set up a new theatre in Britain." Even if that had happened, however, I do not believe the outcome would have been what that writer expected, for Gordon Craig, at the beginning of his career, was a great instigator, perhaps also an ardent teacher, but although he comes from famous stage stock, he is no "actor," if we use this term not only in its usual meaning but also literally as a man of action. Worst of all, he is no organizer, and the theatre requires organization and action just as much as inspiration and art if it is to flourish. Moreover, organization and action in this field can develop only on the foundation of tradition, which makes it a slow and sometimes a painful growth, for it often means a fight against tradition. Nevertheless, tradition there must be if much of value is to be accomplished.

For generations, the English stage has been lacking in such action and organization, except in an entirely commercial way, and, for that reason, even an actor and organizer like Granville Barker, who may be considered

MAX REINHARDT AND HIS THEATRE

Gordon Craig's pupil, not only had an uphill fight all the time, but his appearance and work almost seem to be an isolated episode with no direct forerunner and no direct follower. That is where the importance of a real theatre tradition comes in.

Now Max Reinhardt is not only a really great artist "to his finger tips," a saying which fits his case completely, but he is also what I have just called a great organizer and "actor." Besides all this, he had, when he began, the great good fortune to find, in his field, a long and really living tradition, a tradition which was never entirely lost and of which he himself was partly the product. It is true he started with a fight against that tradition, but that very fight made him strong and sure of himself, and what he fought was, after all, more the tradition gone wrong and stale in character than the old tradition itself.

When he first appeared, a struggle had been going on for several years between the so-called classical style, as represented by the court and municipal theatres all over Germany and Austria, and a naturalistic style which Otto Brahm had inaugurated in Berlin with the help of a band of new actors and playwrights, of whom Gerhart Hauptmann has become the best known. The former, after a long decay, had had a late blossom time in the famous organization of the Meiningers, a troup of players brought together and trained by Duke Georg of Meiningen himself. They toured the whole of Germany and even went abroad several times, spreading the gospel of a kind of academic realism, which had regard more to the letter than the spirit of the text and took no end of trouble and spared no research on surface and "historical" truth, but yet,

[46]

thanks to the enthusiasm and earnestness of all concerned and the really great acting talents among its members, managed to pour a good deal of new life blood into the old molds. On the other hand, Brahm's theatre strove to represent modern life as it was being lived, to show its problems as they were agitating the minds of the people at that time. With the so-called "fourth wall" removed, the spectators were permitted to witness, clandestinely as it were, a "slice of life" unrolling itself before their eyes. Now, as a matter of fact, in spite of there being no "academic" realism here, although this realism itself soon enough took on a decided tinge of academicism, as always happens in all arts in such cases, it was, to a great extent, also a surface realism, a service more of the letter than the spirit. Only, instead of the "grand style" with its big, sweeping, opera manners and effects and all the colors and paraphernalia of an often overcrowded and therefore characterless stage, a subdued tone, almost a whisper at times, and a uniformly gray, drab *milieu* were affected, and these were supposed to take away all staginess from the production and transform it into real life in the eyes of the spectator.

Into this hotly contested fight entered Max Reinhardt in Berlin in 1902 when he opened his Kleines Theater, a little theatre to which, in some measure, the "little theatre" movement even in this country at the present time is indebted. Reinhardt, about whose pre-Berlin career, with its almost humorous beginnings, men like Hermann Bahr have written charming stories, had been a member of Brahm's company several years and in that way had himself gone through the realistic phase of development.

[47]

But, theatre man par excellence that he is, to whom the stage means everything, who is eager to pour all his never-flagging energy, all his overflowing temperament, all his love for movement and color into his work, could not remain long in that sombre school, good as it undoubtedly was for him, if only because it curbed at the beginning a perhaps too exuberant spirit. For Brahm and his followers, the stage was life and all actors were men. In Reinhardt, however, lived the Shakespearean idea of all the world being a stage and all men being players, with all that this belief implies down to the deep irony, self-irony, which, Goethe held, is the sign of the best. Consequently, quite instinctively, he set out to bring stage and life together again in that spirit. It is therefore no wonder that Shakespeare became his god and he, Shakespeare's prophet, a service to which he has given his greatest art and warmest love.

To this fundamental conception of life and stage Reinhardt has held from the beginning, and it has shaped his career and evolution. It and one other marked trait enabled him to become a great producer and at the same time influenced his whole development. That trait is that, for him, art is not only self-expression but conscious impression on the public. To get as near to the public as possible, to gain its ears, its eyes, in fact, all its senses, even its very soul—that, from the very first, has been his fondest endeavor, the very nourishment on which he has fed. The different styles of his productions, the various kinds of stages which he has had built for himself, all have only been means to that end. In the Kleines Theater, auditorium and stage were near to each other,

[48]

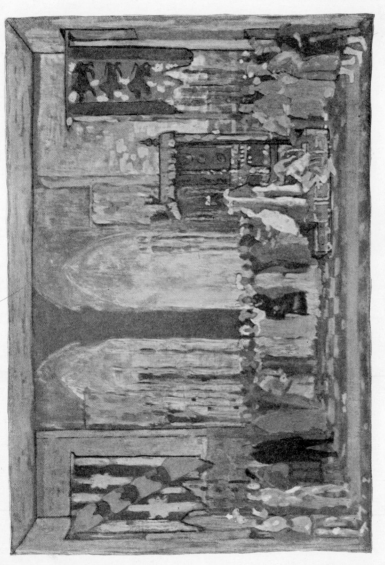

THE PLAY SCENE IN "HAMLET"

AT THE KÜNSTLER THEATER, MUNICH, JUNE-JULY, 1909

Designed by Fritz Erler

and this intimacy he regained when, later, he opened his
Kammerspiele. In his Deutsches Theater he often used
front and apron stages, and he had a revolving stage built
into it to do away with long stops in which the public
might easily escape from the spell that he had laid on it.
Then he went into the arena of a circus, had a circus re-
modeled into an imposing new theatre with a great apron
stage, a theatre whose most characteristic note is the
strongly marked unity of stage and auditorium. In this
theatre, the Grosses Schauspielhaus, he gave, with others,
the antique drama, but, as it were, adapted to the mood
of our times; that is to say, the hearers were no longer
mere spectators; they were, in reality, an enlarged chorus
and, as such, became themselves players, swayed hither
and thither by the rising and receding tides of the tremendous drama taking place in their very midst. Next,
he even went into the market place, like the strolling
players of old, and there, in front of a church, he acted,
as a kind of pageant, the old morality play "Everyman."
And while, in London, for his production of "The
Miracle," he turned a theatre, stage and auditorium into
a Gothic cathedral with all its mystery of rising columns,
of shimmering stained glass and deep shadows; in Salzburg his production of "The Great World-Theatre" by
Hugo von Hofmannsthal in the summer of 1922 took
place inside a wonderful church itself, thus, in fact, returning to the very beginnings of the European drama,
for, at that time, scenes from the Bible were enacted in
the churches as a kind of religious exercise on certain
festival days. There is a plan on foot for the erection
of a great festival playhouse at Salzburg, where Reinhardt

now has his home in the beautiful old baroque castle of Leopoldskron at the foot of lovely mountains. In this playhouse, Hans Poelzig, architect of the Grosses Schauspielhaus in Berlin—the circus which was changed into a theatre—sees, as in a fairy dream, stage and auditorium united under one sky, as it were, flooded with light as mysterious as the Milky Way high in the heavens, while the outside is meant to create, in everyone approaching it, the instinctive feeling of treading on holy ground in reverential mood. Like most great artists in any art whatever, Reinhardt has moved toward simplicity of representation, elimination of details, and, at the same time, deepening of substance. Whoever is rich in himself can afford to do with little, almost nothing, and yet what he does will have the appearance and the effect of richness and depth. Reinhardt can now, if need be or if it suits him, play on an almost empty platform like the one in the Redoutensaal in Vienna, and, with the help of a few accessories indicating mood and period of the play performed, he can draw his audience with him perhaps even more spellbound than if it watched a more elaborate production. Of course, only the master can do this; the imitator would fail miserably, for he would miss just those subtle little touches which create richness by stimulating the imagination and setting associations in motion. The master only may be an ascetic and seem the richer for it. An "academic" simplicity would soon be as tedious as any other academicism.

Personality is everything, and personality means being alive all the time. Reinhardt is that to an almost incredible extent. He does not repeat himself. Every

"A WINTER'S TALE"

At the Deutsches Theater, September, 1906

A Sketch for a Street Scene by Emil Orlik

"THE MERCHANT OF VENICE"

At the Künstler Theater, Munich, June-August, 1910

Two Costume Plates Designed by Wilhelm Hengeler for the Prince of Aragon
and One for Lorenzo

new work is attacked with an open mind and mastered
with its own weapon, so to speak. His is a receptive
mind, but, although he takes mental and artistic nourishment from every side, he makes everything his own. Many
have been the influences that have played upon him, and
he has taken many a thing from others, but he has woven
all into his own fabric, making use, quite as a matter of
course, of the privilege of the great to turn to his own
account whoever and whatever comes into the orbit in
which he swings.

Considering all this, it might be inferred that Reinhardt is one of those selfish producers who use the plays
that they choose merely as a means of showing themselves
off. Nothing is further from the truth. Here, too, his
real greatness shines out clearly. *"Ich dien"* (I serve),
in the coat of arms of the Prince of Wales, might be written in the coat of arms of every true artist and great man.
Reinhardt is quite content to serve the play and its author.
He does not force his own personality and predilections
on them. His endeavor, as ought to be that of every real
producer, is to bring out the mood and atmosphere of
the play in such a way as to force the audience into it
and keep it there during the action as completely as possible.

How Reinhardt used different forms of the stage for
that purpose has been shown. Now it is time to discuss
the way in which his treatment of the *mise-en-scène* serves
the same purpose. The first large production which
made him famous in Berlin and the whole of Germany
was that of "A Midsummer Night's Dream." Until that
time he had not attempted any Shakesperean play with the

[51]

exception of "The Merry Wives of Windsor." Although his methods, since 1905, have changed greatly, his intentions were the same then as during his whole career. The choice of play alone was characteristic and a sort of challenge as well. Hence poetry, imagination, light fancy and romance were to live again on the stage, and all the arts were to take part in this revival. Music, which underlies all of Shakespeare's works and especially this play in the woods, was to cast its wonderful spell again over the spectators. In this there was an approach to opera, but in the form of Wagner's *"Gesammtkunstwerk,"* a work of all the arts toward which Reinhardt always has been drawn. To achieve this, the pictorial arts, color and light, were, of course, of the greatest importance, and Reinhardt, in the case of "A Midsummer Night's Dream," employed them with the main idea of creating the mood and atmosphere of endless woods, now threatening, now sheltering, full of mysterious sounds and beings. Its trees were plastic, the whole representation was not yet symbolic, but the mood was caught, and the public found itself transplanted, as if by a magician's wand, underneath the cool shadows of gigantic trees, and it opened eyes and hearts to receive the message of the poet. One year later Ibsen's "Ghosts" was produced. If Reinhardt's first poetical production had still been treated in a more or less naturalistic way, this grim, apparently realistic piece received a very different treatment. Reinhardt asked the Scandinavian artist, Edvard Munch, one of the great forerunners of the expressionistic movement, to design the setting for him, and already in 1906 we had a scene that used outward forms only for the purpose of

[52]

SCHMIDTBONN'S "THE WRATH OF ACHILLES"

A Design for a Setting by Ernst Stern for the Production at the
Deutsches Theater, January, 1912

deepening the central mood of the play by the way in which it arranged its lines: vertical most of them, horizontals, and curves, repeating the play and clash of ideas, as it were, in a play and clash of lines. Symbolic also was the way in which the room, although it looked out on a fjord, was shut in like a prison by sharply pointed, threatening mountains, piercing and almost expelling the sky, and, with it, freedom and hope. Every line, every mass of space, height, width—all played their appointed parts in this relentless modern drama of fate, and the figures moving in it, almost as if driven by some unknown force, seemed to be placed there by fate itself. They were like necessary spots in the design of the whole scene, like an accent in a bar of music. Reinhardt later staged several of Strindberg's plays in the same mood, but always with a fresh vision, as is his wont, for formulas are the sign of the pupil, not of the master.

The same fruitful year brought "A Winter's Tale." It was in 1904 that Gordon Craig, at the invitation of Count Kessler, had gone to Germany with his designs for "Hamlet," of which one scene is illustrated in the book named. The whole Craig was already visible in it: his insistence on the overwhelming height and expansion of space as compared with the insignificant figures of the mere players. The seed which he had sown had borne fruit. In most of Reinhardt's scenes for "A Winter's Tale" the strongest emphasis was laid on the proportions between the stage settings—generally a towering mass of lines—and the figures. But Reinhardt is not a man of one idea, although most certainly a man of one purpose. Style, as such, never had an appeal for him. "What is in a style?" might rightly be asked. Not the particular style but the element of individual life in an artist's work is what counts eventually. Reinhardt was never a follower of the realistic, the impressionistic, or the expressionistic style; he took points from each of them, molding them to his own use. Just because of that, he, on his part, has given a great deal of stimulus to the art movements of the last twenty years. Thus it came that his scene in Bohemia in "A Winter's Tale," designed for him by Emil Orlik, is a tremendous contrast to the other parts of that play. It is not realistic either, but is just like what a festival in a fairy book would be: full of childlike fantasy, bright colors, gayety, movement. He found in Shakespeare himself the poet and dramatist who refuses to put his plays into the Procrustean bed of a single style, but rejoices, on the contrary, in the fullness of life, movement and fancy.

That is the reason why it is impossible to trace a sort of straight stylistic development in Reinhardt's art. He does not let himself be pinned down. He seems to be a realist today, a stylist tomorrow, and both at the same time on the day after, and all the time the only thing that he really seeks is to show life in all its manifestations, its roundness, its movement, its colors, its music. Once he appeared to be threatened with the fate of becoming a stylist. That was when the people of the Munich Künstler Theater invited him to take over their "relief stage," on which they—artists, not *scenic* artists that they were—had tried to change plays into a series of moving relief pictures. One still comes across, now and then, similar performances of, may I say, "high-brow" dancers

[54]

REINHARDT'S MOLIÈRE STAGE

A Permanent Setting Used for the Production of "George Dandin"

At the Deutsches Theater, April, 1912

MOLIÈRE'S "LE MALADE IMAGINAIRE"

AT THE KAMMERSPIELE, MARCH, 1916

A Series of Costume Designs by Ernst Stern

who affect a "relief dance" as if derived from a relief on an Egyptian tomb.   Reinhardt survived the ordeal and, as with every great artist, the handicap only helped him to new and finer creations.   Where a similar stage arrangement was in the right place, in Molière's comedies for instance, with their pronounced style and, as it were, marionette mood, he built his "Molière stage" on which, in silhouette fashion against a formal garden pavilion, his actors moved somewhat as if they were enclosed in a relief.

Reinhardt knew far too well that the pictorial arts must not be masters but only helpers on the stage.   So he surrounded himself with artists who could enter into his own spirit and execute his intentions almost as if they and he were one in mind and eye.   The principal artist on his staff is Ernst Stern, a pupil of Franz von Stuck, about whose versatile and fanciful art Oskar Bie has written a richly illustrated book.   Impressive scenic pictures were made for him also by Professor Alfred Roller, a marvelous innovator, under Gustav Mahler, of the Vienna Opera, so far as scenery was concerned.   Other artists are Fritz Erler, Wilhelm Dietz and Emil Orlik.

To characterize Reinhardt fully as a producer it would, of course, be necessary to show how he works with his, as he rightly expresses it, "finest material," the actors. That, however, would lead us too far for the purpose of this chapter.   Suffice it to say that here, too, he respects the other artists, his main endeavor being toward a perfect ensemble of which he is the leader, not the dictator. There is a characteristic etching by Orlik, "Reinhardt at Rehearsal."   In it he is seen with hand raised, his face set, and his eyes glowing: truly, the artist at work. Like a great conductor leading his orchestra he looks, and perhaps that is the best way to describe him and his work. This statement is explained when one watches his chorus scenes which, rightly, have brought him almost his greatest fame. Here he does change into the dictator. *His* will penetrates all these players, *his* feeling pulses through them all, with *his* voice they all shout. When we see these masses of humanity changed into one being, as it were, torn between passionate hate or love, fear or joy, as in "Julius Cæsar," "Oedipus Rex," "Danton" or "The Miracle," a terrible thought suddenly strikes us: Was not the whole world recently such a mass of humanity, such a "theatre chorus," when the dreadful tragedy of the late war was staged? Was it not merely such a shouting, gesticulating mass driven by instinct, it knew not why nor whither? Truly, indeed, the stage is the symbol of life. Is it to be wondered at, then, that an artist like Max Reinhardt gives, almost to the exclusion of other interests, all his passion, all his love to these boards which, as Schiller says, mean the world?

Chapter V

THE THEATRE THROUGH REINHARDT'S EYES

BY MAX REINHARDT

I

ON THE ART OF THE THEATRE

THE stage represents the most powerful and direct form of art. The most powerful, because it appeals not to the individual only, but to the public in general, and because it has the power of mastering and influencing that public. Every other art presupposes that he who receives has a certain amount of knowledge, a musical ear, a well-trained eye, and so forth. Every other art, therefore, appeals chiefly to the individual, while the theatre presupposes nothing and, in its best productions, addresses itself both to the most cultured individual and to the great masses. No one knew better and felt more keenly what is essential in dramatic art than Shakespeare. "Hamlet," with a wealth of thought unequalled by any other work of art, has the power to satisfy the highest intellectual demands; it touches the deepest human problems; and, at the same time, it fascinates the simplest and most naïve among the audience, by an exciting and

[57]

intensive action and by holding up to the world an image of its very self.

The drama is the most direct art, because neither letters nor tones, neither stone, nor wood, nor canvas, are its medium for expression, but man himself. It dies with the actor on the stage. And yet it is immortal, because it has its source in an elementary and passionate desire which is innate in man and is always born again in him. It manifests itself even in the child, whose play is alive with creative joy; and it lives in the adult, whether he be an artist or a spectator. It is, so to speak, an indomitable desire to transform oneself, a demonic impulse to disclose oneself. All who are present in the theatre—on the stage or in the audience—strive, consciously or unconsciously, to enhance themselves, to forget themselves, to rise above themselves. They seek that ecstasy, that intoxication, which, at other times, only drugs can give them. It is difficult to understand, therefore, why the State and other powerful agencies, who think it their mission to further all the other arts, should neglect the theatre alone, when it might be of incomparable usefulness to them. It is difficult to understand why they spend exorbitant sums for libraries, museums, schools and other educational institutions, but evidently belittle the value of the theatre, endanger its very existence by levying excessive taxes and thus leave this wonderful instrument in the hands of speculators, who make of it a more or less profitable business. In ancient Greece and Rome, the State itself supported the theatre and cultivated it with the greatest of care. The performances in those theatres were festivals for the whole nation, simul-

[58]

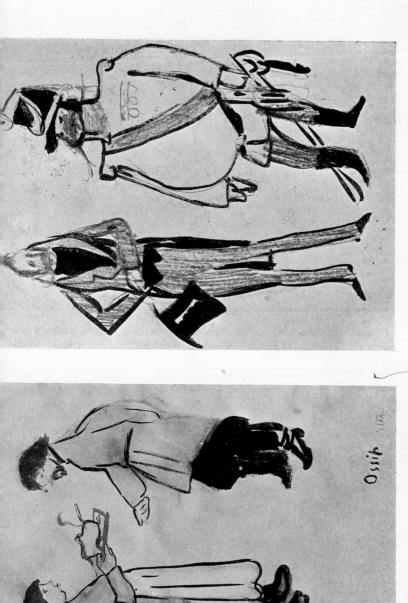

FOUR COSTUME SKETCHES BY ERNST STERN FOR GOGOL'S "THE INSPECTOR GENERAL"

At the Deutsches Theater, March, 1907

The Characteristic Dome on the Horizon Dominates This Village Street Scene in
Tolstoy's "The Power of Darkness"

A Group from Tolstoy's "The First Distiller"
(Left to right) Alexander Moissi, Hermann Thimig and Gusti Pünkösdy

RUSSIA SEEN THROUGH REINHARDT'S EYES

taneously amusement and religious ceremony. The Church to whom we owe the greatest masterpieces of art in all its forms, to whom also the renaissance of our present theatre is due, must have recognized, in its wonderful ingenuity, the power of the drama, when, in wise appreciation, it placed side by side the most sacred things and the profane farce of the devil and the trader, so as to draw even the most simple-minded under its sway. Only the Puritanism of later days succeeded in expelling the drama once more from the Church.

In Europe, the Vienna Opera (subsidized by the Imperial court), the Comédie Française, founded by Louis XIV, and the Burg Theater have been the strong bulwarks of the art theatre. Many German rulers placed the theatre almost at the centre of their interests, and it was the little royal theatre in Meiningen which in its time inspired a reform of the dramatic art. In England, the theatre never flourished more richly than under Queen Elizabeth; and the greatest theatrical genius, Shakespeare, was surrounded by a surprisingly wide circle of dramatic writers. In America, however, neither the Government nor any of the numerous philanthropic captains of industry have ever patronized the theatre. This circumstance explains many of the fundamental differences between the European and the American theatre. When I say this, I do not mean unconditionally to advocate support by the State or any other authority. The influence those authorities would thereby gain over the theatre, has its disadvantages, as well. The opera, with its voluminous and complicated apparatus, consisting of singers, musicians, dancers and chorus, can hardly prosper without additional funds. /A playhouse, on the other hand, should, in my opinion, be able to support itself without any subsidy, even when it presents a highly artistic program. The greatest disadvantages, of course, prevail where mere business considerations dominate. For more than half a century and under three directors—L'Arronge, Brahm and myself—the Deutsches Theater in Berlin has held to strictly artistic principles, always centering its main interest on building up a valuable repertory, on presenting a continually changing program, on attracting young talents, and on gathering a first class ensemble. During all that time it was operated without any additional funds from the State, the City or private patrons; and, nevertheless, in addition it yielded considerable profits./

Today, in my opinion, men of means should take the places of kings and princes and erect a theatre on a sound basis, which should be able to follow its artistic aims, free from all considerations of a purely commercial character. In doing so, they would accomplish more for the commonwealth than by buying pictures. Besides, it would cost them much less, since a theatre which does not pursue only the business side, would do the best business. Such a theatre ought to have a school connected with it which should train its future acting material; it ought to have its own staff of artists, a permanent ensemble, its own workshops where stage decorations and costumes could be manufactured at comparatively low cost. The Deutsches Theater in Berlin, and also the Moscow Art Theatre were founded on that principle. In Russia, these general principles are still further enhanced by the deep, almost religious devotion of the individual artist to the engrossing cause, an attitude which makes the achievements of the Russians so outstanding.

In extreme contrast to this point of view stands the star system, which makes the creation of an artistic theatre impossible. The individual star, who tyrannizes a theatre with his moods, who financially and artistically represses everything and everybody around him, who does not look for good plays but for star rôles, is the most dangerous enemy of the essentially composite art of the theatre. The star who finds his field of activity today here, tomorrow there, who skims the cream of everything, permits nothing else to grow up beside him; and the mere business manager who speculates with that star—these are the two most terrible diseases which threaten the present theatre with decay.

II

ON THE IMPORTANCE OF THE ACTOR

Today and for all time, man must stand at the centre of all theatrical art, man as actor. Where the actor is also a dramatic writer, he has the power to create a world according to his own image, thus awakening the drama to its highest form of life, like Shakespeare and Molière. Whosoever has anything to do with the theatre should be an actor. Whether or not he practices the art of acting is of secondary importance. Many great playwrights, teachers of the dramatic art, theatre managers, were actors without ever having played on the stage. / Only when the

[61]

director, the stage manager, the poet, the dramatic teacher, the scenic artist, the musician, are all actors, when everyone on the stage and everyone in the audience is an actor, and joins in the play, then, and only then, the theatre fulfils its highest mission.

III

ON THE FILM

It is evident that the film, as an art, is still in its infancy. After a flying start, its present stagnation is a serious matter. It seems to be caught in a bad rut, which makes any further development along its present lines rather improbable. Whither is that ever-increasing staging of masses to lead, those buildings, dressed-up circus animals, acrobats? There is no denying that a few ingenious individuals like Chaplin, Griffith, Coogan and others, have attained very striking results in this young art. They are the pioneers who, consciously or not, have built the first bridges from a mere film industry to true film art. These, however, are not achievements of that form of art itself, but the marvellous attainments of a few individuals. They are hints of the possibilities latent in the developing art of the moving picture.

What are the causes of this sterility? The art of the film in its present form does not thrive on its own resources and its own strength, although both are available in great abundance. That art is rooted and vegetates on foreign soil. It is a parasite (and, by the way, a

[62]

THE FESTIVAL WHICH THE KAISER TRIED TO STOP

The Guillotine Scene in the Breslau Festspiel by Gerhart Hauptmann, Produced by Reinhardt in the Summer of 1913,
from Designs by Ernst Stern, to Commemorate the Centenary of Victory over Napoleon

A GROUP FROM THE BRESLAU FESTSPIEL

Mars Handles Napoleon Like a Puppet in Hauptmann's Festival Play Whic[h]
Treated Royalty Without Gloves

rather dangerous parasite, at that) of the theatre, of literature, of music, of painting, and so forth. There is no creative film literature; only more or less arbitrary adaptations of dramas, novels, sentimental or detective stories and the like. For this reason, the film can not dispense with the excessive use of the word, although freedom from the word is one of its chief potential characteristics. Entire chapters from the novel have to be thrown in between the pictures, only proving the weakness of the picture which should be able alone to convey its full meaning. Film actors, too, use the same means of expression as on the stage, although the latter is based on entirely different principles, on the spoken word and on action, concise in time and place. Or they abandon all finer differentiation in expression and limit themselves to presenting the external development of the story. And yet the wonderful possibilities of enlargement and close-up especially adapt the film for the dramatic representation of what goes on within the actor. The manager who is capable of making the actor actually live his part, without resorting to the same technique of expression which he uses on the stage, and which necessarily appears exaggerated in the film, will open up unlimited and undreamed possibilities for interpreting the life of the soul. Music borrowed from operas, concerts, dancing melodies, can not save the film from that unfortunate dumbness which is its fate through uncongenial composition and form of representation. Often it is no art at all in scenario and performance. The film must create its own new adequate mode of expression. It must open up new springs of composition, performance and music, must live on its own soil,

[63]

without borrowing everywhere else. It must stand on
its own foundation, so that it can dispense entirely with
the photographed word.

We know that Shakespeare selected his costumes (viz.
the costumes of his time) with the greatest of care; and
a single annotation in the stage-manager's book like the
one that "Macduff pulls his hat deep over his eyes" when
he hears the news of the death of his wife and his children, tells us more than all words can do.

IV

ON THE LIVING THEATRE

It would be a theory as barbaric as it is incompatible
with the principles of theatrical art, to measure with the
same yard stick, to press into the same mold, the wonderful wealth of the world's literature. The mere suggestion of such an attempt, is a typical example of pedantic
scholasticism. There is no one form of theatre which
is the only true artistic form. Let good actors today play
in a barn or in a theatre, tomorrow at an inn or inside a
church, or, in the Devil's name, even on an expressionistic
stage: if the place corresponds with the play, something
wonderful will be the outcome. All depends on realizing the specific atmosphere of a play, and on making the
play live. And yet, do not banish from the temple merely
the traders and money-mongers, but also the over-zealous
high priests who desire to rob the theatre of all its brilliancy and sensuousness, who would like nothing better

than to turn it into a preacher's pulpit, who swear by the written word, and who after having murdered the spirit of that word, would like to press it back again into its place in the book.

Just the contrary is the true mission of the theatre. Its task is to lift the word out of the sepulchre of the book, to breathe life into it, to fill it with blood, with the blood of today, and thus to bring it into living contact with ourselves, so that we may receive it and let it bear fruit in us. Such is the only way; there is no other. All roads which do not lead into life, lead us astray, whatever their name may be. Life is the incomparable and most valuable possession of the theatre. Dress it up in any manner you wish, the cloak will have to fall when the eternal human comes to the fore, when, in the height of ecstasy, we find and embrace each other. The noble dead of a hundred, of four hundred, of a thousand years ago, arise again on the boards. It is this eternal wonder of resurrection which sanctifies the stage.

Therefore, do not write out prescriptions, but give to the actor and his work the atmosphere in which they can breathe more freely and more deeply. Do not spare stage properties and machinery where they are needed, but do not impose them on a play that does not need them. Our standard must not be to act a play as it was acted in the days of its author. To establish such facts is the task of the learned historian, and is of value only for the museum. How to make a play live in our time, that is decisive for us. The Catholic Church which aims at the highest, the most spiritual, the most supernatural, does so by means which appeal directly to the senses. It over-

[65]

whelms us with the pathos of its temples towering in the sky; it surrounds us with the mystical dimness of its cathedrals; it charms our eye with wonderful masterpieces of art, with the brilliancy of its colored windows, with the lustre of thousands of candles, which reflect their light in golden objects and vessels. It fills our ear with music and song and the sound of the thundering organ. It stupefies us by the odor of the incense. Its priests stride in rich and precious robes. And in such a sphere of sensuousness, the highest and the most holy reveals itself to us. We reveal ourselves, and we find the way to our innermost being, the way to concentration, to exaltation, to spiritualization.

The church, especially the Catholic Church, is the very cradle of our modern theatre. Therefore, down with the iconoclasts at any cost! They cheat the theatre out of its eternal bliss.

Chapter VI

REINHARDT THE ACTOR

BY HUGO VON HOFMANNSTHAL

(English Translation by Joseph Dick)

["Specialist in elderly character rôles," is Kommer's sum-
ary of Reinhardt as an actor in his early twenties. Paul
·gband characterizes him at this period of his career as "a
·en character player led by high artistic judgment and strong
·otional instinct" and he lists among the young player's
·vored elders: Ibsen's kind old Foldal; Hauptmann's old
·umert in "The Weavers"; Tolstoy's phlegmatic Akim;
·sen's hypocritical Engstrand; his philosopher, Mortensgard;
·uptmann's shrewd boatsman of the Spree, Wulkow; Dreyer's
·nny head-master, Störmer; Gorky's philosophic pilgrim,
·ka, in "The Lower Depths"; and the wily title rôle in Beer-
·fmann's "Graf von Charolais" ("The Count of Charolais").
·Reinhardt as an actor was a passing phase, however, for
· soon found that his imaginative ambition refused to respect
·s restricted channel and with the acquisition of one stage
·ter another, he permitted the rôle of *regisseur* to dwarf, ab-
·b, and finally extinguish the narrower craft. The aptitude
·r that craft, however, was not lost in the larger rôle, for it
·rmed a psychological basis for brilliant achievement in the
·acting realm of the *regisseur*, as von Hofmannsthal so ably
·presses it in this chapter.—THE EDITOR.]

IT is difficult to write about a producer like Max Rein-
·rdt, because, in order to understand him, one must an-

[67]

alyze his astonishing personality. His great influen
upon the development of the European stage, and the i
spiration he has been, and is still, to playwrights and acto
alike, give interest to an inquiry into the hidden prin
ples that direct his work, and lead to an understanding
that central energy whose vibrations have been felt f
beyond the shores of Europe.

This central energy is, in truth, the soul of a high
gifted actor, who, unable to realize fully his dramatic co
ceptions within the compass of his own body, does
through the bodies of others. This type of genius close
resembles that other peculiarly compounded one, the dr
matic poet, who also is something of an actor; and tl
more he is an actor, the more he approaches greatness
a dramatist. The dramatic poet weaves his pattern o
of events and characters; he does this by creating an
lusion out of dovetailed rôles and connected, powerf
dramatic situations. The divine inspiration that casts
spell upon the work is, of course, the secret of the creati
genius. I am well aware that all this does not apply
the creative genius of Shakespeare or of Molière, but on
to their particular situation and to the form in which the
poetic genius manifests itself; a form so very differe
from that which holds the hymnic thoughts of a Shell
or Whitman, or the epic invention of a Richardson
Balzac.

The twin-brother of the born dramatic poet is the bo
producer. But the latter's position is more peculiar sti.
and fate's handicap which prevents him from being wh
he otherwise would have been is, in his case, even greate
perhaps this is so in order that his productive powers m

HAMLET AND THE GHOST OF HIS FATHER ON THE PARAPET

HAMLET AT THE GRAVE OF OPHELIA
The Kuppelhorizont Makes Possible a Bleak North Sea Sky for Horizon

TWO SCENES FROM "HAMLET"

AT THE DEUTSCHES THEATER, OCTOBER, 1909

"HAMLET"

AT THE GROSSES SCHAUSPIELHAUS

A Design for the Scene on the Parapet by Ernst Stern

e stored up in a source to be tapped later. If the dra-
1atic poet's visions are representative, such as the actor
xpresses by appropriate movements of his body—a means
f expression denied to the poet—and if, instead, his mas-
ry of language furnishes him the means of being
super-actor and of making others, who are gifted with
1e requisite physical attributes, represent his concep-
ons, then the position of the producing genius is still
1ore anomalous, for he is denied even the power of lan-
uage for creative purposes. Analogously, the dramatist
ompels his contemporaries and posterity to realize his
hantasms, just as the producer imposes his personal,
1dividual conception. He does this by conveying his
wn more pronounced interpretations through the chan-
el of the poet's intentions.

A greater paradox than Diderot's "Paradoxe du
omédien" is the position of the poet-producer. There
oes not seem to be any place for him in the scheme of
1e theatre; yet he occupies a place. The position of the
ader of an orchestra, between the composer and the per-
orming members, is similar; in both cases powers of in-
rpretation are necessary; powers which, in rare instances,
1ay rise to creative genius. It is thus possible to com-
1re men like Reinhardt and Stanislavsky with Nikisch
1d Toscanini. But the leader of an orchestra is, after
1, only a shadow of the theatrical producer.

A view of Reinhardt's artistic activity during the last
ve or ten years shows a wealth of creative achievement.
einhardt does not confine himself to certain styles; his
1tholicity is amazing. Within a few years his interpre-
tions have embraced half of the dramatic literature of

[69]

the world. Shakespeare's gloomiest tragedies and h
airiest comedies; Aeschylus' "Orestes" and Aristophane
"Lysistrata"; Molière, Goldoni and Gozzi; Goethe an
Schiller; also Strindberg, Tolstoy, Tchehoff, Knut Han
sun, Gorky and Tristan Bernard; an operetta, a ballet, an
a portentously gloomy problem-play, the first work o
a young German contemporary. How is it possible t
stage all these in close succession without doing violenc
to some of them; to give each its due, and yet to impa
to each by some subtle touch the unmistakable characte
of a Reinhardt production? It seems like sheer magic
One can not explain creative gifts; they astonish one, an
would keep one in perpetual astonishment were one ca
pable of long-sustained emotion.

The key of the mystery may perhaps be this: the dra
matic text is a thing incomplete; and the greater the dra
matic poet, the more incomplete the text. It was Schill
who said that the born dramatist should work very har
but should only sketch. Schiller said of himself that h
had not enough talent to work in that manner. In th
works of dramatists like Shakespeare and Calderon, a ma
ture judgment can perceive that with all their wonderfu
completeness, they still retain a certain sketchiness; ho
well these masters knew when to stop and what to leav
unsaid! Here, indeed, is the difference between dramat
and epic poetry. "Macbeth" has about twenty thousan
words; "Clarissa Harlowe" or "David Copperfield" prol
ably ten times as many. In spite of this, "Macbeth" i
terprets a world fully as complete and rich as do those tw
novels. Is "Hamlet" any less profound than "Don Qui

[70]

As Engstrand in Ibsen's "Ghosts"   As Luka in Gorky's "The Lower   As Itzig in "Der Graf von Charolais"
Depths"

MAX REINHARDT AS AN ACTOR IN THREE OF HIS MOST IMPORTANT RÔLES

RUSSIA SEEN THROUGH GERMAN EYES

Maxim Gorky's "The Lower Depths" ("Nachtasyl") as Produced by Reinhardt, with
Himself in the Rôle of Luka at the Kleines Theater January, 1903

ote" or the "Odyssey"; is "Le Misanthrope" to be held lighter than the "Princesse de Clèves"?

The novelist's purpose is to reproduce all of his subject in words; and the imagination of his readers, as was the case with the audience of the ancient rhapsodists, is merely receptive, passive. The dramatist, on the contrary, fails of his purpose unless he succeeds in making the audience as well as the actors his collaborators. The audience is the descendant of the chorus of antiquity, which was a dancing and singing crowd surrounding the protagonist, the sacrificed hero, and suffering and rejoicing with him. The audience, in fact, is an enlarged chorus; it is a fellow-actor, playing and being played upon. That is why in a drama things should be merely indicated; the sympathetic imagination of the audience should not be fettered, while the imagination of a quiescent reader should, on the contrary, be controlled by the words of the novel. This explains the necessity in a novel of delineations of psychology, descriptions of scenes of action, and the need of furnishing all other external and internal details. In the drama all these things are imaginatively realized by the audience, in accordance with the Aristotelean "cleansing of the soul through fear and pity"; all that the poet, the producer, the actor, the decorator and electrician do is to supply a chain of suggestions and stimuli for the purpose of producing illusions of certain categories and degrees. But the means by which this is done are palpable, which is not the case with words, the only means used by the novelist. The dancer's, singer's or actor's expressively animated body, the word spoken in concord with the appropriate gesture, the painted and illuminated stage, the properties—all these things are real to the senses, and are put to the service of a seeming reality. The hand that keeps together all these components of a play must be strong indeed.

To do this, to hold the different parts together, is the work of the producer; it is he who unites them in a balanced whole. For, just as the constituents of the body wait only for death to separate them from each other, so do all the constituents of the stage tend towards separate existence. For the actor detachment means emancipation; Gordon Craig is the type of the emancipated stage-decorator: the dumb show, the pantomime, the festive cortège is in the place of the dramatic whole. The clown, that comedian of the body, long since emancipated himself from the comic actor, his twin brother; in Shakespeare's times they were still one.

Reinhardt greatly loves all these elements of the play. He will not be without them; his hand holds them in a firm grip. He needs them, and makes use of them all; the magic spell cast by the great actor, as well as by the clown's grimace and by the painter's craft. But he subordinates them all to a higher end—to the organized whole.

To Reinhardt the stage is the key to the whole world; nor can one deny that, in the proper hands, it is indeed the key to all things, be they small or large. The playing kitten, the seascape with the willows drooping wistful branches toward the restless waves, or the events of the French Revolution: all these may be understood by mimic intuition only. It may perhaps be said, that this key opens only material, phenomenal problems, and not the spiritual and essential ones. But have we not stripped

A SCENE IN "FAUST I"

AT THE DEUTSCHES THEATER, MARCH, 1909

(Left to Right) Georg Heinrich as Faust and Ernst Lubitsch as Wagner

THE BARGAIN SEALED

Werner Krauss as Mephisto and Eduard von Winterstein as Faust

GRETCHEN AT THE WELL

Camilla Eibenschütz as Gretchen and Ellie Rothe as Lieschen

GOETHE'S "FAUST I"

Werner Krauss as Mephisto and Karl Ebert as Baccalaurius

Ernst Lubitsch as Famulus and Werner Krauss as Mephisto

"FAUST II"

At the Deutsches Theater, February, 1911

SPECTRE SCENE
Werner Krauss (extreme right) as Mephisto; Konrad Veidt (centre) as Faust

THE KAISER SCENE
Alexander Moissi (on throne), the Kaiser; Werner Krauss (seated), Mephisto

"FAUST II"

AT THE DEUTSCHES THEATER, FEBRUARY, 1911, ALFRED ROLLER, DESIGNER

off and left behind us this distinction between outer and inner, between kernel and shell, together with other dualistic concepts of the past centuries?

From all matters and events there does, in fact, emanate something intangible, hovering about the thing that gave it birth, spiritualizing and completing it. This something is the mood of things. A Beethoven sonata, a building, an historic epoch, periods of one's own life, the seasons, the weather, a scene of tragedy; all of these may be said to have their own mood. The more susceptible one is, the more pronounced and the more varied is the spell of his mood. The many delicate nuances of mood are the medium in which the suggestions of the dramatic poet are condensed into seeming reality. Reinhardt is great in the art of feeling, in every drama, in each scene of every drama, the whole power of its varying moods, as well as in the power of drawing these moods into the light, and extending their magic over the audience. Great as Stanislavsky is, not even he can approach Reinhardt in the breadth of his intuition and in the uncanny ability of his imagination to translate dramatic creations into intense dramatic effects. Even when, by reason of a strict, concise, dramatic text, or when, as in operettas, there seems to be but little room for interpretation, his adaptable mind easily accommodates itself to the exigency, makes the most of the smallest opportunity, and raises the performance to a level of liveliness and completeness which is surprising. His work once begun, he forgets all differences of rank; he will not impart to an operetta or a pantomime less of himself than he imparts to a tragedy of Shakespeare or to a play of Schiller. In this, of course, he is a spendthrift; and is influenced only by a principle which I once heard him enunciate: to get the most out of a play, the poet must give elbow-room to the producer, the producer to the actor, and the actor to the audience; for only in the mind of the audience does the circle of effects find its consummation.

"FAUST II"

At the Deutsches Theater, February, 1911

Act IV, Scene XIV, Walpurgis Night, Designed by Alfred Roller

CHAPTER VII

REINHARDT AS STAGE-DIRECTOR

BY ARTHUR KAHANE

[The psychological basis of Reinhardt's rôle as *regisseur*, growing out of his innate equipment as an actor, has been sketched by von Hofmannsthal. An intimate glimpse of the concrete means and processes by which Reinhardt fulfills this rôle of *regisseur* is herewith afforded through the sympathetic and observing eyes of Arthur Kahane, his literary adviser for the last twenty years.—THE EDITOR.]

MAX REINHARDT is the latest great name in the theatrical life of Berlin in particular and of Central Europe at large. In this first quarter of the century, he is the only prominent man who has helped to spread the fame of German theatrical art far beyond the frontiers of the country. It was he who recreated the stage manager's art and carried it up to heights reached by no one before him. Those who have come after him, have been his pupils. Whether intentionally or not, they have imitated him. They have been his disciples; although, in justified rebellion, they may even have pursued opposite paths. Nothing happens on the contemporary German stage, as far as the artistic aspect is concerned, which does not find its source in him, nothing which has not passed through him, nothing which is not done as a protest against him.

MAX REINHARDT AND HIS THEATRE

In one way or another his influence is always present. No one has yet surpassed him. The only one who can perform that feat is Reinhardt himself.

Max Reinhardt left Berlin and Germany, because criticism resulting from lack of understanding has ruined his most cherished achievement, the Grosses Schauspielhaus, which he created and constructed. He left also because, with wise and prophetic intuition, he foresaw the impending breakdown of the artistic theatre, a catastrophe which is now actually in process, and he refused to be a party to that calamity.

Reinhardt made his start as a very successful character actor in Otto Brahm's ensemble at the Deutsches Theater, at that time Germany's foremost theatre. About twenty-five years ago he founded an artistic cabaret, "Schall und Rauch," which he soon transformed into the Kleines Theater, a more intimate playhouse. Here he scored his first great successes with plays by Gorky, Wedekind and Oscar Wilde. Soon after, he was made director of the Neues Theater, where he triumphed with the plays of Shakespeare. In 1905 he became director of the Deutsches Theater, on whose stage he had made his Berlin debut as an actor. Next he conceived the idea of a more intimate playhouse, for chamber-plays, after the analogy of chamber-music, and with that purpose in view he built the Kammerspiele. Finally, in bold contrast, he built the colossal temple of the people's art, the Grosses Schauspielhaus, the so-called "Theatre of the Five Thousand." In the course of many years of work, he had gathered for these three theatres and had trained a wonderful ensemble of the best actors in Germany. By their aid he had pro-

[76]

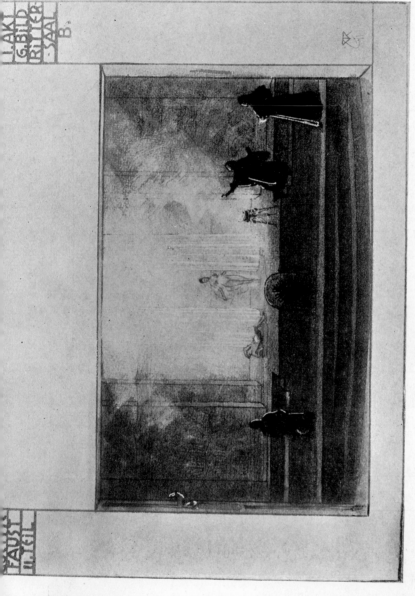

"FAUST II"

At the Deutsches Theater, February, 1911

Act I, Scene VI, The Appearance of Helene, Designed by Alfred Roller

THE SHIMMERING AND TRAGIC BEAUTY OF SPRING

A Setting Designed by Karl Walser for Frank Wedekind's "Frühlingserwachen" ("The

duced a repertory which included everything, from the Greeks, Shakespeare, Calderon, Molière, Gozzi, Goethe, Schiller and Lessing, from the *"Sturm und Drang"* writers of the early nineteenth century, a period of great political upheaval, up to the romanticists, such as Lenz, Kleist and Büchner, to Tolstoy, Strindberg, Wedekind, von Hofmannsthal, Oscar Wilde, Maeterlinck, and down to the most modern playwrights like August Stramm.

No wonder he was loth to see his life-work imperilled by the irresistibly progressing commercialization of the artistic theatre, a process which is visible in the displacement of the ever-changing repertory system by long runs of single plays, in the relaxation of the artistic standard of the ensemble, through "stars." Economic exigencies; diminished appreciation of cultural values, one of the consequences of the war; competition by the financially stronger film industry; resulting corruption and indifference among the actors; growth of labor and other industrial organizations, as detrimental to real art as the trusts of the moneyed interests in the theatrical business—all these factors are digging the grave of the artistic theatre. Reinhardt was wise enough to escape from personal contact with "this terror without end." He left in time. The right moment is waiting for him, and he is waiting for the right moment, to return. Of course, since he left, the German stage of today is lonesome, without a centre, biding its time.

One period of Reinhardt's career, therefore, is closed and in its light it is possible to review his work and personality. Many have done it before, both friends and enemies, with devotion or hatred. Permit me to do it

[77]

with a more intimate perspective. Why should just those who know the real Reinhardt, always remain mute? Such silence and bashfulness may be very discreet and noble. But just because of it, every rumor, spread by friend and foe, crystallizes little by little in false legends and distorts his picture. Foregoing distance and that cold objectivity which is nothing after all but a form of veiled fault-finding, it may be permissible for once to reveal how those closest to him see him, how they view his work, his development, his importance. I am willing to assume whatever blame there may be. Art and artists sometimes need love without disparagement more than they do strict justice.

I shall not speak of Reinhardt's human qualities, unknown to most men and misrepresented by so many. Nor of the qualities which preëminently make him a stage director: his intensity, his industry, his unrelenting energy, his most acute judgment of men, his psychic gifts. I desire to speak only of how his stage-direction became articulate, what avenues of expression he opened up to the theatre, what new conceptions his endeavors have given us of the interrelation between drama and theatre. In doing this, I need not undervalue the importance of other stage-directors, both those who preceded him, and those who disagreed with him. His artistic achievement is of such stature that it should be viewed and judged only by its own results, always taking into account, of course, the background of historic development.

Reinhardt roots firmly in the realistic atmosphere of the nineties. The naturalistic influence of his early years has remained effective throughout his entire development.

[78]

Of course, today realism does not mean everything to him any more; it is no longer a fetish, a creed, a system, an end in itself. It is only a method, a form of expression. True, the first attempt to find his own interpretation of art was a rebellion against the domineering, sober drabness and narrowness of the stage; it was the result of his longing for color and form, for festivity and joy, for purer sensuousness, for expanding rhythm. And yet, during his entire development, through all his fantastic undertakings up to those of the most monumental proportions, a stern appreciation of true reality never left him. When he began to expand the decorative possibilities of the stage, he sought primarily to enhance the dramatic effect by accentuating the reality of the surrounding objects in form, dimensions, etc. Herein lies the explanation of his use of massive walls and doors, of live trees, an attempt to enhance the illusion more for the sake of the actor than for the spectator.

Thus, among the trends of his time, it was naturalism which influenced his development, sharpening his sense for reality, yet simultaneously creating in him a longing for an art more fanciful. Another important factor in his growth was the strong tendency in all fields of artistic endeavor, to do justice once more to the material in hand and to recognize no laws but those inherent in the material. Reinhardt's material was the theatre. Not the dramatist alone, not the actor; neither of the two must dominate. The poet's work and the actor; the latter's dynamic power and his reserve, his voice and his silence; and music; and paintings; and dancing; and the building, with all its potential qualities; and the audience, with all its sensitiveness. All these make up his material. He knows its very essence and laws; and he knows that all these factors can and must undergo further development. Therefore, he does not feel bound by the experiences of others. To mention only one phase: how persistent he is in his endeavors to establish a closer contact between stage and audience; how often has he succeeded in making the scene more than an animated window! One purpose he has followed, from the small hall of the Kleines Theater (at that time probably more out of necessity than of choice), through the intimacy of the Kammerspiele, to the monumental expanses of the Grosses Schauspielhaus; from the "Flowery Path" in the pantomime through the forestage in "Hamlet" and "Othello," to the open circus-arena of "Oedipus," a stage without curtain, in the very midst of an audience which almost becomes co-actor, chorus, in the antique manner. All these are steps toward the same aim, conceived and enlarged in intentful consequence. Again and again, this will finds its way, refusing to look upon building and audience as something permanent, unchangeable. These, too, it molds and alters when necessary in order to intensify the effect.

The theatre for the theatre! The theatre which Reinhardt believes in with all the ardor of the builder, with all the devotion the artist has for his material. The theatre which to him is that higher unit wherein all the powers he utilizes coalesce in a process, not of mere addition, but of multiplication. To him, the theatre is not the willing servant of literature, satisfied with producing preconceived scenes in as correct and intelligible a manner as possible. Neither is it an institution with the purpose

SHAKESPEAREAN FARCE IN FORMAL VEIN

"The Comedy of Errors" as Produced at the Kammerspiele, October, 1910

THE BALCONY SCENE FROM "ROMEO AND JULIET"

Alexander Moissi as Romeo and Camilla Eibenschütz as Juliet in the Production at
the Deutsches Theater, January, 1907

of exhibiting individual actors without harmonious coöp-
eration. To him this theatre is far more—an atmos-
pheric, strange, mysterious, wonderful thing, "created to
be seen, prepared to be heard," dependent on and appeal-
ing to the senses. A thing in itself, following its own
laws, its own path. A *theatrum mundi*. A something
which is in intimate contact with the spirit of the age,
always ready to feel, and to make felt, the pulse of the
age, always under its influence and always prepared to
exert its influence. To him, every new production is a
new world which he creates; he views the dramatist's
conception with the eyes of our time, he fills it with the
forces of our time, with his own experiences, his reminiscences of former moods and emotions, his own knowledge
of life and human beings. And he reproduces them in
the hearts of the people of today with all the means his
material offers—colors, forms, sounds. This is the
strongest feature of his art: the directness and freshness
with which he can view every drama, as if it had never
been played before; and the intensity of his conception
with which he intuitively feels the essential character of
a drama. Only this essential character is of importance,
whether it be soul, atmosphere, basic idea, leading motive.
By this essential feature, a dramatic work becomes an
entity, a world in itself. In the true sense, every great
masterpiece means the creation of a new world, an entire
world in itself, strictly limited, rounded-off, constructed
on a great principle, for which the term "idea" is insuf-
ficient. To be an entire world, it needs its own lights
and shadows, its own beauty and ugliness, its heaven and
its hell, its moments of exaltation and of absurdity. But

[81]

only one sun must shine in this masterpiece, a sun which illumines everything out to the remote corners and the fringes. By this one light the masterpiece grows beyond itself, becomes more than accidental, meaningless activity. Let us admit that Reinhardt often treats the action as secondary, in his feeling for the essential. Frequently, his most beautiful achievements have been like fantasies, played on all his instruments as accompaniment to the one principal theme.

By this method of delving into a poetic masterpiece until he has discovered its inmost nature, and then of using all his material as variations of the essential theme, he has found a new principle: that every masterpiece has its own style, in action as well as in decoration. It became his task to harmonize anew all the elements under his control—play, players, decorations—and by their effective interplay to let the true rhythmic style of the drama emerge into the foreground. As one selects for a given part that actor who seems to be uniquely fitted to the rôle (for only the unique event is of real value in art), so Reinhardt selected for a given play that painter whom he considered best fitted for the task. Always, however, he established proper contact between the individual imagination of the painter, the throbbing organism of the whole work, the nature of the actors, and his own basic conceptions. Again and again he has succeeded in forging into one great entity all of the heterogeneous elements. Every one of his creations is a new entity. Every one has achieved something which the stage scarcely knew before Reinhardt: the atmosphere of the work.

Atmosphere has been present in every one of Rein-

A STREET SCENE IN "ROMEO AND JULIET"

A Design by Karl Walser for the Production at the Deutsches Theater, January, 1907

THE TRAGIC FINALE OF "ROMEO AND JULIET"

Camilla Eibenschütz as Juliet and Alexander Moissi as Romeo in the Production at the Deutsches Theater, January, 1907

hardt's productions. Whenever possible, he makes it felt in the first scene. You know from the start what he considers essential; you feel it, like an aura surrounding the characters of his plays. In "A Midsummer Night's Dream," the infatuation of the forest, where human and super-human disport themselves in amorous nonsense. How different the mysterious, unreal fairy woods in "Pelleas"! In "Kabale und Liebe" ("Love and Intrigue"), the dull depressing closeness of those rooms which awakens a great desire for the freedom outside. In "Minna," a serene, amicable, clean, correct hilarity. In "Elektra," confining, cyclopean walls, as inescapable as fate. In "Salome," a night of most fervid, oriental sensuality. In "The Merchant of Venice," the singing, humming city with its elegance and the effervescent joy of life. In "Aglavaine and Sélysette," the melancholy of delicate, sensitive, soulful characters. The low ceiling in the home of the lower middle class family of philistines in "Das Friedensfest" ("The Coming of Peace"), with their self-tortures and animosities. The almost unreal transient impression of the delicate stage pictures of "Frühlingserwachen" ("The Awakening of Spring"). The frolicking, rollicking clownishness of "Twelfth Night." The farcical improvisation of "The Taming of the Shrew," a spirit borrowed direct from the actor Shakespeare. The well-measured, austere grandeur of "Don Carlos." The rococo-rhythm in "Clavigo," peopled with its men-of affairs. The heavenly bliss of enamored folly and of great love in "As You Like It" and "Stella." The mood of minuet in Molière. In the pantomime, "The Miracle," and in the mystery plays, "The Great World-Theatre"

[83]

and "Everyman," the impassioned and ecclesiastic-religious ecstasies of the great masters of the baroque period to whom, as ancestors of his art, Reinhardt feels related in form and sentiment. "King Lear," carried to the extremes of the fabulous and the barbaric. "Hamlet" and "Othello," with the simplest of stage decorations and with all the emphasis on the psychological problems, acted on a forestage in the midst of the audience, so that the faintest mental vibration, the most delicate psychic emotion is transmitted from the actor to the spectator. And then again, on a dark stage, bathed in radiant light, a head, an incessantly laboring, brooding, meditating head—"Faust."

Throughout the entire series, there is a more and more apparent advance toward simplicity, toward the absolutely essential.

Inasmuch as Reinhardt's methods seem to me to have little in common with what is usually considered "stage-management," I should like to sketch, in broad lines, the typical steps he takes before presenting a new play. In the first period, he remains alone with his work, usually on one of his short vacation trips. The work begins on the train. For a time, at least, he is not interrupted by telegrams, reports, the burdens of his office. He desists from all reading which is not related to the new drama and its sphere. Thus he makes it possible to live for weeks alone with his thoughts concentrated on the piece and its characters, until he is thoroughly familiar with them. The result of this activity is a book with stage directions. It begins with a temporary outline for the space which will be necessary. Reinhardt's imagination needs this space as a premise, within which he will create his composition. Then he endeavors, so to speak, to give physical form to the text, describing in the most minute details and in a continuous series all situations, positions and expressions. Thus, by the very reality of his technical means, he re-models and reworks the entire drama, provides lyric para-phrases, scenic directions and hints for the actor.

When this book is finished, the first picture of the en-tire work stands ready before his eyes; also the entire plan for the ensuing preparations, for the dramaturgy, for the music, for the distribution and studying of the parts. The dramaturgist's task is to save as much as possible of the dramatist's original form and arrangement, the only or-ganic form.

Then, still at the working desk, the conferences begin with the painter and the technical manager. Reinhardt indicates the style, the general atmosphere, the main prob-lems of stage-management, the essential requirements of the play. Sketches are then made. Now comes the most difficult task, to arrange and combine the individual scenes so that they can all be placed on the revolving stage. Models are being built, improved, changed. Thus entire homes, houses, towns are constructed. The stage-manager becomes almost an architect. Both arts, after all, have a great deal in common. The greatest advantage of these activities on the revolving stage, it seems to me, lies in the fact that the scenic-manager is compelled to repeat the inner architecture of a play with the parallel construction of his external pictures; he is forced "to live in the totality of the drama."

Letters to the composer. All parts which require music are indicated. Their sense and meaning are explained in the most minute details—a continuous interpretation which, once more, analyzes the finer texture of the drama, this time considered from the standpoint of its musical possibilities. Here, perhaps, is the most attractive, the most interesting, period; for in nothing does Reinhardt come closer to the spirit of a dramatic masterpiece than through music, probably because the element of music is very strong in him, stronger than his sense of color.

Distribution of rôles. When choosing the most appropriate style, the human material at one's disposal has to be considered. The actor who plays in everyday, unadorned manner requires "real" scenery. The actor who is blessed with grace and beautiful gesture, whose voice is of musical timbre, requires a characteristic style. The realistic gesture, the artist of many changes, must not play before stylized curtains. The actor of finest psychic variations can not act before huge monumental scenery. An actor whose strength lies in suppressed passion, in animated silence, requires more reality in the surroundings than one whose most distinctive art is the spoken word. Reinhardt is always ready to consider the wishes of the actors, if they are mature artists who know their own qualifications; for a passionate joy in the rôle is half the battle. Of course, between actor and manager there exists a natural divergence of tendencies; the actor attempts to demonstrate, with all the means in his control, the full range of his nature; the manager demands from him only that which he, and nobody else, can do, not what he can do as well or a little better than another. Reinhardt desires to spur the actor on, however, within his limitations, to reach beyond himself, always to push on to new surprises and developments of his nature. Out of this divergence arises the incessant struggle between actor and manager, a struggle which begins when the parts are assigned and which is decided at the rehearsals, by the victory of the stronger. In Reinhardt's case, the stronger one is usually Reinhardt.

Finally, after all this preliminary work, rehearsal begins. The imaginary picture is to be transposed into reality. At the same time, reality is called on to revise the picture which the imagination has conceived. It is not Reinhardt's desire to preserve tenaciously this original conception in all its details and to let it gradually petrify. Instead, he aims to transpose it into real, organic life and to nurture it from all available fountains. Therefore, from the experiences gathered at the daily rehearsals, he molds his own vision. Therefore, he trains every actor individually. If one of them is unable to follow Reinhardt's path and chooses his own, the master does not object and is satisfied at finding him his proper place in the ensemble. Sometimes he even alters the entire work to conform with the actor's work. In such cases, he often stimulates the actor, within his individual mode to achievements of which the latter has never dreamed. He leads everyone to disclose his innermost nature. He forces everyone to give his very best, to use all available means —now by most intensive labor during rehearsals, then by individual study after the rehearsals; here by opposition, there by chagrin, by nervousness. In the end, everyone, even the least, gives more than he himself believed he possessed. The same holds true with the masses, the

[87]

chorus, which at first are trained with the precision of an orchestra, separate from other rehearsals, and which later are added to the entire picture and swept away by the intensity of the whole. Every succeeding rehearsal brings new changes, new suggestions for more eloquent effects. Thus, the work is never finished, not even at the dress rehearsal. What is more, on the day of the first performance, Reinhardt cuts, changes, abandons, so that an atmosphere of most intense energy remains and increases, up to the final hour before the curtain rises.

Reinhardt's importance as a stage-director, it seems to me, comprises these factors: that he has rebuilt the theatre on its own true foundations; that he masters, in the widest sense, his material, viz. the theatre; that he opens up fresh possibilities for this material; that in his own work, he has found a new and individual connection with the dramatist's work and finally, that throughout his entire endeavors, a desire has been present, as of a Prometheus, to create his own world. In sum, he has succeeded in expressing his own personality and his own experiences in the creation of a real world, a world in which there is everything: beauty and hideousness, heaven and hell, angel's wings and cloven hoofs. Just like any true world, even that of our dear Lord, Reinhardt's theatre world is imperfect: but it is a world.

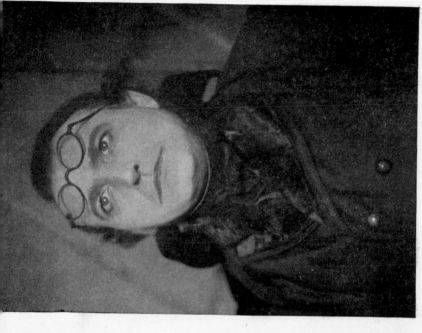

As Robespierre in Rolland's "Danton"

Photographs by Zander & Labisch, Berlin

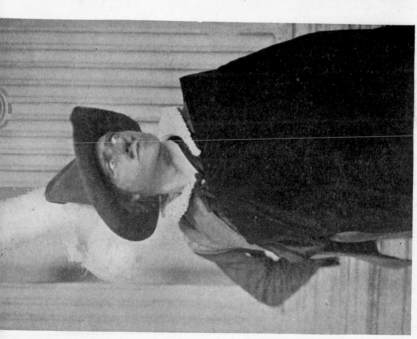

As Cyrano de Bergerac

WERNER KRAUSS IN TWO CONTRASTING FRENCH RÔLES

As Shylock in "The Merchant of Venice"　　　As King Lear

Photographs by Zander & Labisch, Berlin

WERNER KRAUSS IN TWO SHAKESPEAREAN RÔLES

Chapter VIII

THE REINHARDT MACHINE

BY MARSDEN HARTLEY

[The Reinhardt Machine has been a byword of the European theatre for many years. Its reputation lost little time in spreading to America. To the continental mind, it was a curiosity with its far-flung organization, enlisting the staffs of three institutional stages and numberless guest enterprises and traveling companies. To the American mind, it typified the spirit of efficient organization, which, strangely enough, we have developed everywhere except in our theatre. Perhaps just because of this ironic comparison and contrast, it remained for an American artist and critic living abroad, like Marsden Hartley, to write of the Machine and its significance with illuminating perspective.—THE EDITOR.]

IT seems a long, long time since we saw that charming first presentation of "Sumurûn" by the Reinhardt company at the Casino Theatre in New York. Until then we were ignorant of that kind of simplicity, that kind of directness, that kind of theatrical relativity. And that idea of having the actors come up formally or informally out of the audience, so interesting then, had never been presented before in the modern style and surely never before in America. It was all new, agreeable, delightful, and illusory in the best theatrical sense.

[89]

MAX REINHARDT AND HIS THEATRE

It seems, I repeat, a long time since then, and it even seems a huge gap since nineteen fourteen and fifteen when I heard here in Berlin those wheels of the Reinhardt theatrical mill grind out five hours of elaborated "Faust," literally on wheels. And I do not know whether in any other place in the world there is a theatre in which everything is produced on a revolving stage, as well as whole cycles of Shakespeare, the long "Blue Bird," and no end of smaller dramatic tricks of the modern stage.

I suppose that certainly in none of the countries I have lived in during the stretch of these years, has there ever been, since the time of pioneers like Augustin Daly, a greater and more powerful ensemble than was to be seen nightly at the Deutsches Theater here in Berlin. A long list of names is necessary to show this aspect of it alone, and I can register through memory only the major of them, names such as Max Pallenberg, Alexander Moissi, Paul Wegener, Wilhelm Winterstein, Werner Krauss, Gertrud Eysoldt, Else Heims, Maria Fein, Tilla Durieux, Leopoldine Konstantin, Maria Carmi, with an extended list of names that I do not now recall. It was in all best respects a real first grade theatrical machine with all the perfections, the regularities and the defects of a machine, perhaps too well organized. It gave, I mean to say, almost too powerfully the great dramas of the classics, as well as those more or less important plays of the moderns; and the labor involved for its director as well as its staff must have been tremendous, not to say endless.

I admit I am much more in sympathy with the "perishable" than with the "durable" theatre as expressed so attractively by Gordon Craig. I learn from this phrase alone, "the perishable theatre," why I like the American theatre more than any other I have seen, and I wish I could feel somewhere within me the same degree of praise or at least personal response for this powerful demonstration of "the durable theatre" or for any other German idea of the theatre, where if they do invariably present a marvellously working machine, with countless technical novelties, I am always left in a state of exhaustion with the severity of the handling and the seriousness with which the idea of the theatre is taken here. But I must interpose, of course, in defense of the idea of durable, as well as in defense of the idea of perishable, that my eye and mind call for trivial excitements of the moment, and I am not qualified to sit for hours and listen to the grinding out of human philosophy and the effects of boring human conflict for the sake of a producer's skill.

I have seen nothing of Reinhardt's personal presentations since "The Blue Bird," save "Orpheus in the Underworld" of Offenbach, nothing of the Reinhardt idea since the "Faust" and Shakespeare days of the Deutsches Theater in nineteen fourteen and fifteen, other than that quite unusual pantomime, "The Miracle" of Karl Vollmoeller, given in the gigantic Zirkus Busch, one of the forerunners of the most gigantic theatrical machine in the world, the Grosses Schauspielhaus. And what comes to me now is the memory of the most powerful capacity for taking infinite theatrical pains, which becomes, according to this application of the adage, theatrical genius. No one can possibly deny this genius to Reinhardt, the strongest influence in the last and the present decade—in Europe certainly, and most probably in the world.

MAX REINHARDT AND HIS THEATRE

I am not one who approves utterly of the German idea of the stage, of the solid forms worked out by this machine. That does not mean that I do not respect its thoroughness, its capacity for making huge units out of simple ideas or out of great spectacles. There is no denying that the Reinhardt influence is the most important and the most valuable one from the general theatrical point of view, and will without doubt have no legitimate successor. It has had thousands of illegitimate imitators, the illegitimate imitations being perhaps most conspicuous on our own New York stage. There is no question whatever that all this technical rendering is of devout importance to the young producer, but I do maintain that the result will not be the same with us; it must not have the symbolic stress peculiar to the spirit of Reinhardt as well as peculiar to the Teutonic soul in general.

Reinhardt has probably handled the largest theatrical quantities outside of wars, volcanic eruptions, fires, railroad wrecks, and the like equivalents in the spontaneous theatre, and he is, of course, entitled to high praises for his mechanical knowledge and use of these factors. I suppose there is no theatre in Europe today that may not be called a Reinhardt theatre, in one way or another. The mere intervention of cubism and cubistic relativities does not change the prevailing note and the permanent effect on the mind. That is, of course, taking liberties with anyone who has a passionate preference for a Jacques Copeau, or the still newer intervention of the Moscow Art Theatre, in all probability closer to the idea of the mechanical theatre which is pure photography of human experience. And one can say equally that there is no theatre in existence which is not a Gordon Craig theatre, since every prevailing genius of the stage has at one time or another made reference to and direct use of the Craig idea of space and mass and movement. And I am relieved with Craig's idea of the durable and the perishable, as well as with my own feeling for the spontaneous. I only know that I can not hold out a performance of the durable theatre, because I am always and everlastingly made to believe that life is terrible, that life is important, and that we are forever to be reminded of ourselves and our spiritual and moral and intellectual perversities.

But this is not to say that the Reinhardt influence has not been and is not probably the greatest influence of these last fifteen and probably the next fifteen or fifty years, for who can say or lay a finger on the precise moment when an influence has ceased to exercise its power? The Reinhardt machine is a powerful machine, and has spread a technical gospel which can not readily be discarded, and probably from the mechanical point of view is the greatest that ever has been invented.

In other words, Reinhardt has directed a machine that has applied, more greatly and more hugely than any one before him, every known idea that could come to the practical working theatre. But I have never been able to accustom myself, I merely wish to say, to the graveyard appearance and solidity of stage forms. I have always the feeling that the performance is being done just outside the *Kirchhof* where the mourners are waiting to lay away the well remembered dead; and I myself seem like one of them, for the audience is there out in the dark beyond the terrible "fourth wall" which the theatrical genius must work so laboriously to pierce, ready to lay its own coronal of leaves and tie its little band of black upon a superficial sleeve. But there is the crystallization of the Reinhardt impulse, the Reinhardt ambition, the Reinhardt triumph before us, and no room for questioning. Reinhardt did upset the stage of his time by remaking it in terms of a new theatrical language, which, if it seems to us now somewhat mechanical, somewhat rhetorical in its insistence, still retains its Miltonian power to impress the theatrically inclined. And it is through him that the theatrical machine of modern times has been made workable, solid, and dare I say again, almost depressingly workable. One longs for the accidental that happens through sheer childishness, shining pleasantly out over the lights, instead of all this ponderous buckling of an after all easily fitting and pleasant shoe.

Reinhardt has the great gift to impress seriously, Cohan to impress radiantly and lightly. But when I hear that Reinhardt loved the lights of Broadway and that he was amazed to see how much real acting talent there is in America, I realize that Reinhardt, being human, does enjoy theatrical ideas quite the opposite of his own, that having the symbolical wish is no special hindrance toward the enjoyment of the trivial, and I please myself with the thought that in the end, many things please, many things may interest, many things amuse, though after all one's own way is the best way, and while Reinhardt keeps to the historical size and the mural value of theatrical ideas, I return to the good lights of Broadway and to all those graceful and radiant silhouettes which we know as the American musical comedy or the Revue, with a per-

As Henry IV

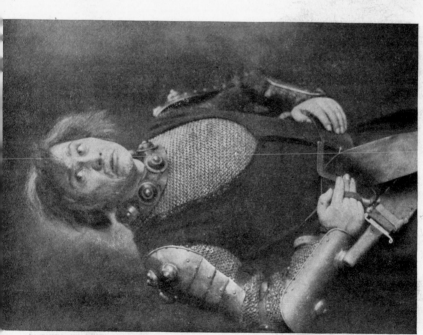

As Macbeth

Becker & Maass, Berlin

PAUL WEGENER IN TWO OF HIS MOST CELEBRATED RÔLES

Photographs by Becker & Maass, Berlin

ALEXANDER MOISSI

sonal satisfaction, as well as a definite personal need for release from all that is meant and attained by the solid, durable theatre.

In Europe, I am reminded constantly of the fabulous country to which I belong, and to which all hounded and driven souls in this part of the world are eager to flee, the land where flowers and fruits are made out of silver and gold, and human eyes have the light of blue white diamonds from Kimberley in them.

After having inspected all the mechanism of the Reinhardt machine in its entirety here in Berlin, from dungeons to ceilings, noted with amazement the astounding organization of mechanics as instituted in the Grosses Schauspielhaus alone, looking down from the electrician's loft through his own peephole—down, down there among the stalactites of the huge ceiling behind which all the lights are concealed, noting the little black dots created by the vast public, and the small square section of the huge orchestra, noted, as I say, all the vastness of the machinery, the various layers of telescope flooring surrounding the revolving stage itself, the huge dome, with those enormous sections of apparatus for creating effects upon the horizon, and far up in the higher regions the complicated machinery for creating moving and stationary cloud effects, with special electrical machinery for the stars alone, the great organ on one side of the stage, the electrical loft upon the left with its incomprehensible keyboards looking like elaborated linotype machines, no end of switches and wheels—my thoughts return to the little man at the back of it all, he who saw the idea to the surface, and saw it through to its present magnificent end, and I can only

[95]

say with the rest of the world, "remarkable little man, this man Reinhardt, tiny little human being with the huge theatrical mentality. Without question the greatest theatrical mentality of all time from the practical working point of view." For no one has produced theatrical volume and theatrical quantity in a more marvellous way than he, none has taken the earlier forms and made them over into terms suitable to our times, and made a new language out of them for the days in which we live—the days of the mechanical era, into which he has introduced a great mechanical invention out of an old and simple toy.

And I came to wondering why, with all these vast toys at his disposal, the spirit of the man forsook it, and only hints of the mind remained. Did he weary of his terrible labors, did he weary of producing so much theatric organism, so many first rate theatrical talents which are now dispersed in all the best theatres of Berlin? Did he long for rest from his great labors, or for new spaces to conquer, new tempers, new spiritual renderings of ideas old to him, new problems to exercise old powers? Or does he perhaps wish for the rest of his life just to sit quietly on a hill watching nature carrying out her own well-organized effects in the most perfect theatre of all, the spontaneous theatre?

My own mind wandered out from all this theatricality to the new eruptions of Aetna, and returned to the stage door of the Deutsches Theater, where, in the shadow of the early evening, stood a blue black raven with scrutinizing eyes, while "Potash and Perlmutter" was being indifferently rendered inside.

"Who is this young melancholy actor, this relative

[96]

As Salome in Oscar Wilde's Tragedy

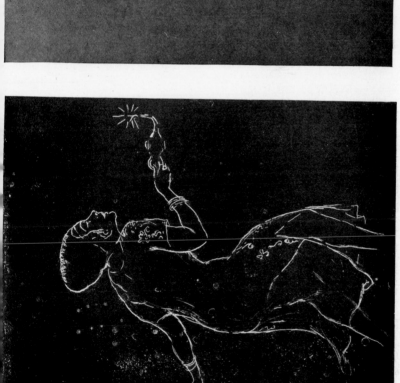

In "The Legend of Joseph"

From an Original Lithograph by Emil Orlik

TWO ASPECTS OF THE PASSIONATE ART OF TILLA DURIEUX

Photographs by Becker & Maass, Berlin

LEOPOLDINE KONSTANTIN

LEOPOLDINE KONSTANTIN AND JOHANNA TERWIN

of him who sat above the bust of Pallas quoting that one terrible word over and over again to the frightened corners of that magical chamber?" And the usher who had shown us over the Reinhardt theatrical plant so generously and patiently replied, "He is the friend of the master mechanic, and he will remain here at this door until his friend calls for him, and he knows that he will come without fail."

The contrast between this actor in the spontaneous theatre and the greatest theatrical machine of the world was inspiring and restful and my mind went over almost sentimentally to the little black bird that brought me so much relief for the imagination, after having seen this majestic theatrical ship at anchor waiting for the captain who perhaps will never come again.

I shall never forget the little black bird, when many other events will pass away from the memory, and I returned to contemplation of this little man of fifty, thinking that in the end it is perhaps only little men that do the big things of the world, since it is little men who have so often made and destroyed nations, those powerful actors in the spontaneous theatre called the world.

It is no small accomplishment—this greatest theatrical machine in all the world, triumph of the years that have been, triumph of the many years that are to come, without question bearing its everlasting influence on the practical rendition of the imaginative problems of the dramatic and poetic mind.

CHAPTER IX

REINHARDT AND THE ACTOR

[Although his reforms in stage settings, mechanism and lighting and his revolutionary experiments in the general technique and theory of the theatre, have absorbed the major part of the attention devoted to Reinhardt for the last twenty years, there is little doubt that his talent for discovering and training actors for his ensemble is an even more important factor in his substantial and continuing success. Without the actor, mechanism is mute and theories still theories. The importance of this subject, therefore, justifies its treatment by several hands who can approach it from divergent angles, ranging from the intimate relationships between the *regisseur* and the individual actor to his molding of the impersonal crowds of the chorus in his mass productions. This symposium is introduced by Gertrud Eysoldt, one of the most important of Reinhardt's discoveries among untrained acting talent and one of the most celebrated of the "Reinhardt actors," and it is continued by other associates and critics from first hand experience and observation.—The Editor.]

I

HOW REINHARDT WORKS WITH HIS ACTORS

BY GERTRUD EYSOLDT

MORNING. The rehearsal is about to begin. Daylight in the dusty morning-gray of the theatre. A groping through the dark rows of the parquet, hands feeling

Photographs by Becker & Maass, Berlin

CAMILLA EIBENSCHÜTZ

In Karl Vollmoeller's Version of Carlo Gozzi's "Turandot"

AGNES SORMA

In the Title Rôle of Lessing's "Minna von Barnhelm"

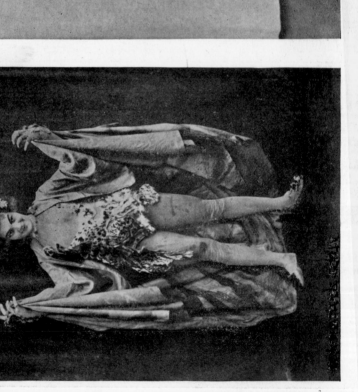

Photographs by Becker & Maass, Berlin

As a Courtesan in "The Comedy of Errors"

As Puck in "A Midsummer Night's Dream"

their way along the back of the seats. The eyes blind with darkness. The stage ahead a light cutout in a hazy blue glow. A faded daylight falls in streaks from above through the flies. The stage is empty—two scene walls, fastened together, are leaning against one side. This emptiness of the stage. Its purity. So touching to the actor. Like a stretched but untouched canvas for the painter.

The actors come one after another. Slow, ill-humored, drowsy. Reserve in every feature. The attitude of saving up for something. Complete inertia. Reinhardt's face and figure reveal themselves through the dark in front of the first row parquet seats. The actors blink down at him with sidewise glances. Something stirs within them, although they seem indifferent. There is a blending of the fighting spirit and unrest. Reinhardt has his book in his hand. His features are apathetic. Morning pushes all of these night-folk wearily ahead of her. Fantasy is settled all about, absolutely motionless. And we know we must set her free. We are afraid. Great energy is needed for that. What you win in the prosiness of a morning rehearsal lives doubly in the inspiration of the night. The artificial light that now illuminates the stage insufficiently for the rehearsal does not awaken the evening mood—the streaks of daylight cut through it. And yet this hostility of the daylight that breaks in everywhere upon the brain and seeks to tear your inner life to pieces, at last fires you by contrast. Suddenly you understand how the deepest sorrows flit like shadows over white plaster at sunny noontide through the indifferent, hurrying crowd.

[99]

MAX REINHARDT AND HIS THEATRE

Reinhardt calls us out of our first lethargy. We begin hesitatingly. Shy. Listening within ourselves. Our voices sound strange to us. A sudden tone awakens us, the familiar tone of our own voices. Timidly the rhythm begins. Reinhardt's eye flashes encouraging interest. He speaks in a low voice, as you call to one who is waking from sleep. His glances are more firmly fixed on his players; we begin to move about. Again that inward hesitation. Reinhardt takes up his book, we listen— partly restless, lest we do not understand; partly timid, in affected opposition. Our hesitancy makes us feel ashamed. We lose our hold, we lack suggestive power, and we suffer. Reinhardt makes believe he lagged behind in his attention and gives us time to rally our strength. He wishes to be considerate. But the minute a sound in our voices betrays a rising of our spirits, he holds on to it tenaciously, and will not let it go. No falling back! He tortures us, drives us forward, resolves every doubt. He makes us repeat. Once more we hold the reins in our hands—tighten and loosen them, until we realize the rhythm of the pace. Once we are under way, all our repressions melt away. A rhythm of intensity and exhaustion swings us in a circle. Reinhardt grasps it, and molds it. We give ourselves up to the play. We sense our partner, his face, his eyes, his hands, his figure, his wooing, his hostility, his hopes and his strife. Reinhardt brings voices into contact, creates distances. He keeps up our enthusiasm, forces us back into the beat of the rhythm. On leaving the scene, we drop exhausted into a chair in the background, trying to quiet the tumult within us, so that we will not waste it on meaningless objects

[100]

outside the play in which we live. We control our features. And by the time we step once more on the stage, we have regained self-mastery. Relieved from all constraint, we are free in action and gracefully dance the light pace of speech. Reinhardt has his book. We have our parts. Each of us has brought his own, has studied and committed it and carries it in momentous hands. And book, and rôles, and ideas are transformed here by the stream of new minds they meet, are given new lines written in blood. Letters and thoughts become feelings— feelings, pictures in our souls. The rare wine plunges us, too, into an ocean of unreality. These dreams against the empty canvas of the stage are beautiful and vivid. Out of the morphia of inspiration, open new dimensions of the universe. We wish to live in them, we try to give them real forms. Our unsteady feet seek solid ground. Now table and chair, wall and stairway are thrust upon us; color surrounds us. This is the realm where our imagination will have to live. We give warmth to lifeless objects. The railing of the stairway is the only object by which we measure our sorrow, our pride. The chair invites our trembling knees, a window laughs love to our lips. Wind and trees speak to us. Restlessly creation stirs in us, flows into us, and forms us. Nothing has a right on the stage unless we, the actors, force it to life.

On tip-toes, one of the stage hands approaches Reinhardt and asks, over the footlights: "The red carpet is going to act, too, isn't it?" And in those words he reveals the true spirit of the theatre.

There is a deep meaning in childish play. The puzzle column of illustrated papers shows pictures with the

words: "Where is the hunter?" or "Where is the hare?"
I should like to draw a picture like this of the actors of the
Deutsches Theater, and write under it: "Where is Reinhardt?" He is there, make no mistake! In ethereal
form, between the figures on the stage, hidden in the trunk
of a tree, or in a cloud, in the outlines of a Moissi, a
Wegener, a Höflich. He peeps out of Schildkraut's
sleeve, and you see his profile in the helpless droop of the
head of a Pallenberg. He is there in the midst of them.
They are visible and you see him through their being.
They materialize him. Thus he leads a mysterious existence. He creates distances, so that objects do not col-
lide in space; then he fills the space between these objects.
He who has been with him for a while will eventually find him; though to discover him, you will have to
turn and turn the picture, and glance at it from a distance,
out of the corner of your eye. Reinhardt and his work
always remain in the background, and intentionally so,
because as he said so beautifully: "The final, the most
satisfying impression my stage affords, is never what I
achieve by working and rehearsing with the actors; it is
the actor's own personality, the secret of his being."

This expression reveals Reinhardt's own secret; the
intensity of his sensory vision which reaches far beyond
the limits of the merely visible out to dimensions where,
in art as well as in life, the mysterious realm of the infinite rises out of the gloom. There he becomes the great
magician who plays treasures into our hands. With all
his senses vibrating with conscious life, he frees the senses
of the actor. Full of emotion, he passes on to us light,
form, color and sound, and rejoices at the echo he finds

[102]

HANS WASSMANN

As Sir Toby Belch in "Twelfth Night" at the Deutsches
Theater, October, 1907

ELSE ECKERSBERG AS ILSELILL IN GERHART HAUPTMANN'S "SCHLUCK UND JAU"

Photographs by Becker & Maass, Berlin

LUCIE HÖFLICH AS GRETCHEN IN THE PRISON SCENE IN GOETHE'S "FAUST I"

TWO OF REINHARDT'S ACTRESSES IN CHARACTERISTIC RÔLES

in us. It is his joy to recreate in us his own self, multiform, protean. He lives in our blood, and deep is the contact between him and his actor. Yet only those who are true artists can own him. Weak talents dissolve his power to an impersonal void. And he knows it. He instinctively seeks the artist. Whoever departs from him without any deep personal experience, has never sensed him. Openly and secretly, we are happy in his presence. We doubt ourselves when his faith in us is shaken. We rebel when he takes no notice of us. And finally we calmly wait for him, because we realize he will come for us. At times, he is faithful to us against his own will, which begrudges the influence we have on him, and then our mutual hatred is spelled out in secret and passionate signs. Thus we face each other at rehearsals, both sides heavily laden by the first, the deepest element of our art—emotion.

II

REINHARDT PRECEPTOR OF POET AND PLAYER

BY DR. RICHARD BEER-HOFMANN

(English Translation by Lucie R. Sayler)

While others become dull as their general knowledge and special science grow greater, Reinhardt has a vitality which always makes him face a new task wholly fresh, as if it were the unique event of his life.

His strength lies perhaps in that he is closely related to the poet, and just as a poet is unable to write the same thing twice, because he simply can not endure it; just as

[103]

God, as the type of creator, would not be able to create two beings, two leaves, alike, because it would bore him, so Reinhardt would probably be paralyzed if he should be required to repeat himself. A poet, if he really is a poet, can not take the material which he saw in a certain manner in, say, 1901, and rewrite it five years later exactly as he wrote it five years before, because he himself must have changed or at least developed in these five years.

Reinhardt used often to say to me that I was a born *regisseur*. I replied to him then: "You are mistaken, I am only a born poet." That Reinhardt should say this to me is due to the fact that he has grasped something which of late years has been rather forgotten, namely, that the source of all artistic creation is *imagination*. And so Reinhardt, when he feels imagination in the poet, and since he realizes how much he himself is dependent on imagination, says to him, as the highest praise he can offer, "You are a *regisseur*."

His suggestive influence on the actor is therefore so great because the actor feels that someone is listening to him who is not only a teacher or doctor who can help him, but that someone is sitting there below who will always be as carried away as the naïve public when the actor succeeds. Whence it happens that the actor also feels that Reinhardt notices a hundred things, besides, which escape the public, and that he is thankful for them. And he knows, too, that whatever success he will have in the evening, he has had his most responsive public in Reinhardt at rehearsals.

I find that Reinhardt has had the worst influence on many poets. For many poets who have no very strong vision of their own and no precise conception of how the figures of the characters whom they let talk should actually look, write scenes consisting for the most part of dialogue, without thinking of what the atmosphere of these scenes, and their pictorial, musical, and spiritual values must be. When they see these scenes put on the stage by Reinhardt, they are so astonished to observe things which existed only on paper (and would have remained only on paper if they had not had the good luck to be produced by Reinhardt) acquire so much actual life, music, atmosphere and soul, that they (the poets) depend entirely on Reinhardt from then on, and make only outlines, with the assurance that Reinhardt will supply what is wanting in poetry. And Reinhardt himself has received these plays not unwillingly, for he found therein the opportunity to do what he wished in the depth of his heart to do, and did: be a poet or at least collaborate in the creation of poetry. But I repeat that he exercised the worst influence over these poets, for they were probably not real poets.

The others, however, the real poets, owe him a great deal. For when they give their plays to the public under other auspices, they have the feeling that they will be in great measure misinterpreted, and that it will not even help to have a great actor take part in them, for the actor can express only his own rôle; he can not control the whole play. Here they have the comfort of knowing that there is an administrator who is determined to carry out not only the poet's last will, but his wishes from first to last, and to translate the poetic vision into stage vision so that not only none of the spiritual effect is lost, but it gains a new and surprising illumination.

MAX REINHARDT AND HIS THEATRE

It is worth noting that actors who came to Reinhardt without name, often won a reputation in a short time, which they again lost as soon as they left Reinhardt. For a while what they had learned retained its influence, but as soon as they fell into the hands of other *regisseurs,* or worked without a *regisseur,* a great part of their power, and likewise of their fame, was lost.

Reinhardt has the happiest way of changing his method with one and the same actor during the study of the same rôle. Under conditions which force him to do as he, Reinhardt, wishes, he will drive him to desperation, make him discouraged, until he has brought him into the direction he wants him to go: then with a casual, enthusiastic word of praise he will set the actor on his feet again in such a way that he goes into the work with stronger intensity than before.

Reinhardt does not insist always on his own will, but often brings out original ideas on the part of the actor, born of the latter's individuality, which he then, with renunciation, permits to supersede his own earlier wish.

He does not prepare for the actor a warm or a cold shower-bath or massage, but each of his rehearsals is like a steam-bath in which the actor goes from one to the other, complains often about his treatment, but at the end leaves the bath with the feeling that he has become a new man.

I understand actors to be instruments that easily become out of tune, and that they can give their best only when the strongest vitality and confidence can be given to them. I remember one incident, at which I was not present, but which was told to me later. An actress, until

MAIDI CHRISTIANS

In the Title Rôle of Lessing's "Minna von Barnhelm"

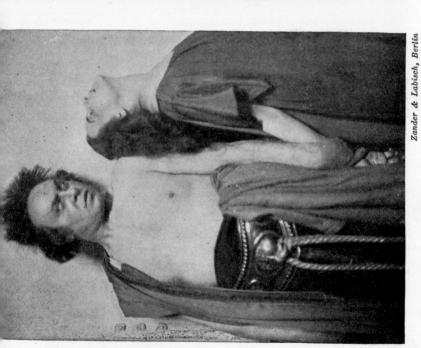

EMIL JANNINGS AS CREON AND MAIDI CHRISTIANS
AS ANTIGONE

In "Antigone" by Walter Hasenclever

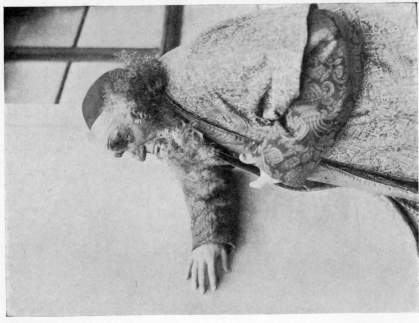

RUDOLF SCHILDKRAUT

In Schmidtbonn's "Der Verlorene Sohn" ("The Prodigal

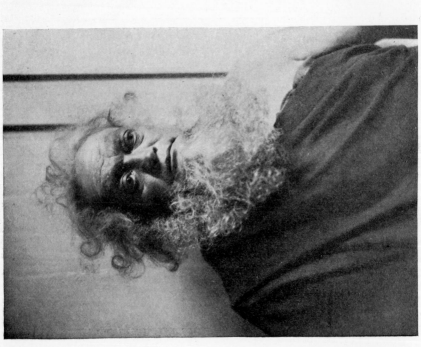

ALBERT BASSERMANN

As Shylock in "The Merchant of Venice"

then unknown, on whom high hopes were placed (her name is Wangel, and she has since left the theatre and given herself entirely to a religious movement similar to the Salvation Army), received for the first time a decisive rôle in a play, one of Oscar Wilde's, if I am not mistaken. She was so anxious and excited that in the first two acts she scarcely spoke intelligibly, and it was feared that the play—it was a première—would be a failure because of her. Reinhardt went into her dressing-room, shook her hand and said: "It will be a great success for you. The feeling in the audience is distinctly enthusiastic for you. Only go on!—perhaps a trifle louder." If that was not true at the end of those two acts, it had become truth by the end of the last one.

III

REINHARDT AND THE YOUNG ACTOR

BY ERNST DEUTSCH

Even the greatest genius among actors falls short in his personality alone, of all the suggestive power he needs. Costume, scenery, light effects, support him. He soon realizes, however, that his achievement is nothing but a step upward on an endless ladder. No matter how ambitious and enthusiastic he may be, he feels that he needs help to attain the top. And the day comes when he sees the helping hand. He faces one who is so rich that he can afford to be a spendthrift. The nature of this wealth is nothing but the immense suggestive power which he communicates to the actor, thus enhancing to a phenomenal degree the latter's means of expression—suggestion. On facing Reinhardt, the young actor never feels overwhelmed or weakened. On the contrary, it is a process of transplantation like the budding of a tree with a sprout of superior culture.

IV

THE ARTISTS OF THE DEUTSCHES THEATER

BY WILLI HANDL

Reinhardt's stage art has only one soul and meaning: acting. Its development comes from within itself; it has no direction, no tendency; its strength, its motives, its art, are there for its own sake and serve only its own purpose. Thus the value and importance of the individual member of the ensemble grow with his own personality and out of it. The object of the revolution which Reinhardt brought about in the theatre, made the theatre its own master, gave it a worthy artistic purpose of its own. And that is the source of his manifold activities, of his continually growing wealth of achievement, of fresh promises which do not seem yet to be exhausted. Inner growth and depth have no set goal; every one carries the laws of his own development within himself; they are his secret. And where personality is the foundation, as in Reinhardt's drama, a corresponding form and style emerge quite naturally. All Reinhardt asks is that every one working with him be himself and keep on developing his

[108]

artistic faculties, in order that he may become richer, more expressive of what is beautiful in him, and more and more qualified for a stage which lives—and only for one of that kind.

Thus the group of artists around Reinhardt is a growing unit of free, independent individuals. Common work binds them from production to production. As a unit, however, they have no systematic organization. Besides, there is a continuous development and transformation.

Gertrud Eysoldt's art is conscious; a radiant, restless spirit, which controls voice and bodily gestures so that they obey the directing will almost blindly and instinctively.

Alexander Moissi is all lightning and flame, by blood inheritance from Dalmatia and Italy. Every sound of his voice, which is soft as a 'cello, every motion of his aristocratic slender body, is dictated by the imperious impulse to live in joy and beauty.

The opposite of Moissi, possessor of an almost magic mutability, is Friedrich Kayssler whose nature is strong and steady, and whose art accentuates and brings to the surface what he is and what he desires to be. He is unequalled in rôles of reserved, self-reliant virility.

Paul Wegener, with his muscular physique and highly-wrought nerves, embodies powerful expression and subtle sensibility, thus reflecting the ideal of our time.

Lucie Höflich, always delightful and at her ease in look, laughter and gesture; always direct in her plastic humor as well as in deep, tragic emotion.

Else Heims' inner gracefulness reveals itself in the

mildness of her grief and in the touching charm of her smile.

Eduard von Winterstein, who struggles for expression against the proud reserve of his genuine nature, and who is at his best in interpreting harsh defiance, mingled with undaunted kindness.

Hans Wassmann's comic parts, mad in their hilarity, are deepened by a melancholy touch of warm sympathy for human deficiencies.

Victor Arnold, a comedian of fantastic grotesqueness, is a master in giving expression to his most foolhardy fancies.

Paul Biensfeld, without fantastic arabesques in his nature, is simple and natural also in the conception of his rôles.

Wilhelm Diegelmann always conceives his comic figures—full of powerful earthborn reality—from the angle of their lack of balance, thus preventing them from being taken seriously in normal surroundings.

Adele Sandrock, whose artistic resource has always been her powerful temperament, rises to a tragic zenith in moments of passionate emotion.

The art of Rudolf Schildkraut, master of detail in character drawing, unites keenness of thought with temperamental warmth and energy.

In Camilla Eibenschütz, temperamental spontaneity mingles with conscious expression, and her erotic wit is likely to make a parody of a rôle which she herself plays with naïve serenity.

Tilla Durieux' art does not analyze, but embodies a

As King Lear, from a Drawing by August M. Frohlich

As Shylock in "The Merchant of Venice"

Hänse Herrmann, Berlin

RUDOLF SCHILDKRAUT IN TWO OF HIS MOST CELEBRATED SHAKESPEREAN RÔLES

RUDOLF SCHILDKRAUT

higher humanity, which, superior in intelligence, equanimity and self-consciousness, lives in a cultured reserve.

V

THE ACTOR OF REINHARDT'S ENSEMBLE

BY CARL HEINE

Every stage represents the individuality of its manager, especially when the dramatic text is not the sole factor of importance, but is only one of the means to a desired end. This is especially true of Reinhardt's stage—due not only to the strong influence which Reinhardt exerts on the actor but to the individual training the actor receives under Reinhardt and to the latter's individual conception of his art.

When Reinhardt began to follow the accepted principles of modern painting, that is, to consider light the primary source of all colors and to make use of light for his scenic effects, he laid the final stone to his edifice. Only by the synthesis and analysis of all form through light, did he achieve that highest form of expression which is his aim: the cooperation of all factors toward a common goal. At last it was possible to give to the hard outlines of tone, speech, gesture and motion, that flowing smoothness, that vague, dimly-defined, limitless atmosphere which is always startlingly effective, inasmuch as it distracts the eye from inconsequential detail to the infinite whole. Since that invisible vibration is present in Rein-

[111]

hardt's conception of this world, only he can educate the actor so as to adjust him to the total picture. Of that picture, Reinhardt's performances reveal distinctly only that which should be visible at the moment. Yet the uniform rhythm must not be lost. Only he can fit into the ensemble who has experienced within himself how an apparently isolated characterization serves a common end. Reinhardt's success in making this point clear to the actor, and in coaxing out of him his best qualities, even those most insignificant, is due to his ability to force the actor "to work out his own salvation."

Reinhardt persuades the actor of his own free will to surrender to the ensemble; this power of suggestion springs from the conciseness with which every figure stands before his eyes as an effective part of the total picture which he has worked out with untiring zeal. These children of his imagination, Reinhardt lays before his actor during the first rehearsal. With the patience and the keen senses of an Indian, he sneaks around the actor, and lures him into the mask of the figure he is to represent. Nourished thus through the channels of all his senses with the food prepared for him, the actor gradually grows into his task; and, released in his mind from having to give conscious support to the whole, he is able, by the inspired will of his leader, to reach the uppermost range of his possibilities in materializing the rôle given to him. Knowing that his capital will yield him generous returns, every actor submits unconditionally to Reinhardt, with the result that the least important actor of his ensemble is superior, in a sense, to the best who come from a different school.

VI

REINHARDT'S MANAGEMENT OF THE CHORUS

BY JULIUS BAB

Reinhardt's great achievement is his success, through cultural instinct and a talent for organization, in uniting the kindred elements of modern painting, poetry and stage art to a modern form of drama. Reinhardt created the neo-romantic drama, and with it a form of expression which was a demand, a necessity, of the present time. The most striking, the most original aspect of his work, is his management of the chorus.

The actor Reinhardt had two essential gifts: great inventive skill in describing a man's surroundings by hundreds of characteristic gestures and actions; and an almost frightening, sudden, explosive power, a mighty forceful accentuation.

These same fundamental qualities—an imagination rich in new ideas and pantomimic forms of expression, and a clear, powerful theatrical accentuation—reveal their most complete development in Reinhardt's handling of the chorus. The naturalistic school had tried to give to the uniform "exercises" of the chorus the appearance of a more natural agility and vivacity. It was Reinhardt, however, and only Reinhardt, who poured the fire of a passionate will into the dead mass of supers, "liquefied" it, and molded it into manifold fantastic forms.

Shakespeare, especially, has many scenes in which,

[113]

at times, great masses of people dominate the stage. In this realm Reinhardt's imaginative resources are inexhaustible. Reinhardt's chorus in "Twelfth Night" is full of burlesque gaiety. The scene at the inn in Schiller's "The Robbers" is magnificent. And so is the finale of "Lysistrata." While the masses on the stage dance and sing and embrace and celebrate, the drowsy city in the background awakens, morning dawns, distant sounds and noises mingle with the laughter of the frolicking crowd and rise to a roar, until orgiastic shrieks burst out on every hand like the giant wave of a flood breaking through the dunes.

In "Oedipus and the Sphinx," the chorus opposing Creon is divided into four groups with voices of different pitch. Each one of these groups, is a perfect unison, while all four together form a well-tuned ensemble, differentiated and harmonious at the same time.

Where the chorus is meant to be an effective background, too, its ecstatic shriek in unison has something elemental in it. In "The Merchant of Venice," it breaks the atmosphere of breathless tension, when Portia's speech suddenly takes its decisive turn. In the court scene in "A Winter's Tale," the excitement at the entrance of the queen, announced by a few words which run from mouth to mouth, suddenly engulfs the whole crowd, which foams with love and rage until it is beyond control—and then that shriek! Here an unrivalled talent for organization has made a mass of impersonal human material into an instrument of most powerful expression.

It has been said—and maybe not without reason—that in some of Reinhardt's settings, the individual actor's art is subdued by the overwhelming power which the manager Reinhardt lends to the chorus. But that is avoidable only where actors of great elemental personality maintain their balance with this great elemental stage manager. This disproportion should certainly be remedied by raising the standard of the personality of the actor —as Reinhardt tries to do by training—never by laming an imaginative power like that of Reinhardt in his management of his chorus.

CHAPTER X

REINHARDT AT REHEARSAL

BY HEINZ HERALD

[The art of the theatre is characterized by a peculiar human relationship, an intimate adjustment of one personality to another, which reaches its most fruitful, unusual and interesting phase in the process of rehearsal. But since rehearsals are usually conducted behind doors closed to the critics and since the actor does not always have the proper perspective to visualize this process objectively, it has been wholly neglected too often in writing about the work of great producing artists. Reinhardt has been fortunate enough to have several men in the literary division of his Machine whose labors have brought them in close contact with the rehearsal stage and yet have kept them far from the narrowing experience of actual participation and whose critical gifts enable them to report and interpret what they have seen. One of these literary advisers, Arthur Kahane, has already spoken on this subject in general terms, but Heinz Herald approaches it from a concrete and human viewpoint which brings to life the director at work among his artists.—THE EDITOR.]

To present a picture of the entire world, or at least a reflected picture of it, is a characteristic longing of our contemporary theatre. To this end, it invites the cooperation of the other arts, painting and music, and drafts to its service the highly advanced technique of our day, as

a means only, of course, to the artistic purpose. The
spiritual, not the technical influence, must dominate.
With a style of its own for each play, our stage, to be sure,
needs a highly developed technique, which, in turn, calls
for the hand of the stage manager to master it. In his
brain, the vision of the finished play must live, while he,
step by step, leads the way to its materialization.

Reinhardt was endowed with the strength and courage to attempt the reconstruction of the theatre of our
time. He is not *a*, he is *the* stage manager of his day.
Seldom has a man so completely identified himself as he
has done with the demand of an epoch, with the task in
hand. Parallels for this phenomenon we find only in the
dramatist Shakespeare, in the critic Lessing. Every
worthy achievement of the present-day theatre, every substantial promise of the theatre of the future, is, in some
way, connected with Reinhardt. And no stage of tomorrow will be able to dispense with a manager in the sense
with which Reinhardt's activity has invested the profession.

Reinhardt goes about for years with a finished or almost finished outline for a production in his mind. On
occasion—after conferences with the painter, the dramatic instructor, the musical adviser—he delays the première again and again; sometimes, if the results do not
satisfy him, even after the last rehearsal. His book of
stage directions is about the most thorough example of
its kind in existence. It represents "a complete, detailed
paraphrase of the play in the stage manager's language."
Side by side with the original text, condensed and sometimes made up of different versions and translations (Reinhardt avoids all versions and translations which destroy

the poetic rhythm)—he compiles his own text, the stage manager's text, which is often much more voluminous than the original. Everything has been taken into consideration, from the most important feature to the least: the atmosphere of every scene, of every conversation in that scene, of every sentence in that conversation. Expression, intonation, every position of the actor, every emotion, the indication of every interval, the effect on the other actors—all these details are mapped out in clear, concise words. At the beginning of each scene, there is a minute description of all the decorations, generally accompanied by drawings, together with a sketch of the stage with full explanations; there is an accurate description of the costume for every new actor, all the crossings within a scene are not only mentioned, but also sketched; the lighting and all the changes in the illumination are described; there are notes on the significance, expression, length, and volume of the music; notes on the different noises; and notes on the way in which the change of scenes is to proceed. The book of stage directions, the playbook, which contains all these elements, reminds me of a closely woven rug; in its explanations, it is a complete work without any gaps.

Now begin the conferences with the scenic artist, the dramatic instructor, the chief technician, and eventually with the composer. Reinhardt's manner of dealing with his designer differs greatly according to the personality of that artist, according to the play, and according to his own relation to it. Sometimes, Reinhardt hands only the play to the painter and expects him first to give his own ideas in regard to the scenery. Then again, he explains

[118]

Photographs by Zander & Labisch, Berlin

REINHARDT AMONG HIS COLLABORATORS

A Rehearsal Group Before the World Premiere of "Der Rosenkavalier" in Dresden, January, 1911. (Standing left to right) Max Reinhardt, Regisseur; Hugo von Hofmannsthal, Librettist; Alfred Roller, Designer. (Seated left to right) Graf Seebach, General Manager; Richard Strauss, Composer; von Schuch, Music Director.

REHEARSING AT BRESLAU

Reinhardt (seated at table) directing preparations for the "Jarhundertfestspiel 1813," produced during the Summer of 1913, with Gerhart Hauptmann, author of the pageant, standing above him, and Einar Nilson, Musical Adviser, at the far end of the table.

REINHARDT AT A REHEARSAL OF "ŒDIPUS" IN THE CIRCUS

From an Original Etching by Emil Orlik

a rough draft of his plan. A third time, the painter faces a project completely outlined, with the form of every chair designed by Reinhardt himself. Sometimes, manager and painter get together and lay out their plans in common. That is Reinhardt's way of working with Ernst Stern, because they are familiar with each other's methods. Thus the fundamental idea for the decorations in "Macbeth"—a decorative scheme more closely connected with the inner idea of the play than usual, belongs to Reinhardt: the detailed execution is Stern's; while the technical execution is the work of Dvorsky, Reinhardt's technical adviser.

The costumes, next, have to be adapted to the character of the play. They must be harmonious in their own colors. Stern, for instance, who is usually in charge of the pictorial side of a production, uses for his scenery only a limited number of colors—a scale of certain colors, excluding all the rest, for the purposes of the play in hand, as if they did not exist. From the start, care must be taken, that the sketches of the different scenes harmonize. The space on the revolving stage is extremely limited and must be used to the best advantage. Then the decorations must be executed, the costumes made. Reinhardt has found out that the details of the decorations are best made "at home" and therefore has provided his theatre with large shops, which turn out excellent work. This circumstance of his shops alone, has given Reinhardt an opportunity to experiment freely. It is his principle to consider old forms and rules as necessary and useful checks, but to shake them off energetically when his impulse to do so becomes imperious. The fascination which novelty exerts over Reinhardt, which makes him clair-voyant in the application of the latest technical achievements, and gives him the courage on occasion to break through the conventional form of our normal stage, has been attacked from many sides by those who forget that we owe to Reinhardt's activity and to his vital example, the widely acknowledged dramatic progress of the last fifteen years.

The rehearsals, of course, have started long before—as a rule simultaneously with the execution of the decorations. Reinhardt has always considered his work with the actor as the most important part of the process of production. He therefore dedicates much more time to it than to all the rest of the work put together. Already in his book of stage directions, he has laid the greatest stress on the actor's work. From the very beginning, he reckons with his actors, makes them the basis, so to say, for the elaboration of his dramatic figures, permits his artistic speculations occasionally to be influenced by their personalities—only, of course, when they are individualities. Actors of little individuality, he forms and molds to fit his vision of the complete play. How near to his heart is this chief task of the stage manager, only he can realize who has had an opportunity to observe Reinhardt at rehearsals, day and night; who has witnessed his untiring zeal, his devotion, his alertness, his diplomacy, and his wrath, which is rare; who knows that, outside rehearsals, he studies entire rôles, sentence by sentence, with the individual actors, or successfully influences them in the course of a conversation. He who knows his way of mastering and inspiring great crowds of supers, almost without raising his voice, how he arouses their enthusiasm for the work, welds the masses into a great powerful unit, and yet permits every member to retain his individuality—only he will understand the impressive effect produced by these enormous choruses. At rehearsals, Reinhardt is a clown at a given moment: in the next a loving sweetheart; in the third, a warrior among a hundred others. Yet he always remains the manager. Even during the last twenty-four hours between the dress rehearsal and the first performance, he still confers, experiments, changes, eliminates certain parts which, after all, do not seem to be sufficiently important or which the actor may not be able to master completely. For him rehearsal does not cease until the curtain rises.

Actors more than any of the theatre's craftsmen profit by or miss the assisting hand of a stage manager. I have never heard Reinhardt's actors speak in any but the highest terms of veneration and loving admiration of his work at rehearsal. Reinhardt may leave quite different impressions on one who watches him at two different rehearsals. He has days when he does not speak, seems almost dumb, when you see him sitting there in his characteristic position, with his head resting heavily on his hand. If on a day like that, he says anything at all, his words emerge hesitatingly and with a jerk, as if he were under a strain. He seems to be all eye and ear, and to take in everything that goes on around him. Sometimes, it is true, after at least a day's interval, the gates of his soul suddenly open and we see before us a different person, one who has completely thrown off his fetters.

While he is rather uncommunicative and reserved by

nature, at such hours of perfect inner relaxation, he radiates an exhilarating influence, difficult to describe. Moments like these reveal the strength which holds the reins, the will which forces everything within the sphere of his imagination. Yet in minor details he is not stubborn. Moments like these reveal, too, how he inspires the individual actor, how he intensifies him, gives him ideas, and helps his soul to find the way to the surface.

When you hear those short, clear, concise directions, which carry without difficulty in the largest arena, you realize the conciseness of his orders, the plastic form of his visions, the stress of the intellectual work which is being done here. Yet Reinhardt never loses himself in ecstasy. Even at moments when his inner fire glows strongest, he appears perfectly calm and permits no thoughtless or inexact word to cross his lips. He knows how to explain his wishes to his co-workers, especially to his actors, through the slightest gesture, the shortest word, a mere intonation, thus letting his intentions, so to speak, shine through a gesture, a word, a sound. For instance, as part of his singular technique, which is the servant of his creative mind, he whispers a word in a way that lends the actor the right intonation.

Sometimes, of course, this perfect, almost unnatural outer calmness leaves him and the flame of passion overwhelms him, without robbing him of control over his speech and gestures. Then it happens that he acts part after part, without forgetting a single characteristic word or feature. At such moments, we get a glimpse of the world this artist carries within himself, and of the way in which, with the full weight of his will, he imposes his

SCHIGOLCH (WERNER KRAUSS) AND A YOUNG GIRL   LULU (GERTRUD EYSOLDT) AND SCHIGOLCH (WERNER KRAUSS)

TWO SCENES IN REINHARDT'S PRODUCTION OF FRANK WEDEKIND'S "THE BOX OF PANDORA"

From Original Lithographs by Emil Orlik

GERTRUD EYSOLDT AS LULU   EMIL JANNINGS AS RODRIGO QUAST

FRANK WEDEKIND'S "THE BOX OF PANDORA"

Two of the Leading Characters in Reinhardt's Production

mental conception on the material in hand; while, in spite of all his victories, he has not escaped the tragic fate of the artist: the realization that the glowing pictures of his imagination do not take perfect form in the blunt material of the theatre.

CHAPTER XI

MUSIC UNDER REINHARDT

BY EINAR NILSON

[The use of music by Reinhardt to enhance his dramatic effect is so characteristic of his work as a producing artist that it deserves a chapter by itself. The logical hand to trace the psychological motives involved, the technical means utilized and the esthetic results achieved is that of Einar Nilson, the young Swedish composer and conductor who has been associated with Reinhardt as his musical adviser for over fifteen years. Nilson first came into Reinhardt's orchestra before the days at the Deutsches Theater and assumed charge shortly after the removal to Schumannstrasse. Since then he has reorchestrated many scores, besides writing the music for "Everyman," "The Great World-Theatre," "Orestes," "George Dandin," "Rappelkopf," "As You Like It," "Much Ado About Nothing," and many other works by Shakespeare, Molière and Strindberg. He has accompanied Reinhardt as conductor on all of his guest seasons abroad and has re-orchestrated Humperdinck's score for the American production of "The Miracle."—THE EDITOR.]

COLLABORATION with Reinhardt is interesting to the musician, because new perspectives invariably unfold during rehearsals. The proximity of this producer to the essential values of music is an impression that persists and grows. He has drafted music into the service of the theatre as no one else had done before him. Sometimes it actually seems that Reinhardt falls back on music whenever the other crafts of the theatre prove powerless to gain an effect he desires.

How much Reinhardt considers music a part of the performance, is implicit in one fact alone: the different position he gives to the orchestra in different productions. In the plays of Raimund and Nestroy and in all farces, the conductor and the musicians with their instruments and lights must be in front of the stage in sight of the audience. In "A Midsummer Night's Dream," the music has its source below, invisible; everything seems to rise out of this musical undertone. In "Much Ado About Nothing," all the bushes and hedges on the stage seem to resound with music. On account of the strongly accentuated musical atmosphere of many of Shakespeare's plays, Reinhardt frequently likes to place the musicians in costume in full view on the stage, so that these small orchestras become a part of the picture. In Molière, he brings before the curtains his musicians, also properly costumed and led by costumed flunkeys, and there he groups them around an old spinet.

Reinhardt uses music not only as accompaniment, but also for another very important purpose: unification of the production. Music plays during the act intermissions and subdues the rumble of the machinery of the revolving stage. Large orchestras and choruses did not always prove sufficient, and so he installed an organ in the Deutsches Theater.

In his production book, Reinhardt includes everything essential for the composer and conductor: the at-

[125]

mosphere of the scene, its duration, the quality of the
music that appears desirable. Thus he invariably obtains
just the music which will be best adapted to his scenic
conceptions—Humperdinck's tender accompaniment to
the love scenes in "Twelfth Night"; Leo Blech's county
fair music in "The Taming of the Shrew"; primitive, almost barbaric melodies in "King Lear." In cases like
these, Reinhardt's fine feeling for the artistic expression
of a period, either sends him back to the old music, or
else he asks a composer to write music for him in the
spirit of the particular period involved. Examples of
the first method may be seen in his use of old French melodies for Molière and for the ballet (Rameau and Lully),
as well as old Welsh dances which he weaves into the action of "Henry IV," creating an atmosphere of warmth
and comfort in the scene at the inn. The second method
was tested in "Everyman," which had music reminiscent
of medieval melodies. A task still more important than
that of service as undertone, accompaniment and bridging of intervals, was imposed upon music by Reinhardt
when, in "The Comedy of Errors," he used it to set the
rhythm for the entire play. In this connection, too, the
music for ballet and pantomime deserves mention, for,
inspired by the action, it identifies itself fully with the
story and, in its turn, becomes the key to every motion
and gesture of the players.

Even where music remains in the background, it has
important functions to fulfil in Reinhardt's productions.
Thus Chopin's C Sharp Minor Impromptu on the piano,
sounding through the storm, contributes vividly to the
ghostly atmosphere of Strindberg's "The Pelican."

"TWO SHEPHERDESSES"

A Setting for a Ballet by Hugo von Hofsmannthal, Designed by Ernst Stern

Thus the subdued music, which in Sternheim's version of Molière's "L'Avare" accompanies the dressing scene of the young roué Cléant, not only gives more life to the pantomimic action, but also, quite automatically, accentuates the rhythm of every gesture of the valets attendant on their master. Thus again, in "The Merchant of Venice," the carnival life of the Venice lanes and canals is depicted most happily by the violins in the distance, intermingled with songs and suppressed shouts of joy which merge into Gratiano's merry catch.

Here we enter upon a territory where Reinhardt has executed decisive reforms: the wide range of stage sounds and noises. No one before him had any idea of the significance of different sounds as aids to characteristic atmosphere on the stage. These sounds, which Reinhardt heard when he first read the play, are often very hard to reproduce and their materialization encounters technical difficulties. Reinhardt composes them as they rise and fall, mount to a climax and die away, just as you would write a symphony. Either they stand out alone as in "Macbeth," where the night of the murder is suggested to our minds by a deep rolling sound produced by the organ, intermingled with the ghastly shrieks of the screech-owl. Or else they are combined with other means of expression. Thus the effectiveness of great mass scenes is enhanced by simultaneously striking and holding several deep tones on the organ which have but few vibrations. These sounds, especially when supported by the roll of the low-tuned kettle-drums, produce a prolonged noise resembling thunder, which seems to come directly from the masses on the stage.

[127]

MAX REINHARDT AND HIS THEATRE

Especially in the Arena, whose vast dimensions demand something to fill them, Reinhardt uses musical sounds to the limit. The performances of "Orestes," "Oedipus Rex," "Everyman" and "The Miracle" are opened by trumpets, the sounding of gongs, and the ringing of bells. Where productions like these are not also accompanied by actual music, their atmosphere is effectively enhanced by sounds and noises from an orchestra with a complete outfit of percussion instruments, trombones, cymbals, triangles, muffled horns, basses and harmonium.

The Arena, the "theatre of the five thousand," requires music much more than any other form of the theatre. Every aspect of it calls for music. The space itself with its colossal dimensions must never for a moment be left dead and dumb. The character of the scene, cold, immutable, monumental, can find nothing like everchanging music to create the impression of detail and shading. The specific type of public in the Arena can be reached only by what is clear and of the most general import. How could that effect be attained better than by music? Also, the intrinsic nature of the play in the Arena, always that of a festival, calls for music.

All forms of music are at home in the Arena: absolute orchestral and vocal music, as well as music which accompanies and interprets the action on the stage, either as rhythmic foundation for the chorus or as stage sounds. As Reinhardt's musical adviser for all his Arena performances, I have had an excellent opportunity to observe to what extent the dramatic and musical atmosphere can be influenced by the latter. It seems to me that Reinhardt

[128]

ENGELBERT HUMPERDINCK

Composer of "The Miracle," "Hänsel and Gretel" and "Königskinder"

EINAR NILSON

Swedish Composer and Musical Adviser to Reinhardt

"ARIADNE AUF NAXOS"

STUTTGART, OCTOBER, 1912

Two Sketches by Ernst Stern of Reinhardt's Production of the Opera by
Richard Strauss and Hugo von Hofmannsthal

has discovered here a source of new possibilities, which may be of great importance for the development and dramatic effect of theatre music in the future.

The principle involved is this: to render the atmosphere of a play not only through word, gesture, line and color, but also through sound, by laying musical stress on the voices of the masses and on sounds emanating from inanimate objects, by tuning them to each other and linking them to an inner harmony. In addition to accentuating through musical means such noises as the squeaking of a door on its hinges, the clatter of hoofs, the clash of arms, the roar of the sea—musical sounds can be used broadly to express the threatening growl of dissatisfied masses, or to intensify an atmosphere of awe, the source of which remains a mystery to the audience. What spectator realizes that the inexplicable, subdued trembling and vibration which he imagines he hears in his own awe-stricken soul while watching an inexorable tragedy, has been imposed on his imagination by the hautboy sounding its F sharp?

In reality, all of these problems are nothing else than an attempt to intensify and simplify the effectiveness of dramatic expression—more so in the Arena than in the ordinary theatre. And that is why every new performance in the Arena brings to the musician new problems and new solutions of problems.

A special feature of the music on Reinhardt's stage is the *spoken* chorus which he builds up like a composer. Examples thereof are to be found in "Die Braut von Messina" ("The Bride of Messina"), in "Oedipus and the Sphinx," in "Oedipus Rex" and in "Orestes." Here he has written what amounts to an actual score. The speakers are divided into groups which correspond to the singing voices of a choir. By omitting several words, a given sentence of the text is shortened for that group which is to join in later, and so on from group to group, until, at a given moment, the entire chorus is heard in full, powerful unison. All this is no matter of mere chance, but is exactly graded as to the intensity and pitch of the tone. This spoken score is accentuated by sounds from different musical instruments, consisting chiefly of open chords on harps, sustained chords on stringed instruments, the peals of the organ and the thundering of percussion instruments, grouped in a manner similar to the arrangement of the speaking chorus which they accompany. The exact laws of musical compositions, it is true, are not always followed, and in the nature of things, can not be followed. The important point to remember is that this aspect of Reinhardt's work is truly musical in nature.

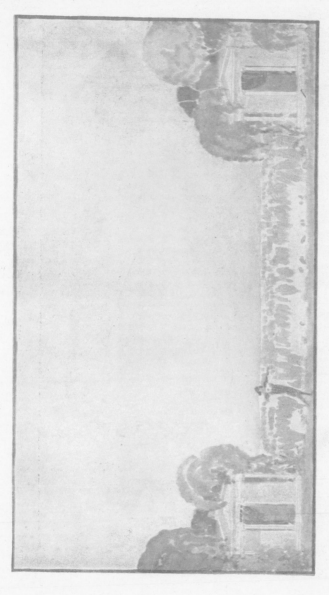

OFFENBACH'S "ORPHEUS IN THE UNDERWORLD"

COPENHAGEN, FEBRUARY, 1921

A Setting for Act I, Scene I, A Landscape in the Neighborhood of Thebes

Designed by Max Rée

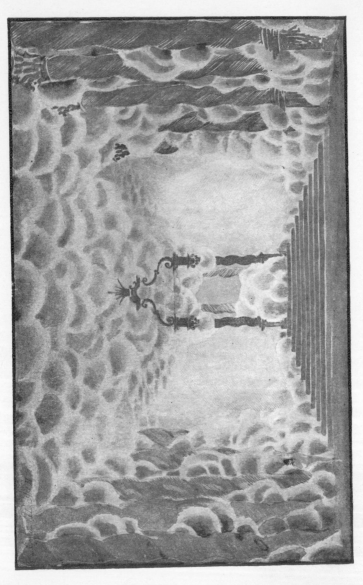

OFFENBACH'S "ORPHEUS IN THE UNDERWORLD"

COPENHAGEN, FEBRUARY, 1921

A Setting for Act 1, Scene 2, Olympus

Designed by Max Rée

Chapter XII

REINHARDT AND THE SCENIC ARTIST

[Just as stage settings have been the battle-ground of the whole so-called new movement in the theatre, so with Reinhardt, the question of scenery has been the moot point among his critics and the angle from which he has been viciously attacked. Scenic investiture is the most obvious aspect of a reborn theatre and, therefore, has monopolized comment and controversy. It has its legitimate place in the dramatic renaissance, a fact which Reinhardt promptly recognized; but with his broad view of the many-sided art of the theatre, he has seldom permitted it to engross more than its rightful realm. Angles of this problem emerge in almost every chapter, most notably in Maximilian Harden's tribute to Reinhardt's genius in Chapter XVII, but I have gathered here two pertinent studies of the subject by co-workers, Alfred Roller, Viennese artist who has designed many of his productions, and Max Osborne, an able Berlin art critic, together with an appreciation by the English critic and friend of Reinhardt and Salzburg, Professor E. J. Dent, celebrated authority on Mozart.—THE EDITOR.]

I

THE SPIRIT OF EXPERIMENT

BY ALFRED ROLLER

WHEN I work on stage decorations with Reinhardt, I am less interested in the results of our activity—the per-

[131]

formances themselves—than in the perspectives and the ideal opportunities to give form to the drama in question. These opportunities recur continually, due to Reinhardt's unprejudiced, daring and uncompromising way of approaching the difficulties in setting a play.

The average stage manager who, either from pride, laziness, or subconscious realization of his deficiency, turns down everything which differs from what he has learned and from what is being done, who believes in a standardized way of stage setting, and who considers the theatre in general and its work (not that of the poet) as something final—this familiar "shrewd, experienced, ingenious stage manager," who does not know that every work of art must follow its own laws of stage setting, completely paralyzes the creative artist. Reinhardt's lavishly expended energy; his unmechanical way of working, his zeal in sounding the work itself for the style in which it has to be expressed; his youthful vitality, which would like best to invent a new way of acting for every individual dramatic production on which he lays hand— all this makes cooperation with him the most exciting, most passionate pleasure for me that I have ever experienced, except—and then even in still higher degree— when working under Gustav Mahler's direction.

In view of that pleasure, the greater or lesser success of the individual experiment means little to me. None of us is satisfied with our present way of playing theatre. Only a progressive development can help us find a better one. Now that we have fixed our attention on staging a play and giving it a decorative equipment, we must proceed over the top of the hill. To turn around would only

HUGO VON HOFMANNSTHAL'S "ŒDIPUS AND THE SPHINX"

A Costume Sketch by Alfred Roller

retard our progress, to give up the pursuit would be no solution. It is Reinhardt's merit to have accelerated the pace of this inevitable development by his untiring work and his genuine experiments, and thus to have brought within nearer reach the possibility of a new conception of the stage.

Besides, what else can we do at a time when the billboards are full of dramatic productions of all the centuries, written under the most varied circumstances; at a time, when the modern drama as yet has no individual and uniform scenic principles to offer?

If ever a strong, uniform modern form of production should come our way, then, and only then, we shall also find a method of our own to stage the masterpieces of the past.

II

STAGE AND SCENERY

BY MAX OSBORNE

In the Kleines Theater and the Neues Theater, Reinhardt made his first attempt to apply to the stage the results of modern artistic culture. The Meiningers transplanted Piloty's style of painting to the stage, while the naturalistic school created a realistic stage, copying Uhde's, Israel's and Liebermann's paintings of petty, impoverished people. After the cleansing bath of the naturalistic regime, which left behind a conscientious care in the arrangement of the scenic frame, the influence of new and different styles made itself felt in stage decorations. The artists began to discard their aristocratic isolation and helped once more to solve practical problems. Free art and applied art joined hands again. The artists designed furniture, rugs, tapestries, paper-hangings, embroideries. They provided the interior decoration of rooms and halls and whole houses, thus sowing new seeds in a thousand ways. They also began to be interested in stage scenery and effects, illumination and costume. Practical and artistic principles united to produce the modern stage picture. This new art replaced scientifically studied historic detail with the artist's recreative vision of past periods, shifting the attention of the public from minute accurate objectivity to the larger lines and to the spirit of the whole period in question.

Reinhardt's setting of "The Lower Depths" showed an independent way of studying and recreating a period in the realistic manner. Wilde's "Salome" already reflects the newly-acquired freedom in applying historic coloring, using these elements only to give the desired characteristic touch to that flower of modern refinement. All this was attained by experiment; Reinhardt's and Vallentin's ingenious instincts made the suggestions while Impekoven's decorative studio executed the new plans with great talent and understanding. The first major document of the youngest style of creative imagination was "Pelléas and Mélisande"—a fairyland with wide-open, questioning eyes, a world of mystery and fathomless depth, illumined for a brief moment by a ray of light. And in Impekoven's decorations, the same mighty contrasts as in Maeterlinck's poetry: The castle—vast, threatening, gloomy space; wide, empty halls; and narrow, dark passages. The

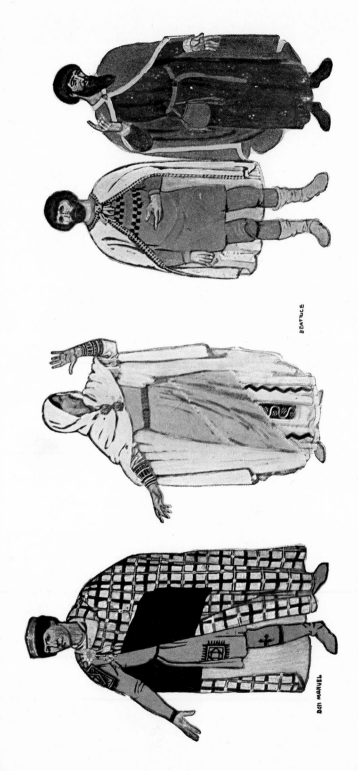

BEATRICE

DON MANUEL

SCHILLER'S "THE BRIDE OF MESSINA"

At the Künstler Theater, Munich

Costume Plates for Four of the Characters by Wilhelm Dietz

garden—a dream of luxurious green with vibrating yellow
light and murmuring fountains. The costumes, too, fitted
into the scenic setting, designed by Lovis Corinth, the first
greater painter working for Reinhardt. The principles of
modern art are strongly emphasized: commanding form
and isolating outlines; the flowing lines of the Pre-
Raphaelites; decorative, fantastic landscapes, like Leisti-
kow's; free, flat surface, alternating with ornamental designs, without any historic reminiscences as background;
an illusion of space, attained, not by crowding in as many
details as possible, but by a few definite carefully selected
features; contrasting light effects, which did away with
the stage as a panorama; and above all, a new and
courageous use of color. The sculptor, Max Kruse, and
the painter, Corinth, designed new scenic decorations for
"Salome," "a sultry Oriental fantasy," and for von Hofmannsthal's "Elektra." A new strength had thrown over-
board all stale conventions. The usual rococo scenery for
"Minna von Barnhelm" was changed to the simpler atmosphere of about 1760, with old Menzel giving suggestions where Frederick the Great was involved. Slevogt
created an historic fantasy for "The Merry Wives of
Windsor" and Karl Walser made designs of laughing and
dancing vivacity for Nestroy's "Einen jux will er sich
machen" ("He Wants to Play a Joke"), Rüderer's "Morgenröte" ("Dawn"), and Bernard Shaw's "Caesar and
Cleopatra." Since 1906, Ernst Stern's versatile pencil
has created a series of humorous and serious stage pictures, and has been Reinhardt's mainstay, although Rée,
Roller, Orlik, Dietz and others have varied this aspect of
his stage.

Meanwhile, a genuine craze for decorative work had taken possession of the theatre. The new delight in color, in light, in the restless exploration of modern technical expedients for scenic and stage effects, in the revolving stage as a useful factor in this brilliant and inspiring dreamland. "A Midsummer Night's Dream," "The Merchant of Venice"! Yet, realizing the danger lurking in exaggeration, modern stage artists took refuge in a simple, well-defined style and made the stage picture, which so far had aimed at illusion, appear merely a suggestive help to the imagination of the audience. The English added new impulses through Gordon Craig, who proposed draperies and contrasts of light and shadow, as an ideal background for the stage. Traces of these new tendencies are found in "Oedipus" (1906), and in Emil Orlik's decorations for "A Winter's Tale." In 1907, Maeterlinck's "Aglavaine and Sélysette" provided a new opportunity to apply these principles of simplicity and moderation. Here the rooms are walled off by wide flowing draperies of dark purple color, with openings in them instead of doors, while the scenes in the park and on the tower, after sketches by Ludwig von Hofmann, are removed from a commonplace atmosphere by a severe decorative form language, and the costumes and stage effects are free fantasies on contemporary models with a slight romantic touch, suggestive of the Belgian Fernand Knopff's modern studies in mysticism.

The first season at the Munich Künstler Theater, in the summer of 1908, continued this development and helped to clarify its laws: the desire to create an apparent uniformity among otherwise variable scenes, following

"A WINTER'S TALE"

<small>At the Deutsches Theater, September, 1906</small>

A Scene Designed by Emil Orlik for the Sheep Shearing Festival

the principle of the leading motive which, by comparatively few characteristic alterations, can satisfy any local requirements; language of ornaments and interior architecture which contemporary taste applies to fantastic and historical objects; and, above all, the use of light for contrasts in atmosphere to an extent never before dreamed.

During the winter 1907-08, Reinhardt devoted special attention to overcoming the space limitations entailed by the revolving stage. The setting of "Faust," bravely redeemed by Roller from the Kaulbach-Lietzenmayer style of illustration, disclosed South German influence and rich effectiveness in the strong concentration of the light.

These years of pioneer activity and the later ones during which experiment was consolidated and applied have taught us how old problems reconsidered may become new inspirations; how we may alternate sparkling life and a severe set style, realistic illusion and modern decorative forms heedless of the laws of any epoch, pleasure in detail and ascetic reserve—always according to the requirements of the words of the dramatist which they serve; how such service must be kept under control; how overemphasis in decoration and stage management may be avoided.

III

THE STAGE PICTURE

BY E. J. DENT

The German theatre sets out to produce the maximum number of plays at the minimum of cost; the English theatre aims at the maximum of profit with the minimum

[137]

of plays. It is hardly surprising, therefore, that ideas of production which are by now the commonplaces of the German stage should be almost unknown in England. It seems even scarcely worth while to write about them when the social and economic conditions of the theatre in England make it almost unthinkable that they should ever bear fruit there. For modern German experiments, even the most modern, are inseparably connected with the old traditions of the German stage, however sharply they may at times run counter to them. Court patronage gave Germany the repertory system and the tradition of building theatres on a liberal scale. The ground plan of the ordinary German theatre, old or new, shows that however large the area of the auditorium, that of the stage is generally much larger. If the theatre has a revolving stage, the revolving circle is more or less equal in diameter to the circle round which the auditorium is planned. English theatres are built to hold the largest possible number of spectators. To this end, cloak-rooms and foyers are sacrificed as far as authority permits, and the same applies to the stage and dressing-rooms. The English producer is perpetually confronted with the inconveniences of a cramped space, and he expends all his skill in trying to create the illusion that the stage is illimitable. The German producer, with a vast space at his disposal, prefers to utilize only a very small proportion of it.

The genius of Reinhardt is typically German. Many of the ideas associated with his name originated in other brains, but Reinhardt was the man who grasped them and organized them. To Wagner above all he owes the conception of the theatre as a union of all the arts. He is

GLOUCESTER'S ROOM

EXTERIOR OF THE CASTLE

TWO SETTINGS FROM "KING LEAR"

AT THE DEUTSCHES THEATER, SEPTEMBER, 1908

From Designs by Karl Czeschka

A Street Scene

The Fair

"THE WUPPERS," BY ELSE LASKER-SCHÜLER

Two Settings in Modernist Vein by Ernst Stern for a Production Made for
Das Junge Deutschland, April, 1919

the nearest that the world has yet succeeded in producing to Gordon Craig's ideal of a stage director. If he falls short of perfection, it is as the actor dressed in his clothes falls short of the ideal drawn on paper by the designer. Reinhardt is typically German, not in his creative power, but in his power to appreciate. He is a man of business, but he respects art and learning; he knows that the things of the mind can be turned to commercial purposes. It is this combination of the practical and the artistic which has made him the widest influence of the German stage at the present day. His influence is, generally speaking, an influence for good; but unless he has still the acquisitive power to absorb yet newer ideas, his day is done. The English theatre might learn much from him; the German theatre has swallowed him and almost completely digested him. In a few years time his methods will be simply the normal average tradition.

The revolving stage was invented by Lautenschlager of Munich in order to produce Mozart's operas at the Residenz Theater there. The adaptable proscenium was the feature of the Munich Künstler Theater. These two devices are the foundation of Reinhardt's decorative system. The revolving stage solved the problem, not only of "Don Giovanni," but of Shakespeare, and, above all, of "Faust." It is rightly inevitable that all the methods of the German theatre should be centered on "Faust"; that all technical devices of staging, acting, music or anything else, should be regarded as means to its performance; and that this play of all plays should set the example to playwrights, producers and everyone connected with the theatre. The turn-table can give quick changes, but it limits the available area of the stage. It does not necessarily mean that every scene has to be set in a quarter of the circle; the area of the circle can be distributed among the various scenes as the designer pleases. But it undoubtedly makes for a small scene rather than a large one, and it has always been Reinhardt's tendency to design small scenes. The climax was reached in his recent production of the "Urfaust."

The "Urfaust" is a series of scenes for "Faust," sketched by Goethe in 1774-75 when quite a young man. He destroyed the manuscript, but about a century later there came to light a copy made by a lady-in-waiting at the Court of Weimar. It is a fragment of great historical interest, the performance of which would be very appropriate at a special Goethe festival or as an illustration to university lectures on the poet. It was performed at Frankfurt, Goethe's birthplace, in 1918; Reinhardt produced it at the Deutsches Theater in the autumn of 1920. His idea was to make the play into a series of old Flemish pictures. The stage opening was reduced to a width of about nine feet; it was framed in a neo-Gothic arch of rather clumsy design, the traceries of which could be adapted to any height. The depth of the stage was about equal to its width. Several of the scenes were most effective and impressive. Faust sat at his study table facing the audience, in front of him Reinhardt's inevitable shaded lamp casting a light on the actor's face; the spirits appeared high above, Mephistopheles at one side. The Gothic proscenium alone was enough to suggest the cathedral; all one saw was a pillar and a black wall, with a number of women kneeling on steps, all with their backs

GOETHE'S "URFAUST" AT THE DEUTSCHES THEATER, OCTOBER, 1920

A Design by Ernst Stern for the Garden Scene

toward the audience, and all closely packed together. How valuable the small stage is when closely packed with figures appeared forcibly in the cellar-scene. Here the roof was brought down so low that it was barely possible to stand upright; at the back of the stage a staircase led upwards to one side. In this confined space sat four men, shouting, singing, belching, drinking, roaring, quarreling. The vivid reality of the scene was unbearable; one imagined oneself as close to the actors as they were to each other. At other times one felt that the play had been sacrificed to the picture. Gretchen looked like a Madonna by Memling, and stood habitually in a Memling attitude. The formal garden had a golden sky for background; and the same golden sky appeared through Gretchen's window. They were exquisite tableaux, but they made a picture-book, not a play.

It might well be replied that the "Urfaust" is not a play but a sketch-book, and that this was the right way to treat it. Yet I can not help feeling that the play was performed as an excuse for the pictures, instead of the pictures being designed as a background to the play. This is the inevitable danger of such methods as Reinhardt's. He honestly values "Art," i. e., painting and architecture, and therefore employs real "artists" to work for him. He wants the stage to look like a picture in a gallery; if the audience can recognize that, they will call his theatre artistic. It is perfectly true that these methods do often make for a tense concentration on essentials. It has been pointed out that the early Italian painters often represented religious scenes as they saw them represented on the religious stage. Giotto's "Annunciation" takes

[141]

place not in a real house, but in a *luogo deputato* such as was made for the medieval drama. Accordingly some producers in Germany are urging a return to medievalism, and exhibiting Italian primitives as the models for modern stage decoration. This movement is due in part to the revival of interest in the medieval stage itself, not so much on artistic as on ethical grounds. Its danger lies in its tendency to convert the theatre into a museum. There is a great fascination about the reproduction of pictures on the stage, but when attention is distracted from the play and its actors, it does not really matter much whether the scenery is by Giotto or by Hawes Craven. Moissi, Reinhardt's most popular actor, said long ago that he would like to see all scenery abolished and all costumes reduced to a sort of stage uniform.

Reinhardt's literary henchmen make much talk of the medieval stage and of the classical Greek theatre in connection with the Grosses Schauspielhaus. It is to be a theatre for the people, a festival playhouse, a rite of worship, of purification and of joy. In actual fact, the building is a clever piece of scenery, suggesting a temporary exhibition building rather than a shrine of austere art. Its plan is neither antique nor medieval but resembles the masque-stage of Callot's well-known picture.

For the realistic handling of crowds it is appropriate, but for nothing else. A lady told me that she enjoyed seeing Romain Rolland's "Danton" there because she had lived through the same scenes during the revolution in Berlin. Her artistic attitude differs little from that of her English sister who would like to ask her favorite actor to tea. Georg Kaiser's "Europa," which might have

"THE MERCHANT OF VENICE"

At the Künstler Theater, Munich, June-August, 1910

A Costume Plate Designed by Wilhelm Hengeler for the Rôle of Shylock to Be
Played by Rudolf Schildkraut
The Custom of Pasting Textiles on the Costume Plate, Now Widely in Vogue in
America, Has Long Been Used by Reinhardt's Scenic Artists

been a delicately amusing idyll, was produced as a mixture of musical comedy and circus. The resonance of the building magnifies every cough or shuffle into a roar, and the only way in which the actors can make themselves heard is to bawl louder than ever they did in the days of the old Court Theatre. Reinhardt never conferred a greater benefit on the German stage than when he created the Kammerspiele. The Grosses Schauspielhaus is a belated product of pre-revolutionary German megalomania. But the revolution in the theatre has already begun.

CHAPTER XIII

REINHARDT'S THEATRES

["Architecture keeps pace with the problems of its time,"
says Hermann Dernburg, "creating new forms for housing
new phenomena." This fact is the secret underlying the chain
of structures and sites in which Reinhardt has exhibited the
developing phases of his art. He has supplied the phenomena
while others, with his collaboration, have built, altered, or
remodelled the new forms to house these phenomena. Count-
ing his career as beginning in a large way at the Deutsches
Theater, Reinhardt took over what others had built but proceeded to equip the old structure with mechanism to meet the
demands of a new time. He soon felt the need of a smaller
and more intimate hall, however, as Heinz Herald explains,
and the result was the Kammerspiele. Herald has been connected with the Reinhardt theatres in a literary capacity for
many years, is author of two books—"Max Reinhardt" and
"Reinhardt und seine Bühne," and is, therefore, qualified to
speak about these stages and the development of Reinhardt's
theatre homes. En route to his long-cherished "Theatre of the
Five Thousand," which he finally achieved in the Grosses
Schauspielhaus, Reinhardt developed the technique of the
Arena productions and pressed into temporary and makeshift
service such huge enclosures as Olympia in London and the
Berlin circuses, Busch and Schumann. The technical phases of
this period are sympathetically set forth by Robert Breuer, an
authority on decorative art. The phenomenon of dramatic
masses finally found a concrete form to house it in the Grosses
Schauspielhaus which was opened with Romain Rolland's

[144]

Zander & Labisch, Berlin

REVOLUTIONARY ELOQUENCE FILLS THE VAST REACHES OF THE GROSSES SCHAUSPIELHAUS

A Scene from Romain Rolland's "Danton," Produced in February, 1920

THE GROSSES SCHAUSPIELHAUS, BERLIN

"Danton," February 14, 1920. Although marred by a flaw here and there in conception and execution, this vast bank of seats with the stage thrust out into their midst and all hooded by a dome of illuminated stalactites, is one of the most challenging and inspiring temples the drama has ever possessed. In fact, it is drama in itself, dwarfing any but the master dramatists and their works. Out of the storm of controversy it has aroused, I choose the tribute by Rudolf Borchardt, a German poet and critic, as most nearly approximating my own feelings.

Reinhardt's theatres do not cease with his Berlin trio, which he left to their own resources in 1921, for wherever Reinhardt goes, he takes the theatre with him. Vienna: Maria Theresia's ballroom: Theater in dem Redoutensaal. Salzburg: the Domplatz and the Kollegienkirche: the site of modern mystery plays in front of and inside of the Cathedral. These aspects of Reinhardt's theatre homes will be treated fully in succeeding chapters.—THE EDITOR.]

I

THE DEUTSCHES THEATER

BY HEINZ HERALD

BERLIN's theatrical leadership of Germany dates back to the erection of the Deutsches Theater in 1883. It was then that the post of command passed from Vienna, the city of the Burg Theater, to the youthful capital of the north and to the stage which Adolf L'Arronge had just founded. When this new and important period of German poetry and dramatic art introduced the era of naturalism, Otto Brahm, its most eminent herald and representative in the theatrical world, took over the Deutsches

Theater. He was followed by Lindau, who after a short and soon forgotten reign, passed it on to Reinhardt.

Thus, Reinhardt entered on historic ground, consecrated by the noblest and most vital performances of two theatrical generations. This fact must be admitted even by those who are opposed in principle to the now obsolete naturalistic theatre, and who believe that Reinhardt was the first theatrical artist in the full sense of the word and that he gave the art of the stage a start in a new direction, the only direction suitable to our time. Reinhardt's assumption of the Deutsches Theater had the advantage for him of being considered symbolic by his contemporaries, who had become accustomed to see in the productions of this theatre the most important expression of modern stage art. This circumstance, coming at the moment when he introduced himself to the broad public, assured for him that public's confidence without which no one connected with the theatre can achieve greatly.

Another advantage of a subtler nature was that his work at the Deutsches Theater forced him to counsel with his own soul. And it may have helped him overcome many of those unpleasant hours which are the lot of all of us. Here the inner relationship of everything may have become clear to him. Here he stood with both feet on ground which was the result of long development and which he always respected, in spite of the strong consciousness of his own individuality and of the new mission which he was destined to fulfil.

Between the theatre of the three hundred, the Kammerspiele, and the theatre of the five thousand, the Arena or the Grosses Schauspielhaus, stands the theatre of the thousand: the Deutsches Theater. Reinhardt erected the Kammerspiele and the Grosses Schauspielhaus to have a home on the one hand for plays of too intimate a charm, and on the other for those of too broad a sweep, to find the proper resonance at the Deutsches Theater. Here at the Deutsches Theater, he made the majority of his productions—those which called neither for the warm intimacy of the Kammerspiele nor for the gigantic vaulted ring of the Grosses Schauspielhaus. Reinhardt's aim in founding the Kammerspiele and the Grosses Schauspielhaus was not to dethrone the existing theatre form, the theatre of the thousand, which had stood many a test and earned so many laurels for the art of the stage. His desire was to have stages which could be used where that theatre form did not suffice. The Kammerspiele will be a theatre for the few; the performances in the Grosses Schauspielhaus, something festive, out of the ordinary. But for everything else, in spite of the architectural deficiencies of the building, at which Reinhardt more than once has taken offense, the stage of the Deutsches Theater has always been a valuable instrument for his plans.

II

THE KAMMERSPIELE

BY HEINZ HERALD

I remember an incident which took place at a rehearsal directed by Reinhardt. They were performing one of those reticent plays whose effectiveness lies in the

[147]

strictly inward impression it produces on the spectator. In that play was a scene of the most passionate, most vital emotion under an unruffled surface, acted by a man and woman only. When the scene was over, Reinhardt, in his quiet way, remarked to the two actors: "It was wonderful for me, but unfortunately the spectators are not sitting on the stage as I do." It was then I realized more than ever how Reinhardt had conceived the idea of the Kammerspiele, or rather the problem whose solution in the present Kammerspiele is perhaps not final.

Reinhardt always liked a small theatre. The name of his first stage was "Kleines Theater," and it was exactly what its name implied. When, on moving to the Deutsches Theater, he gave up that stage, he did not wait long before he built a smaller, more intimate, more quiet house for which he selected the name of Kammerspiele. This brought him a step nearer to the principle of the *Kammerspiel* or chamber play. Here is a small hall without galleries and with stage scarcely separated from the auditorium panelled in warm brown. In this hall, at the same time cozy and solemn, the lights are not extinguished suddenly, but there is a gradual passing from light to darkness. Thus everything in this little playhouse is calculated to prepare and to maintain an atmosphere of concentration.

Reinhardt has made the effort also to give the foyer, to which the spectator repairs during the intermissions, a character that will not wrench him from the atmosphere with which the play has surrounded him. His main purpose in building the Kammerspiele, however, was to create a new relation between the actor and his public, between

Ernst Wasmuth, Berlin

A VISTA THROUGH THE FOYERS

Zander & Labisch, Berlin

A VIEW OF THE AUDITORIUM AND CEILING

THE GROSSES SCHAUSPIELHAUS, BERLIN, FROM TWO ANGLES

THE GROSSES SCHAUSPIELHAUS, BERLIN

A Fantastic Conception of the Great Auditorium and Stage with Its Exciting Play
of Light, from the Pencil of the Artist, Hahlo

the stage and the auditorium, to intensify the contact, to erect a broader and stronger bridge between the two.

The Kammerspiele and the Grosses Schauspielhaus are Reinhardt's last respectful bow to "style." Every actor of Reinhardt's ensemble knows that it is one thing to play at the Kammerspiele, and another to play at the Deutsches Theater, and something still different to play in the Grosses Schauspielhaus. What, at the Kammerspiele, is a mere relaxation of the fingers, must become a motion of the hand at the Deutsches Theater, a lifting of the arm in the Grosses Schauspielhaus. A clearly pronounced word at the Kammerspiele has no accent at the Deutsches Theater, and becomes a whisper in the Grosses Schauspielhaus. The spectator does not realize these technical factors, but this differentiation is necessary to create the same feeling in the spectator in the three different auditoriums. In the same way, the spectator little realizes that the actor, emptying a cup at a pantomime, must, in order to produce similar effects, put that cup to his mouth with twice as wide a gesture as he would in a drama.

Still another factor, aside from the building in which the play is enacted, is the determining influence on the theatrical form, on the drama itself. A play has in itself the laws which determine its form of expression: the relative intensity and scope of the style, gesture and other elements. "Orestes," to give a striking example, is as little adapted to the chamber play style, as "Ghosts" is to the wide gesture of the Arena. At former performances of chamber plays in the ordinary theatre, manager and actors had to make up their minds to act them more

[149]

broadly than they were meant to be acted. That, of course, prevented any exhaustive display of their charm, shut them off from achieving their full effectiveness on a badly adapted stage. The Kammerspiele has done away with that false proportion. Here the theatre itself as well as the play calls for subdued expression.

This can be attested by many positive and negative examples. Positive proofs are at hand among hundreds of plays by Ibsen, Strindberg, Maeterlinck, Shaw, Wedekind, Hauptmann, Schnitzler and many others which found a fitting and satisfactory home on this stage, although they were almost impossible on any other stage. Negative proofs were certain plays which, because of their structure and their setting, prescribing intensity of expression, did not seem to feel at home at the Kammerspiele. In so extended an enterprise as the Reinhardt stages, readjustment is occasionally necessary. Thus for mere formal reasons, a play must be transplanted sometimes from the Kammerspiele to the Deutsches Theater or vice versa. Excepting a few plays which keep the balance and may be performed on either of the two stages, it is interesting to observe whether its new atmosphere enhances or harms a play, whether that play so far has been in the right or the wrong place. Then we shall know immediately whether the play in question is a chamber play—or not. Under this test, "Frühlingserwachen" ("The Awakening of Spring"), can not stand the cooler air of the larger theatre, while "Nathan the Wise" only there unfolds its full effectiveness.

Perhaps Reinhardt's *Kammerspiel* problem has not yet found its final solution in the erection of the theatre

carrying that name. There are indications that he has
not yet discovered the form of theatre where not the
slightest radiation of the actor's expressive power is lost
on the way from the stage to the auditorium. The will
to deepest theatrical concentration, which created the
Kleines Theater and later the Kammerspiele, will characterize that new theatre form more than ever. If he
really desires it, Reinhardt will reach this third stage also
on his way to the perfect materialization of the *Kammerspiel* idea. He is not one of those who permit themselves
to be enticed from the path which they have recognized
as the right one; he is not one of those who lower their
flag. Thus far, in spite of all difficulties, he has always
created for his theatre the form which his inner vision
has revealed to him as the right one.

III

THE DRAMATIC VALUE OF SPACE AND THE MASSES

BY ROBERT BREUER

Looking at the framed stage is somewhat similar to
looking through a telescope or a microscope. On lifting
your head, you are back in the world of reality. In the
Arena, the spectator himself undergoes a transformation;
he becomes an actor. The drama has broken through
the wall that separated it from real, everyday life; it
has stepped right into the centre and radiates a magnetic
power of attraction that draws everything toward it. The
masses gathered around it become a frame, a sounding

board. Herein lies the secret effectiveness of the Arena, it is built out of the masses of the people, the thousands around become the mute chorus, a wall against which the powerful waves of the drama throw themselves only to float back again to the centre, back and forth in alternating rhythm. The drama has come into our midst; a human ring of thousands is caught up into an exalted experience; the action progresses within live walls. And this live theatre ring is a unique creation, filled with voices and music and floods of light. While the framed stage has a tendency to analyze, the Arena makes the concrete part of life appear still more concrete. And by permitting an awe-inspiring fate to fulfil itself within a circle of commonplace human beings, the tragic is enhanced to the monumental. The ring of thousands feels as if the actors had emerged from its own midst, as if they were merely expressing visibly what it is acting itself.

Thus the Arena is the medium which opens the soul of the people once more to the drama and makes this very soul visible. This is a fruit which only time can ripen. The form which art takes at a given period depends, too, on economic development. The emancipation of the masses claims the drama as the highest expression of its own life.

The framed stage like the framed picture seeks to accentuate perspective. In the Arena, this condition is altered, for the eye is not focused in one direction. Here the different planes can not be arranged one behind the other; they must stand one above the other. It is not a mere chance that the three plane mystery stage comes into its rights again at a time when the art of painting also

SCHILLER'S "THE BRIDE OF MESSINA"

AT THE KÜNSTLER THEATER, MUNICH

A Design for a Setting by Wilhelm Dietz

ignores frame and perspective, and arranges its planes likewise one above the other. What has been accomplished in the Arena by Roller, Ferdinand Hodler achieved before him in painting. Rhythm defeated the illusion. Piloty's development of a linear parallelism into modern monumentality is due to the same motives as the flight of the drama from the prison of scenic illusion into the clear cut style of the Arena. There is no monumentality without the clearest structure of the separate parts, without a clear, definite theme and without a code of laws for the different variations. The Ancients knew this. So did the Egyptians, Giotto and the architects of the Cologne Cathedral. In his wish to evolve pure form, to give style to the rhythm, Hodler stripped nature of all accidental aspects, and redeemed the typical, the essential in her. And it is a similar redemption of the figures, from the narrow and romantic maze of the stage and their exaltation into a concentrated pathos, into a rhythmic accentuation of what rises out of the ring of the thousands, at which the stage aims when it is arranged in different planes.

IV

THE GROSSES SCHAUSPIELHAUS

BY RUDOLF BORCHARDT

The distinguishing features between the Grosses Schauspielhaus and other theatres are not only conceptions of size and figures. Whether a theatre holds one or ten thousand people, means little more for that theatre than one or ten thousand subscribers mean to a newspaper, or one or ten thousand purchasers mean for a novel. Such figures concern the cash box, but intellectual criticism refuses to take them into consideration.

I do not believe that the people as a whole are more stupid and barbaric, more vulgar, more brutal, than during any "golden age" of the past. Yet I do believe that the so-called educated classes, the rich and very rich and the people of distinction have gradually landed at the bottom of an abyss of stupidity, banality and impotent lack of judgment, as low as no period before ever reached, no matter how miserable. I am convinced, therefore, that the dolled-up, half-educated *plebs* of today have lost their right to have a theatre of their own, such as three preceding generations of highly educated ancestors possessed. The time is ripe now for theatrical amusements after the manner of England and France; for their long runs; for their silly "hits of the season," as manufactured according to prescription by literary artisans; for the operetta and the movie. The level of later Rome, later London, later Paris, has been reached. Poetry as such, the drama in particular, have lost their footing in the average theatre.

At the same time, the misfortunes and impoverishment of our nation have reduced most of the theatres of the capital and practically all of those in the provinces to so low an economic standard that they can no longer move freely nor undertake any new enterprise in their competition with the film. To the depraved taste of that public which formerly attended the good theatres, the film appeals not only culturally and artistically; but eco-

THE DEUTSCHES THEATER, BERLIN

Famous Old Playhouse in Courtyard off the Schumannstrasse, Scene of Many of
Reinhardt's Triumphs

THE KAMMERSPIELE, BERLIN

Intimate Theatre Built by Reinhardt Adjoining the Deutsches Theater

Two Interior Scenes

Two Exterior Scenes

THE SECRETS OF THE REVOLVING STAGE REVEALED

A Model of the Turntable at the Deutsches Theater from Two Angles, Showing
Settings for Four Scenes of "King Henry IV" in Place and Ready
to be Disclosed in Succession to the Audience

nomically, too, it is better adapted to their reduced financial condition. The people nowadays have to be satisfied with theatrical performances which, owing to the mechanical process of mass reproduction, are much cheaper.

Is the German theatre lost? Has our drama been destroyed? The German drama which, in elective affinity, comprises the drama of all times and nations, the only drama in which the Greek, Spanish, English and French plays still live, though they died long ago in their native countries? Is all this dead, only because German money is worth nothing, because the rich in Germany have lost their fortunes while the bourgeoisie have lost their culture—dead, though dramatic conceptions still live and find form in the brains of German writers? Though thousands of Germans are loth to miss Shakespeare and Calderon, Kleist and Goethe, "Le Misanthrope" and "The Robbers," "The Jewess of Toledo" and "Everyman"? The poor and the poorest, students, former officers, impoverished girls who now have to do sewing and office work, ambitious working men, men with gray heads and young souls, widows whose only consolation is the small library left behind by the beloved dead, glowing youth, the whole chaos of a heart-breaking but not heart-broken time which fights its way from out of the darkness up to the stars, a generation which consciously feels that it is a drama in itself and is unwilling to die under any circumstances—why should it die here?

Reinhardt's new theatre is an appeal to the extreme courage to meet an almost hopeless, unprecedented situation by equally unprecedented means and to grasp a state of affairs on the downward grade, turn it around and force

[155]

it once more up to the peak. Every appeal to courage first awakens the chorus of cowards. All we heard during this theatre's entire first year was cowardice of opinion, the fear of having to change one's opinions, fear of facing the new situation and of passing judgment on this gigantic new project. On every hand, these cowards stopped the public at the doors of the enormous red building, attempted to drag it away and to give it no time to look and to think for itself. Accordingly, it became almost an act of treason to visit this theatre, to lend your pure soul to the shameful crime perpetrated here against the German past and the true spirit of the drama. The public, however, could not be misled for any length of time; whether with a good or a bad conscience, it has come to that house and has taken possession of it. With or without reasons, or reasoning, with or without realizing the importance of the deed which has been accomplished, it firmly stands by its new theatre and nothing can drive it away. Max Reinhardt has pushed the critics aside and has won the people. His theatre is today's historic event, the fight against it is the last remnant of sentiment and resentment. Not only is that stage an historic event, but so is the audience in the amphitheatre, the new people, the new public. This public which is still in creation and does not know yet whether a sensational or a vital impulse makes it sit there; whether it came to be amused and vulgarized or to undergo a great transformation; whether that stage, those actors, that method of performing a play in an empty space, are only a new sensation or a necessary step into the new land of the theatre; whether they mean a reaching out for an effect of the cheapest sort, or the process of taking the

SCHILLER'S "THE ROBBERS"

At the Grosses Schauspielhaus, September, 1921

A Design for a Setting by Kurt Richter

SCHILLER'S "THE ROBBERS"

At the Grosses Schauspielhaus, September, 1921

A Design for a Setting by Kurt Richter

drama from the hands of its usurper, the individual, and giving it back to its legitimate owner, the great, sacred mass of the people—this public is entitled to its rights, in the full sense of the word. It has a right to hear and to have proof that it did well by tearing up the newspapers and by coming into this theatre; that it, the public, is maturer and wiser, braver and freer, than the critics who pretend to lead it; that its inner relation to the courage, the instinct, the genius, which erected this theatre at the moment of utmost danger, is nearer and deeper than that of the whole offended pack of high brows, who measure that genius by the standard of bygone days. For this new public, as well as the genius, are the immortal part of a genuine humanity, Out of those who cling to the opinion that the former theatre can still be saved, and who for this very reason oppose the new one, speaks the narrow-mindedness of their epoch, the traditional prejudice of mere academic principles, without imagination and passionate love, which mistakes the means for the end and defends them where all vital necessity has long died.

That is why I started by speaking of numbers and measures, and that is why I return to them. The large house is not the old stage with a seating capacity of ten times the former size: such a compromise of bad taste could be made only by those who would generously admit people without means to the door of the educated bourgeois classes and who called into existence such hybrids as the "people's theatres." The stage of the Grosses Schauspielhaus is not the kind of stage which presents the same types of performance whether it has an audience

[157]

of five thousand people or whether, with half the auditorium cut off by a partition, it has only five hundred. Here the people are not "admitted"; they own the place. They are not educated from the stage; but they influence that stage. The latter thus attains its most primitive and simplest character, by being reduced to the essential. So that everyone may see what is going on (he who sits high, he who sits awry, he who sits at the side of the building), the stage sacrifices its usual two-dimensional picture which, as such, is visible only to him who faces it. It sacrifices the forestage, the curtain, the rear wall as its background. It sacrifices the scenery and the fly gallery, and breaks up altogether the old box arrangement. It is no more a cut-out; it has become a space. It is no more a flat surface, but has the dimensions of things that live. The former conventional attributes, which made it so easy to give a certain style to a stage, exist no more. The stage has gone back to its beginnings. It is a space for dances, for games, for theatrical action and pageants, as it had been with the German drama of the baroque period.

This, too, is the character of our elder theatre, in its relation to humanity. The only difference is that in former times it just happened to have this form, while the iron grip of economic conditions makes that form indispensable today. Whether this restoration will be a success or not, the German spirit and impulse will have to decide. It depends, as Goethe says, on "the power of man, such as it manifests itself in the poet." The poet will have to show how much of that power lives in him, and how much of the power, common to all, he will be able to summon for his task. Every opportunity has been given to him to tear up the account-book of the past and start anew on the struggle of mastering his time, just as the Athenian and the British poets did before him. The house stands, all seats are taken, the stage is there, such as Goethe imagined it when he said in his famous letter to Kleist that, with Calderon and Shakespeare, he would be sure to win any audience at a fair with two boards laid across two barrels. The Grosses Schauspielhaus is just that and nothing else—in gigantic measure. It admits all that is human, human deficiencies included, and super-human perfection. We have the choice to make it the home of the sublime or of the vulgar. The masses can be won for either; it is all a matter of your loving or despising them. Let us share the courage of him who built it, and let us not shrink from the word "plebeian." This word is less foreign to the sublime than its degenerated form, the "vulgar," which, clothed in cheap finery and studded with the swindler's false jewels, ostentatiously struts up and down the dying stage of the parvenus. In the film, this vulgar public has produced a theatrical method with rights to only those values which had better disappear in this great unfortunate nation, while all that is entitled to live once more faces Fate with the great question—here in the theatre and here alone.

CHAPTER XIV

REINHARDT AND THE FORMAL STAGE

BY KENNETH MACGOWAN

[Of all Reinhardt's theatres and stages none holds more unusual possibilities, none is more indicative of the inclusive range of his vision than the Theater in dem Redoutensaal, the theatre and stage in Vienna's expansive Hofburg which the Austrian Government made out of Maria Theresia's elegant ballroom and which Reinhardt almost immediately seized upon as home for his experiments in formalized dramatic art, at that time engrossing his interest. The analysis of the motives behind his experiments and the forecast of their possibilities are well within the range of the sympathies and observation of Kenneth Macgowan who has become the American protagonist for the various revolutionary tendencies in the art of the theatre.

The subject of Reinhardt and the formal stage, however, requires an additional word on the producer's latest project in this vein. Likewise in Vienna, he proposes to establish Das Theater der Schauspieler in der Josefstadt (the Theatre of the Actors in the Josefstadt). This gem of Austrian baroque architecture had its heyday in the latter part of the eighteenth century and the years had permitted it to sink into decay and oblivion. But Reinhardt's associates are restoring it to its original form and aspect, and in it he expects to continue experiments in the style utilized in the Redoutensaal with a company of his old players organized on a coöperative basis after the manner of the Moscow Art Theatre, and looking toward an ultimate rebirth of the formalized theatre of the *commedia*

[160]

MEDIEVAL INSPIRATION FOR THE LIVING THEATRE

Great Ballet and Caroussel in the Courtyard of the Hofburg, Vienna, January 24, 1667, from an Old Print in Reinhardt's Private Collection

From these Great Festival Productions, Reinhardt has Gained Much of His Inspiration not only for the Formal Theatre as in the Redoutensaal, but for His Mass Productions in Salzburg

A PRODUCTION IN THE SALLE DE SPECTACLE, VERSAILLES, 1745

An Example of the Formal Stage of the Eighteenth Century, from Reinhardt's
Collection of Old Prints

dell'arte, which, originating in Italy, attained perhaps its finest flower in old Vienna.—THE EDITOR.]

IN Vienna on Christmas Day, 1921, there were no matches in the match-stands of the cafés and no paper in the hotel writing rooms. Some of the well-to-do and the recklessly soft-hearted had begun to feel that they could afford to keep pet dogs again; but there were no silk stockings on those most un-Teuton ankles that paraded the Burgring. You may guess, therefore, that there was no butter on the tables of the middle classes, and no milk in the houses of those who, by a curious clairvoyance of language, are called the working people.

Two nights later three or four hundred citizens, with bits of bread and meat wrapped in paper and stowed in their pockets, could be seen seated in a great and splendid ballroom of Maria Theresia's palace, under the light of crystal chandeliers and the glow of priceless Gobelins, watching the first performance, "The Marriage of Figaro," in a theatre a stride ahead of any in Europe.

They had paid good money at one of the doors of that extraordinary old building, the Hofburg, which rambles from the Opera to the Burg Theater half across the shopping district of Vienna. After they had parted from two or three thousand crowns apiece, they had wound up stone stairways between white walls and twists of old ironwork, passed through cloakrooms where princesses once left their wraps, and a supper room where artists may cheerfully go mad over molding, pediment and mirror, and reached at last the Theater in dem Redoutensaal. They found one of the handsomest baroque rooms in Europe holding within its beauty both a stage and an auditorium. A row of Gobelin tapestries filled the lower reaches of the walls. Above were moldings and pilasters, cornices and pargeting, spandrels and pediments, fillets and panelling, an ordered richness of ornament that held suspended in its gray and golden haze mirrors that echoed beauty, and chandeliers radiant with light. At one end of the room, beneath great doors and a balcony which the architect had planned in 1744, was a new structure; it broke the line of the Gobelins, but continued the panelling, freshened to cream and gold, in a curving wall across a platform and in double stairs leading to the balcony. With man's unfailing instinct for the essence of life, the audience promptly indentified this roofless shell as a stage. There was a platform, of course, but there was no proscenium. There were doors and windows in the curving wall, but no woodwings, borders, flats, or backdrops. There was even a something along the front of the platform which might conceal footlights, but there was nothing to be seen that looked more like scenery than a row of screens.

Such is the room in which the forces of the Austrian State Opera House were giving "The Marriage of Figaro" and "The Barber of Seville" in the summer of 1922, and in which Reinhardt began in that fall the most interesting experiment of his most experimental life—the presentation of plays under a unique condition of theatrical intimacy between actor and audience.

It was an odd spectacle—Vienna, then the bankrupt, going lightheartedly out on the most advanced experiment in production yet attempted in Europe. One of its oddest angles was that the man who made an empress's ballroom

THE REDOUTENSAAL IN THE HOFBURG, VIENNA

As Used for a Concert Hall over a Century Ago. From an Old Print in a Portfolio, "Die Catalani," Published in 1821

GOETHE'S "CLAVIGO"

IN THE REDOUTENSAAL, VIENNA, SEPTEMBER, 1922

(Left to right) Luis Rainer as Carlos and Alexander Moissi as Clavigo

Photographs by Reiffenstein, Vienna

GOETHE'S "STELLA"

IN THE REDOUTENSAAL, VIENNA, OCTOBER, 1922

(Left to right) Wilhelm Dieterle as Fernando (standing); Lina Lossen as Cecilie
(at the rear of the bench); Helene Thimig as Stella (seated)

over into a theatre was a socialist—President Adolf Vetter of the Staatstheaterverwaltung, the bureau under the republic which controls the State playhouses. The conversion was not an easy matter. Opponents rose up inside the State theatres and outside them. Vienna was engaged for months upon one of those artistic quarrels from which it is always drawing new health and spirit.

When President Vetter had won his point he plunged briskly ahead at the work of making over the ballroom into a very special kind of theatre without marring its beauty. Part of the old balcony came out, mirrors replaced doors and windows down the sides of the hall, and Oberbaurat Sebastien Heinrich and Alfred Roller, friend and associate of Reinhardt, set to work on the problem of creating a permanent architectural setting for the stage which should harmonize with the lovely room, yet stand out from it significantly enough to centre attention on the acting space. Meantime, President Vetter took another look at the Gobelins which had satisfied Maria Theresia, and decided that they weren't quite good enough; others had to be found. Even now he is a little doubtful about those on the right hand wall.

The work of Roller and the Oberbaurat is admirable. They have continued the molding above the Gobelins, and made it the top of the curving wall which is the background for the stage. This shell is broken at each side by a casement, which holds either a door or a window, and two masked openings. Through one of these, close to the front of the stage, a curtain the height of the wall is run out to hide changes in the screens and furniture upon the stage. At the back, where the shell curves close to the old balcony of the ballroom, the architect has placed a pair of graceful stairways, which meet at the top, and provide, underneath, an exit to the rear. For lighting, there are the foots in their unobtrusive trough, and small floods placed in the gap where the curtain moves; but by far the larger part of the illumination comes from the seven chandeliers in the ceiling of the hall. The chandeliers toward the rear are sometimes turned half down or even off, and strong lamps are hidden in those at the front, but essentially it is the same light which illumines both players and audience.

The light and the formal and permanent character of the stage stamp the Redoutensaal with a character as old as it is fresh. This theatre goes beyond even Copeau's Vieux-Colombier in the attempt to re-establish in our century that active relationship between actor and spectator which existed in the great theatres of other centuries, and towards which the finest minds of the theatre have been striving. Here is a stage freed from all the associations of modern stage-setting, innocent of machinery or illusions, essentially theatrical. Actors must be actors upon its boards. They can not try to represent actual people; they can only present themselves to the audience as artists who will try to give them a vision of reality.

This is comparatively easy in opera. There is no realistic illusion about a valet who sings a soliloquy on his master's more intimate habits. People who quarrel in verse to a merry tune are most unlikely to be mistaken for the neighbors next door. With music and the stage of the Redoutensaal to aid them, the singers of the State Opera managed to give a roughly presentational performance. In direction there was nothing notable to be seen, unless it was the wedding scene in "Figaro" with the Count striding up and down across the front of the stage, opposed in figure and in action to the plaguing women above upon the stairs. The acting possibilities of this stage, however, are very great. Reinhardt saw them vividly in the summer of 1922, while he was making preparations for his four productions in the autumn: "Stella" and "Clavigo," by Goethe, "Dame Kobold," by Calderon, and "Beautiful Women," by Rey. He saw the possibilities and the difficulties of acting also, and he rejoiced that he was to have old and tried associates like Moissi, Thimig and Rainer with him once more when he began his experiment with a theatre far more exacting than the Grosses Schauspielhaus, and a technique of acting very hard to regain after so many years of realism.

So far as there must be indications of time and place upon this stage, the forces of the State Opera made a beginning in experiment. It was not a particularly good beginning, but it showed the opportunities for the artist, and also the limitations. They are very nearly identical. It is the business of the scene designer who works here to draw from the Redoutensaal itself the motifs and colors which he shall add to the permanent setting. It is his privilege, using only these things, to give the scene just the fillip of interest which the play demands.

Alfred Roller, a veteran of the scenic revolt of fifteen years ago, and, next to Reinhardt's artist, Ernst Stern, the most distinguished German scenic designer of his time, made the screens and set pieces for "The Marriage of Figaro" and "The Barber of Seville," as he did later for the productions by Reinhardt. In "The Marriage of Figaro" Roller made the first scene, the servant's room, out of a row of antique screens of faded crimson placed well down stage. Through a door in the central one, you saw green screens, which, in the second scene were to define the room of the wife. With an excellent sense of climax, Roller proceeded from the shallow stage of the first scene to the deeper stage of the second, and finally swept in the whole permanent setting for the wedding in the third scene. More than that, he called the stairs and balcony into play, and finally opened the great doors above the balcony to let us see beyond to a room of crimson hangings and more crystal. The last scene, the garden, was shoddily conceived, with a few uninteresting potted trees, a bad painting of Schönbrunn in the exit under the steps, and a sickly attempt at moonlight from the floodlights and foots. Why not, you wondered, delicate, artificial, gilded hedges along the walls, and fruit trees flattened on espaliers against the steps?

Perhaps the most serious question concerned with the physical arrangements of this stage is whether there should not be some scheme of levels other than floor and balcony. A lower forestage would aid the director in composing his people, and getting movement and variety out of this fixed and therefore limited setting. It would also aid an audience that is seated almost on a flat floor.

The sceptic may find other limitations in the Redoutensaal. And he will be right if he points out that its atmosphere is too sharply artificial in its distinction to permit every sort of play to be given here. Gorky's "The Lower Depths" might be played in the Redoutensaal as

[166]

a literally tremendous "tour de force," but it would be in the face of spiritual war between the background of the stage and the physical horrors of the slums which the play describes. Plays for the Redoutensaal must have some quality of distinction about them, a great, clear, emotion free from the bonds of physical detail, a fantasy or a poetry as shining as crystal, some artificiality of mood, or else an agreement in period with the baroque. You can imagine Racine or Corneille done perfectly here, Euripides only by great genius, "The Weavers" not at all. Nothing could suit Molière better, or Beaumarchais or the Restoration dramatists. Shakespeare could contribute "Twelfth Night" and "A Midsummer Night's Dream," perhaps "Romeo and Juliet," but never "Hamlet." Here, of course, is a perfect stage for Oscar Wilde, a good stage for Somerset Maugham, A. A. Milne, some of Clare Kummer. The Moscow Art Theatre would have no trouble with "The Cherry Orchard." More or less at random, you think of Bahr's "Josephine," "The School for Scandal," "The Sabine Women," "Lysistrata," "The Mollusc," "A Marriage of Convenience," "The Truth," "Prunella," "The Beggar's Opera." The one impossible barrier to performance in the Redoutensaal is atmosphere. If a play is drenched in the emotions of firesides, poppy fields, moonlit gardens or natural physical things, it is impossible here.

These are the limitations of the Redoutensaal, not of its idea. The permanent setting and its enclosing hall can take the shapes of other periods and meet almost every demand of the drama except atmosphere. Ideally the hall should have some sober yet arresting architecture com-

[167]

mon to many periods. A neutral order of this sort might be the blank Roman arches and plain pilasters which are seen so often in modern buildings. The chandeliers might take a form less ornate and less blazing; nuances of lighting, if desirable, might then be achieved. More important, however, would be to have three interchangeable shells and steps. One set of walls should be classical and severe, suited to Greek tragedy, "Julius Cæsar," and, with a bit of brightening, to Shaw's "Cæsar and Cleopatra." Another shell should strike the note of artificial distinction with which the Redoutensaal now echoes. The third should be of dark, paneled wood, to suit Shakespearean tragedy, the comedy of Goldsmith, and modern pieces from "Rosmersholm" to "Getting Married" and from "Alice Sit-by-the-Fire" to "Magda."

The idea of a permanent room in which to act a related repertory is thoroughly applicable even to our peepshow playhouses with their prosceniums. It would be possible to install a shell or room on the stage of any reasonably presentable theatre, such as Henry Miller's, the Little, the Booth, the Plymouth, the Selwyn in New York, the Künstler in Munich, the Volksbühne, the Kammerspiele in Berlin, the Comédie des Champs-Elysées in Paris, St. Martin's in London. The room would have to be formal, probably without a ceiling, and certainly far more like a wall than a room.

Such a compromise seems the only chance America may have of experimenting with the idea of the Redoutensaal. There is nowhere in this country a room so naturally fitted to the purpose by its beauty as was the ballroom of the Hapsburgs. The building of a fresh struc-

THE REDOUTENSAAL, VIENNA, AS MODERN FORMAL THEATRE

A Drawing by Robert Edmond Jones of Maria Theresia's Cream and Crystal Ballroom, with Its Priceless Gobelins, as Used Today by Reinhardt for One of His Latest and Most Successful Experiments

ture is a little too much to ask; for we have hardly the directors or actors to launch unpractised upon such a costly and critical test. It might be risked perhaps, as Frank Lloyd Wright proposed risking it, in a theatre of purely artistic nature far from Broadway. Wright designed for Aline Barnsdall a playhouse to be erected in California, with an adjustable proscenium, a stage with a dome that all but continued over the auditorium, and, upon the stage, a plain curving wall some ten feet high, following the shape of the dome. The nearest analogy to the Redoutensaal that has been actually attempted in America is probably the adaptation which Director Sam Hume and the artists Rudolph Schaeffer and Norman Edwards made of the Greek Theatre in Berkeley, California, for "Romeo and Juliet" and "Twelfth Night." There is a certain significance, however, in the pleasure which our scenic artists seem to get out of a play which gives them only one setting to design, but which requires them to wring from it, by means of lights, many moods and a variety of visual impressions. Lee Simonson's circus greenroom for "He Who Gets Slapped" and Norman-Bel Geddes' sitting room for "The Truth About Blayds" showed how seductive to the artist of the theatre may be the game of playing with lights in a permanent setting.

Approached purely from the point of view of scenic art, or the so-called new stagecraft, the Redoutensaal presents excellent reasons for its existence. Historically it could be defended by a study of the theatre from the Greeks, with their daylit, architectural background, to Georgian times when the stage and the house were both

[169]

lighted by the same chandeliers, and the wide apron, the boxes, and the proscenium made a sort of permanent setting which was varied by the shifting backcloths. But if we go no further back than the days when Craig and Appia were beginning to write, and before their voices and their pencils had won an audience among theatre directors, we shall find the start of an evolutionary development for which the idea of the Redoutensaal provides a plausible climax. In the first decade of the twentieth century, the "flat" was flat indeed, and the painted wing and backdrop ruled. If there was any depth, it was the space between wing and wing, or the false space of painted perspective. Then the ideas of Craig and Appia, making a curious alliance with realism, forced the plastic upon the stage. The solid, three-dimensional setting dominated. When directors and artists began to discover the physical and spiritual limitations of "real" settings which could present nothing bigger than the actual stage space, many went back to the painted flat. It was a different flat, however, one painted with dynamic and expressive design. The third method is seldom quite satisfactory. The living actor, with his three-dimensional being, clashes with the two-dimensional painting. The result is bad from a realistic or illusionistic point of view; and, as soon as we think of the stage in terms of a frank convention, we find that we want the emphasis thrown upon the actor as the more interesting and the more difficult element. We want a defined and permanent artificiality that shall give the actor scope, serve as a *pied-à-terre*, not in a fantastic competition. We can escape plastic and limited reality in the Redoutensaal, while we supply the actor with a

[170]

background that harmonizes with the living character of his body. At the same time we can secure the vivid indication of mood or time or place which we seek, and achieve it more vividly because of the permanence of the main fabric of the stage, and its contrast with the merely indicated setting.

German scene designers and directors move in theory steadily towards what they call the podium, the platform pure and simple, from which the player addresses the audience openly as a player. In practice they tend steadily to try to approach this by driving out as much of changing scenic background as possible. They place something in the middle of the stage, a table, a flight of steps, a pillar, a bed, and they try to eliminate the rest of the stage. Jessner does this in Berlin by using his cyclorama as a neutral boundary without character in itself. Fehling, the director of "Masse-Mensch," uses black curtains, and the artist Krehan by the same means tries to centre our attention on small set pieces placed in the middle of the stage and designed to represent corners of rooms or a sofa by a window. Black curtains appear everywhere in Germany—perhaps as an expression of the mood of the beaten nation, but also unquestionably from a desire to drive out both realism and pretense and to leave as little as possible upon the stage except the actor and the barest and most essential indication of setting. Instead he gets desolation, spiritual negation.

In the Redoutensaal, the actor is backed up by space. It is a positive presence instead of a negative background. Yet it does not obtrude, this splendid room, with its gold and gray, its mirrors and its tapestries. These things float in the back of consciousness, filling what might be a disquieting void or a depressing darkness. Always the cream walls dominate the gray, and always the living actor, driving his message directly at the spectator, dominates them all.

Such is the theatre to which Reinhardt turned from his exile in Salzburg. Master of acting and of actors, of atmosphere and of setting, servant of realism and spectacle, worker in little theatres and in circuses, pioneer of the cabaret and priest of the churchly drama, outstanding figure in every field which the modern theatre has explored, Reinhardt came to the Redoutensaal with an eagerness of spirit which only a thing both old and new could awaken. Here was the Vienna of the centuries, and the theatre of all time. Here were tradition and revolution, wedded in progress. Here was the last experiment. It should lead him back to the fundamentals of the playhouse—to the art of the actor in all the purity of true make-believe.

Chapter XV

REINHARDT'S SALZBURG

BY OLIVER M. SAYLER

UNDER the shadow of the Untersberg and the Gaisberg and the more distant but neighborly protection of the Watzmann and the Hohe Göll, just before the Austrian Tyrol loses itself to the northward in rolling plains, and just across the border from Bavaria, lies the ancient and venerable town of Salzburg to which I have dedicated this volume. The reason for that dedication, as I have indicated, is that Salzburg is not only the home of Max Reinhardt but the cradle and capstone of his art. In a very real sense, Salzburg today is Reinhardt's Salzburg. It is he who has lifted it once more to international repute and importance. Through it as a focal lens, it is possible to view Reinhardt as a man and to examine his ripened theories of the theatre as he has made them concrete and manifest.

Unlike the wild retreats where nature's task resents improvements, cities and towns are products of men and women, the offspring of human civilization. The personality of a race, a clan, a family, or an individual lies behind them and lives through them. Sometimes a single breath of life runs thrilling through them and perpetuates them long after the life itself has ceased to be a vital

[173]

force and has become a dim legend. Thus, Potsdam: Frederick the Great; Assisi: St. Francis; Granada: the Moors; Nikko: the Shogun Iyeyasu. At other times, the vitalizing breath of human personality recurs to give new, potent and contemporary meaning to stones which otherwise would be mere reminders of a glorious but dead past. Thus, Fontainebleau: Francis I, Louis the XVI, Napoleon; Florence: Dante, Lorenzo de Medici, Robert Browning; Geneva: John Calvin, Jean Jacques Rousseau.

To this latter classification belongs Salzburg. First, it was Roman outpost, camp and deathplace of Marcus Aurelius. Then, as the medieval church waxed wise, beautiful and powerful, it became the site of the most lavish and brilliant sacred builders north of the Italian frontier. Later, with the advent of Wolfgang Amadeus Mozart, it was known as the musical fountain-head of Austria and of the world of its time. And now, by the grace of the little man who played his first season in its new municipal theatre and returned to it with all his ripened powers to live and work, it is the Mecca of the contemporary art of the living theatre. The Archbishops Wolf Dietrich and Paris Lodron; Mozart; Reinhardt. To each of these in turn, Salzburg has truly belonged in spirit —most richly to the latest in the line of succession, just because it had belonged so securely to his predecessors, had expressed their spirit so amply, and thereby had laid up for his dynamic and eclectic imagination a fund of tangible and intangible treasure on which he could draw at will—atmosphere and architecture, esthetic theory and civic pride.

The first glimpse of Salzburg with its fortress perched

Paap, Salzburg

IN THE GARDEN AT SCHLOSS LEOPOLDSKRON

Morris Gest and Max Reinhardt Laying Plans for the American Production of "The Miracle," between Eighteenth Century Figures in the Grounds of Reinhardt's Castle

IN THE CHAPEL AT SCHLOSS LEOPOLDSKRON

Reinhardt Rehearsing Lady Diana Manners in the Rôle of the Madonna in "Th
Miracle" in Salzburg, August, 1923

on an eminence as perfect as that of Edinburgh, reveals
nature shaped shrewdly by the human imagination. Im-
pregnable power made beautiful by the hand of the artist.
Extended acquaintance discloses evidence of more than
one imagination, more than one prince, more than one
artist. A hierarchy, a dynasty, of rulers and builders.
Only thus could this nest of imposing structures have
grown in the constricted plot of land between Hohensalzburg and the hurrying flood of the Salzach. Only thus
could the area of twenty city blocks hold relics that engross the attention for weeks without being exhausted.
Salzburg today, Reinhardt's Salzburg, has had a past
which is not only fascinating in itself but which lives
potently once more in its present. Unlike Venice, it is
not a mere monument. The mouths of a former glory,
Reinhardt has discovered, can be taught the language of
today, while they themselves contribute to contemporary
tongues a rare and forgotten accent.

Just what was this elder Salzburg that lay sleeping
but not dead, waiting for a Reinhardt to stir it once more
to creative life? What was it in itself? What are its
implications today? How is it possible to see Reinhardt,
man and artist, more clearly through its focal lens?

Whatever praise or blame is chargeable elsewhere to
the combination of spiritual and temporal rule, the results of such a regime justified it here. The church militant and the state beautiful. There was nothing of the
recluse or the hermit in the religion of the Archbishops
who guided town and duchy through medieval strife, the
Peasants' Rebellion and the Thirty Years' War, as un-
molested as an island in the Atlantic. Nor were mere

power and its resulting safety sufficient in the eyes of these *markgrafs* of Rome. Something deep within them bade them build for the glory of their name and of the Church—to make Salzburg, despite its typically Teutonic fortress, the northernmost Italian city. And if there wasn't room to build, down came an earlier Gothic edifice to make way for the new one in the current baroque.

The age of Wolf Dietrich roughly paralleled the Elizabethan. Paris Lodron built the marble Dom while we were busy piling logs into cabins on Cole's hill and along the James. Abbey and cloister; chapel, church and cathedral; palace and castle; fortifications knitting them all together like a western Kremlin; a tunnel driven like a Gothic arch through the conglomerate rock of the Mönchsberg, the natural eyry on which Hohensalzburg or the *Festung* had been growing gray with age already for six centuries.

But the days of temporal glory for these princes of the church waned and passed. Hohensalzburg was no match for modern cannon, and during the Napoleonic wars, the town on the border was bidden by ephemeral treaties to obey one master after another. Meanwhile, however, a new jewel was set securely and eternally in Salzburg's crown. Alongside art and architecture came music with Mozart, born in a tenement in the narrow Getreidegasse and nurtured in his art in the local court until he was ready for flight to metropolitan Vienna. His memory, persisting here through a century and a half, finally found concrete expression in 1914 in the Mozarteum, an admirably equipped concert hall and music

SCHLOSS LEOPOLDSKRON FROM AN OLD PRINT IN REINHARDT'S COLLECTION

SCHLOSS LEOPOLDSKRON TODAY, WITH HOHENSALZBURG AND THE GAISBERG
IN THE BACKGROUND

TWO VIEWS OF REINHARDT'S CASTLE HOME IN SALZBURG

SCHLOSS LEOPOLDSKRON FROM THE LAKE

Würthle & Sohn, Salzburg

THE MARBLE HALL IN SCHLOSS LEOPOLDSKRON

INTERIOR AND EXTERIOR OF REINHARDT'S CASTLE HOME IN SALZBURG

school, enabling Salzburg to serve as the musical convention city of Central Europe.

When Max Reinhardt determined in his maturity to
return to Austria and the scenes of his professional ap-
prenticeship, he found these varied material and spiritual
remnants from a storied past:

Physical structures abounded, all in reasonably good
repair. There was a stately home at hand in Schloss
Leopoldskron, a castle with its baroque beauty intact
since its erection by the Archbishop Leopold Firmian as
wedding gift to his nephew in 1740, in whose marble hall
and spacious grounds this prince of the theatre could
hold fitting court. With the passing of temporal kings
and princes, there are few men alive who could do more
than rattle around or make vain show of living in such a
milieu. But Reinhardt can and does measure up to its
challenge.

There were theatres—natural theatres, most of them
intended for other uses—standing ready for his vitalizing
imagination. The Domplatz, the huge enclosed square
in front of the Cathedral, which he chose first to favor
with his production of "Everyman" in the open air. The
Kollegienkirche, Fischer von Erlach's pearl of the late
baroque, site of von Hofmannsthal's "The Great World-
Theatre." The musty and mysterious nave of the
Franziskanerkirche, opening and rising into the daylit
choir, which waits impatiently the first production of "The
Miracle" in a real church. The Summer Riding School
with its three tiers of boxes hewn out of the solid rock
of the Mönchsberg and the greensward for sylvan stage,
ready at the whim of Salzburg's first citizen to welcome

"As You Like It." The Winter Riding School, already emergency auditorium for "Everyman," when Salzburg's incessant rain drove the players and spectators indoors from the Domplatz, and scheduled as temporary home of the projected Festival Playhouse in Hellbrunn's meadow. The natural stone theatre in Hellbrunn made to order for eerie performance of "The Tempest."

And finally, the inspiring park of Schloss Hellbrunn itself, scene of the prankish waterworks with their far-famed marionette theatre, strange by-product of a civilization that had time to burn and source of endless delight to this little modern man of action. Here in the meadow-cup, rimmed by the entire bodyguard of protecting mountains, he would build the Festival Playhouse which would capitalize the best of the elder remnants and crystallize the new spirit he himself could contribute to Salzburg's creative annals. He, too, would be a builder, a fashioner of the native conglomerate rock and the marble from the Untersberg, like Dietrich and Lodron and Firmian before him.

Less obvious but more significant and more potent were the spiritual remnants he detected, sleeping but still alive. Lineal descendants of those who had executed the orders of the great builders, a race undiluted by immigration or emigration, contemporary Salzburgers know what art is, what it may be—a vital component of life, something to inspire every-day with a sense of the infinite, not an inert specimen in the glass case of a museum. Art to the Salzburger is not an affectation but a necessity.

Music, too, is taken for granted in the Salzburg scheme of things. Mozart probably would have been Mozart without that atmosphere. Genius like his is independent of encouragement and environment. But, despite the niggardly support of the reigning prince, the musical tradition of the city, fathered like its art by the Church, undoubtedly served as stimulating background. And Mozart in turn, reciprocated by providing relay stimulus for the generations that followed him.

Another tradition with roots in a far past, which merely awaited the Magician's hand to give it eager impetus, was that of peasant play and festival. On their holidays, the villagers from the neighboring mountain towns preserve the old customs of the mysterium, the passion play and the folk dance, executed with the ancient masks handed down from the Middle Ages. On occasion, they still swarm by the thousands into the capital of the duchy in quaint and colorful native gown and headgear to celebrate their games and sports in the old time *Trachtenfest*.

Even less tangible and still more significant is the tradition of civic integrity still dominating the citizenship of Salzburg and cherished with a determination and reserved pride which is unsuspected until emergency spurs it into action. Such an emergency arose several years ago before Reinhardt's return. Without the assured future promised by that event as an alternative choice, the officials and populace of the town faced frankly the project of making it a fabulously prosperous Central European Monte Carlo with gambling pavilion located in the nearby royal castle of Klessheim, and in spite of economic conditions without a ray of hope at the time, they grimly and resentfully turned the proposition down.

MAX REINHARDT AND HIS THEATRE

Finally, waiting Reinhardt's wand, was the natural situation of Salzburg at the heart of the trans-continental arteries of Europe, remnant of the days when Roman and medieval caravans passed through it to the East, a location which was recognized and further assured when builders of railroads routed their tracks through its *Bahnhof*. Tourists knew Salzburg and how to get there, even if they were not always sure whether it was in Germany, Bavaria, Czecho-Slovakia or Austria.

The individual and especially the collective significance of these remnants was not apparent to the outsider. Even the casual tourist probably did not suspect their existence, let alone their exciting import. The general impression that swept through well-travelled Americans when they heard the announcement of Reinhardt's abdication from Berlin and his proposal to make Salzburg the axis of his future activities was that here was a case of preciosity, of his unbridled imagination gone wrong for once. What could it mean but that he was aping Bayreuth and Weimar? Even today, after Reinhardt has proved partially what he can make Salzburg mean, it is impossible to conceive how rich is the promise of his dream without going there and observing it in process of realization. Fully to visualize this picture of the living theatre in the making, is like trying to paint, for one who has never been there, a convincing word canvas of such strange and mysterious crowns of a fabulous civilization as Moscow and Peking.

By an almost miraculous intuition, however, Reinhardt saw the opportunities implicit in these dormant remnants of a glorious past—saw them in the memories

HE MARIONETTE THEATRE AT SCHLOSS HELLBRUNN, SALZBURG

his Tiny Stage, Operated by Water Power and By-product of an Idle Civilization,
is a Source of Constant Delight to the Tireless Reinhardt

Photographs by Würthle & Sohn, Salzburg

THE MUNICIPAL THEATRE, SALZBURG

In This Playhouse, During Its First Season in 1894, Max Reinhardt Made His
Début as an Actor

MEDIEVAL SALZBURG
From an Old Print in Reinhardt's Collection

Würthle & Sohn, Salzburg

SALZBURG TODAY
A View from the Same Vantage Point, the Kapuzinerberg
REINHARDT'S SALZBURG, OLD AND NEW

cherished from his early days in Salzburg as a young actor, memories whose true meaning he fully and really understood only after his wealth of experience in a wide world. The process by which he came to see them, I shall permit him to explain in his own words later. In the course of four years, he has carried realization to the extent of establishing his residence in Salzburg, of entering fully into its life as its first citizen; of making three productions, two ambitious and one intimate, within the town's precincts; of planning numerous other productions; and of projecting on paper the details for a Festival Playhouse which will consolidate and coördinate all of the remnants and traditions of the past as well as his own fresh and original contributions to their spiritually wealthy annals.

In the light of these partially fulfilled dreams, it is possible to obtain an illuminating glimpse of Reinhardt, the man, the citizen, the international force, the artist of the theatre.

Life at Schloss Leopoldskron has all the elements of a figment of a prolific imagination. How little did Archbishop Firmian realize that in laying stone upon stone, in encrusting wall and ceiling with stucco wreaths rich in allegory, in bejewelling each room with a myriad mirrors, he was rearing a palace for a prince of the theatre he hated, such as modern funds and craftsmanship could never hope to approximate! Midway between the medieval lodge in the woods and the overgrown and unwieldy edifice like Fontainebleau and Schönbrunn, Schloss Leopoldskron can be made and is being made cordial and habitable by one with the varied, generous, cosmopolitan taste of Reinhardt. In his hands, a castle has become not a mere museum nor a vain channel for pomp and magnificence but a laboratory and home commensurate with the dreams, the labors, and the diversions of its owner.

Here on winter nights, when the Alpine winds whirl down from the legendary caves of the Untersberg, the prince sits in his library annotating the *Regie* Book for a production he will make, God willing, a year or even five years hence. Here, through long summer days and evenings, prior to the beginning of his own workday at midnight, he walks and talks on shaded paths and sits drinking coffee on the terrace with visitors from the ends of the earth. The problem of getting work done in Leopoldskron seems insuperable unless you too are willing to begin your day at midnight.

From this almost baronial stronghold, a mile and a half from the town but within sight of the *Festung*, Reinhardt keeps in close touch with Salzburg and its civic affairs when he is not directing a guest season in nearby Vienna or distant New York. His favorite route to the town is to tramp hatless in summer the winding path which leads round the fortress with the Nonnberg cloisters at its base. Then in the narrow streets of the town or at table in one of the numerous cafés, he may be seen engaged in earnest conversation with banker and artist and churchman, discussing the details of his latest venture to make Salzburg a living force in the world today.

Not only the work he does and the productions he directs, but also the life he lives, therefore, make Reinhardt and Reinhardt's Salzburg an international magnet

[182]

to attract outstanding personalities from the four corners of the earth. If Reinhardt and his mountain will not come to Mahomet, the Mahomets of the five continents and the seven seas must come to the mountain. A stream of cosmopolitan visitors, acquainted with him intimately or casually or not at all, pours through the hotels of the town, telephones to the Schloss or descends without warning upon the princely domain. And all are welcomed, for Reinhardt can not find it in his heart to deny a single one. Besides, his workday begins at midnight, so why not live until then? The stream reached its peak in the summer of 1923, when plans for "The Miracle" in New York brought half a hundred continental and American artists for consultation, trial and testing; Norman-Bel Geddes, young American designer of the production, with blue prints of the entire project for Reinhardt's review and approval; and, finally, Morris Gest himself, who, with his Russian intensity and American energy, and by aid of a retinue of newspapermen and secretaries, turned the quiet town and the quieter castle into a skyscraper of activity through five crowded days.

To conceive what Reinhardt will ultimately make Salzburg accomplish for him and the theatre of his time, still requires strong faith and a vivid imagination. Thus far he has here found two authentic channels of self-expression, both concerned with the living theatre rather than with that of illusion: one of them by way of the intimate stage, with players and spectators caught up in a single, cordial, close-knit circle; the other by way of the theatre of masses—masses of players, masses of spectators—differing from the former only in its scope and the degree and kind of emotional reactions made possible by that scope. Experiments along the latter line have already become known to fame through the ventures of 1920, 1921, and 1922—"Everyman" and "The Great World-Theatre." The former mood has had single trial in the production of Molière's "Le Malade Imaginaire," in the castle in August, 1923, when Max Pallenberg as Argan swung the lariat of his wit in the carefree manner of the *commedia dell'arte* and ensnared with it not only the rest of the players but the last of a hundred spectators seated luxuriously in Archbishop Firmian's golden chairs round the great blaze in the fireplace of the marble hall at Leopoldskron.

Salzburg's past, therefore, has been made to order for its present under Reinhardt's sponsorship. Its buildings give him provocative stages and auditoriums. Its musical tradition enables him for diversion to entertain and enchant a brilliant audience with chamber-concerts by the Rosé and other quartets in the mellow splendor of the marble hall or to beguile his guests in an upper window of the Residenz with the Haffner-serenade played by torchlight by a quartet of quartets in the courtyard below. That tradition, too, he dreams of calling into more commanding service with productions of the Mozart operas in the Festival Playhouse in Hellbrunn. And the local tradition of folk plays he has already made sufficiently articulate that numerous nearby villages have repeated with success on their peasant stages productions of "Everyman" and "The Great World-Theatre." Little by little, he is gathering together long neglected skeins of human impulse and knitting them once more into a new tradition

[184]

wholly unlike that of which they once before formed a
part. Little by little, he is vitalizing a community, and
that community is revitalizing him, until Rome's Salzburg
and Mozart's Salzburg shall become in truth and for all
time—until another maker of traditions arises—Reinhardt's Salzburg.

Chapter XVI

THE SALZBURG PROJECT

I

IN SEARCH OF A LIVING THEATRE

BY MAX REINHARDT

(English Translation by Lucie R. Sayler)

[No single aspect of Reinhardt's entire career holds more implications for the future—if a confused world ever permits its realization—than the project for the erection of a Festival Playhouse in Reinhardt's home city. To this project which already has three preliminary productions to its credit— "Everyman," "The Great World-Theatre," and "Le Malade Imaginaire"—Reinhardt has devoted the major part of his time and thought for the last three years. It is fitting, therefore, that the story of its genesis and significance be introduced by his own pen. For the first time in his career, he has consented to write here about his own work, a diversion which his preoccupation with the work itself has heretofore prevented. Previous biographers and critics have attempted in vain to elicit from him such self-commentary. Despite the fact that engrossing preparations for "The Miracle" necessitated leaving portions of this chapter in outline form, it is a gesture of respect to his American audience that he has consented to break his rule at all for the sake of the present volume.—THE EDITOR.]

THE SALZBURG PROJECT

THREE great things I learned in Berlin: (1) The secret of work, which is perhaps more foreign to the Austrian than to any other people or nation; the pleasure of work, which is of the most decisive importance in art and in the theatre. (2) Something which only Northern people have (in contrast to the Italian or Latin manner): *a restrained, impenetrable, economical* way of playing, which happened to be very near to my own nature and at the same time of great significance for the Northern literature arising at that time. This is also the key to the production of Shakespeare. (3) Northern literature, then new. Ibsen, Hauptmann, Strindberg.

The whole Berlin period of twenty-five years was filled with the recognition of these three things. And now that I am once more back in Austria, after my wanderings among the Northern landscapes, I feel so thoroughly at home there, that I am essentially conscious that these three great acquisitions do not mean everything for the theatre, though much. Even in that passionate work inspired by the activity of a great city theatre the most precious thing is lost: the sense of play, which was so strong in childhood and can not be dispensed with in art and especially not in the theatre. I am conscious that the Northern manner of playing, which can naturally never be lost but must be cherished solely for the sake of this repertory, hides within itself the danger of leading to impoverishment and fossilization. I realize that the dramatic elements, as they are found in the old Austrian and Bavarian theatre, such as the *commedia dell' arte*, the production of mystery-plays, religious works, French, Spanish and Italian plays, and the musical element in the

[187]

theatre, can not find sufficient nourishment on that stage. And I understand finally that the third subject, literature, has tyrannised too much over the theatre and carried it too far away from its starting-point. Literature easily leads too far into abstraction.

Strongly convinced of all this again in my home landscape, I have felt the desire to create a theatre there where the theatre originated, on Austro-Bavarian soil, in the city where I began my career. Here is a real folk-poetry (Oberammergau, Zell-am-See, etc.), and this poetry does not exist to be read in books, but has sprung from the joy of play. Only thus can the true theatre originate.

Salzburg, because of its situation, its architecture, its past history, Mozart, and the great intelligence and independence of the ecclesiastical circles who have ruled there and consequently have always had much influence, is the natural place for this theatre. A truly festival spot, where all men gather to spend their holidays. Whether it be to climb mountains; or to enjoy the beautiful, almost undisturbed architecture of earlier times, or music. So it was a logical idea to found there a theatre that would be likewise in festival and holiday spirit, that would be built on principles different from those under which a theatre enterprise in a great city suffers, that would be as free as possible from all commercial conditions. I have tried to avoid these myself, and I have never taken a penny up to this time for my own work. I have asked the same of the players and I have not been disappointed. The Festspiel corporation comprises leading people of the idealistic classes. They keep themselves free from any

WERNER KRAUSS IN "EVERYMAN"

HELENE THIMIG IN VON HOFMANNSTHAL'S "THE GREAT
WORLD-THEATRE"

WISDOM AND THE DEVIL IN TWO SALZBURG PRODUCTIONS

MOLIÈRE'S "LE MALADE IMAGINAIRE"

In the Marble Hall of Schloss Leopoldskron

Hansi Niese as Toinette and Max Pallenberg as Argan in Private Performance in
Salzburg, August, 1923

commercial transactions. Great support was found also among the population.

The fundamental idea was: to let the theatre become a festival again, as it was in ancient times and in the Middle Ages under the leadership of the Church, while in the great city it is in most cases rather entertainment and amusement. From my first year in the theatre in Salzburg I remembered the beautiful garden at Hellbrunn and approached the Emperor Francis Joseph on the subject of giving over this park for the erection of a Festspielhaus. The old Emperor willingly agreed with this project and all details were already arranged through the office of the master of ceremonies. But the war and its consequences, and later the abdication of the Imperial house have delayed the carrying out of the original plans, changed them in many details, but have not caused them to be given up, and have rather strengthened them in all essentials.

Next, I studied the extant folk-literature, and many mystery-plays, as these still exist in the Salzburg neighborhood, or have been collected by individuals. And it now became important to find *two people* in particular as helpers in this work. First, a dramatic censor, in the finest sense of this word. Not one who reads plays that have been sent to him and writes refusals, but one who is able to bring to life for our time the rich existing material; to work it over and adapt it to the existing resources, actors and localities. I knew no man who could do this better than the Austrian poet, Hugo von Hofmannsthal, with whom I had already been in close relationship for many years, and who most eagerly agreed to my plan.

[189]

MAX REINHARDT AND HIS THEATRE

The second man who was necessary was a great musician, who could fill this old musical city, Mozart's birthplace, with the music of our time. Strauss was available, for I had had a strong, active connection with him also. Strauss, through my performances, had received the impulse to write his first operas, "Salome" and "Elektra." And I had staged the original productions of "Der Rosenkavalier" and "Ariadne" in Dresden and Stuttgart.

Then from among prominent Salzburg citizens, who had already founded a Mozart Society, a Festspielhaus Committee was formed, which took over the constructive part of the whole plan.

The first active venture under these auspices was the production of "Everyman," with the consent of the Archbishop, in the Domplatz, with the best actors of Germany and Austria. A stage of boards in front of the Cathedral doors. Heralds who announce the play. Entrance of the actors from the neighboring Squares. The bells of all the churches ring. Organ. Choir from the Cathedral. Mystic cries from the church-towers, down from the *Festung* or Fortress and from a greater distance, calling Everyman to death. The Devil springing up from between the spectators' benches to the podium. Faith and the Angel coming out of the Cathedral at the end. The broad Squares fill with a dense crowd of spectators. From the windows of the neighboring monastery, monks and priests: in the first row, the Archbishop and the Cathedral Chapter. Traffic is completely stopped, and the whole city listens and watches breathlessly. Wonderful play of light—first, daylight; then sunset; then finally, torches.

The result was that not only many friends came to see the play, but the whole country population streamed and pressed in from the vicinity. And, most important of all, in the following year, the old mystery-play by von Hofmannsthal was presented in many localities. Especially good productions of it took place in Mondsee, Zell-am-See, and other peasant villages. The year after that it was repeated with a great crowd. A folk-poet put it in dialect and toured with his company in it.

"Everyman," thus, really came to *life*. The Archbishop wept when the Paternoster was spoken. Priests have said that the play was stronger than any sermon, that it had not been handled in such a way as to bring forth an empty old play as a curiosity for a few people interested in historical things, but that the accomplishment of the *regisseur* and his dramatic collaborator had consisted in making this old folk-play really alive, filled with the spirit of today, and once more a community possession for the people. In fact, the giant post-war social revolutions, the new wealth arising everywhere, the dangerous materialism of today, all gave a great contemporary significance and deeply penetrating moral effect to this old play about the death of a rich man.

The second work of the past year was "The Great World-Theatre" by Calderon, likewise in a version of von Hofmannsthal. This work, thanks to the courageous and far-seeing cooperation of the Archbishop, could be played in the church itself—even in the old Jesuit church, the splendid baroque building of Fischer von Erlach, the Kollegienkirche.

Actual original touches of von Hofmannsthal: the

beggar deeply affected by communistic ideas, which are carried *ad absurdum*. Voices of the Angels from high up. Old Gregorian alternating chants. The people seated almost three hours without intermission. Spellbound. The Dance of Death. Here, too, the play really came to *life*. Not a resurrection of history, nothing of the museum, but made contemporary.

The *regisseur's* work was evident, for example, in the Dance of Death. As it appears in the original manuscript, Death was one of the smaller rôles. Since the actor was so rhythmic and sensitive in his physical reaction, I built up a whole dance macabre around him in which death singled out each individual performer, greeted and dismissed him.

The native population coöperated here, too; in the choir and below on the stage. Natives were chosen for many of the rôles: a peasant player from Reichenhall played the Peasant; a citizen of Salzburg, Curiosity. All before sold-out houses. And meanwhile, morning, afternoon and evening, performances of Mozart's works by the Vienna Philharmonic Orchestra with singers from the Vienna Opera under the direction of Richard Strauss. Mozart-Mass in the Cathedral. Concerts in the Mozarteum. Mozart's Haffner-serenade by torchlight in the court of the old Episcopal residence. The famous Austrian Rosé quartet plays in Leopoldskron before American, French, German and Austrian guests. An international public.

Poelzig, the most highly-gifted German architect, builder of the Grosses Schauspielhaus in Berlin, is chosen to build the great Festspielhaus in Hellbrunn. A big

Photographs by Ellinger, Salzburg

THE THEATRE RETURNS TO THE CHURCH

The Kollegienkirche, Salzburg, with a Stage in the Course of Construction before the Altar, and a Scene from von Hofmannsthal's "The Great World-Theatre," as Produced There in August, 1922

The Model for the First Plan, Rejected for a Simpler and Less Rococo Design

Interior of the Second and Current Plan, Showing Auditorium and Stage Arched
by the Same Ceiling

TWO OF HANS POELZIG'S PROJECTED PLANS FOR THE SALZBURG
FESTIVAL PLAYHOUSE

building for mystery-plays and large operas, a small one for Mozart operas and more intimate plays. The cornerstone is laid in 1922 in the presence of the Austrian Government, the Archbishop and others.

Poelzig's project has been delayed through difficulty of obtaining funds necessary to erect such a building today. And yet it has proved fortunate that the project could not be carried out at once, because it was only during that period of practical experiment that the Festspiel idea has become fully and clearly crystallized. So here a costly theatre was not first created and then afterwards the contents sought, but the very reverse was the case.

The original plan contemplated drawing on the wealth of world-literature. Today it is clearly decided that mystery-plays should compose the greater part of the repertory and that old and new music, especially the Mozart operas, should be cherished. For the production of mystery-plays, a baroque, fantastic theatre building like Poelzig's first project is not required, but a severe, holy interior, like a Cathedral. The pathos of height. No extensive mechanism for a stage technique. In the near future Poelzig's project will scarcely be possible to realize. Therefore, Alfred Roller's plan has taken shape to make over for temporary use the old riding-school in the inner city.

MAX REINHARDT AND HIS THEATRE

II

A FESTIVAL PLAYHOUSE IN THE ALPS

BY HERMAN GEORGE SCHEFFAUER

Max Reinhardt is being drawn, perhaps even driven away from Berlin. The amusement tax that breaks the back of theatrical enterprise; feuds of art and feuds of finance between rival directorships; the feeling that a new generation, bred by the war, rude, full of revolt and a lust for conquest, is pounding at the doors he opened and closed—such are a few of the factors in this move.

It may be that Reinhardt has scented a new world to conquer, that he wishes to remove himself to rarer and purer altitudes of activity than Berlin-after-the-war can offer. His eyes are now directed southward to Salzburg in Austria, one of the most beautiful spots in the world, a romantic landscape composed as by Salvator Rosa in his gentler mood. Here, in the ancient and historic park of the Schloss of Hellbrunn, Reinhardt sees a new temple of the drama arise, a spacious and noble fabric, a kind of lay cathedral or cathedral organ, quiring amidst the trees, shining against the snow-clad hills of the Salzkammergut. The thing is as yet only a vision, a project, a committee program, an architect's sketch. Yet it will be born in obedience to the will of the man of action and the desire of the dreamer. And as the expression, as the projection of something for which the soul of Central Europe aches and cries—a refuge, a retreat, a bright tabernacle for the grail of art.

THE SALZBURG PROJECT

A Festspielhaus. Let us divest our minds of the muddy meaning the first two words have acquired in our country, and invest them, as in their original tongue, with a sense of the gravely-joyous, the ceremonial *allegro* of the spirit, of serene and stately delight, of that exaltation of the soul and mind, clarified by the wonders and mysteries of the drama, art and music, revealing themselves against backgrounds of beauty and eternity. If Bayreuth rolls and drones with the spirit of Wagner and a semi-sacerdotal cult and tradition, Salzburg is to chime with the bright and silvery spirit of Mozart, for Salzburg is the city of the master of "Zauberflöte" ("The Magic Flute") —here stands the famous Mozarteum.

The project took its rise as far back as 1916—amidst the ever-present shadows of collapse and dissolution. Possibly some instinct of the salvation, the solace to be found in art was at the root of it, some dim foreboding of the Stygian fate that lowered beyond the battles, even the victorious battles. Will the plays, mysteries, spectacles, masques, oratorios and operas played or presented in the name of the blithe and harmonious Mozart, help to heal up a broken land? Will Reinhardt's wand be able to strike balsam from this Salzburg stone to soothe the wounded breasts of a mutilated people? He who knows the Austrian soul can not doubt this. But it is not for Austria alone nor for Germany that this great structure is to be erected. It is to be a playhouse for the world, a stage for the hopeful and the affirmative in our age and for that which has remained young and valid through past ages. It is to be a place of pilgrimage and devotion.

"The Salzburg Festspielhaus Community" was

founded in August, 1917, and chose this art-anointed spot for the erection of a theatre which was to be free from the tyranny of the box-office, the mere-amusement-mad, the metropolitan mob. An Art Council was appointed to take initial steps—among its members were Hugo von Hofmannsthal, Austria's most distinguished poet; Richard Strauss, the composer; Max Reinhardt, Franz Schalk and Alfred Roller. The site—the southern part of the splendid park belonging to the Schloss of Hellbrunn. Soil and place are propitious. For it was here that Bishop Marcus Sittich of Salzburg, an art-loving, life-loving creator and impresario of feats and festivals, built in 1617 the first open-air theatre in Europe—a charming hemicycle of stone in a lonely spot relieved by a romantic and rocky gorge.

Max Reinhardt had already sent out his feelers towards Salzburg, the old city on the Salzach with its wooded hill crowned by the fortress Hohensalzburg, rising from its heart. During the autumn of 1920 he arranged for a monumental production of "Jedermann" ("Everyman"), on the steps and approaches of the cathedral there. Alexander Moissi, the famous German actor, and a picked troup of players, carried off the old morality with great effect. The setting seemed made for the play, the play for the setting—the bells rang from the steeples, the chanting of the choirs came from within the church. A semi-religious, medieval air dominated the performance and worked its will upon the large audience which stood thronged in the streets and in the windows of the houses in the Domplatz.

Another step has been taken towards the realization

of the Salzburg Festspielhaus—a task that is gigantic in the difficulties that must be overcome, as for example, the raising of funds, the agreements with the state, the enormous expense of all building operations. Two eminent architects, Hans Poelzig of Berlin, the creator of the Grosses Schauspielhaus, and Joseph Hoffmann of Vienna, have been commissioned to make plans and sketches. Poelzig, a gifted craftsman and creator, at once plunged into this grateful task, brought himself in tune with the dramatic, historical, natural and cultural features of the problem. Thus far he has produced two sets of preliminary sketches and models which are characteristic of his bizarre but fascinating genius.

The plan is to comprise a complex of buildings, a living organism of various parts, coördinated and united into a monumental whole. The program of the Salzburg Festspielhaus Community calls for a large festival theatre to seat some two thousand persons, in addition to which there is to be the smaller Mozart Spielhaus, seating some eight hundred. The two theatres are to be surrounded by workshops, studios, rehearsal halls, terraces, arcades and a restaurant.

Poelzig at once dug out the esthetic imperative of this problem. How to interpret the spirit of Mozart—to express that fluent, light, melodious, Ariel-like grace and dignity in architectural terms? A clue, as the art critic Paul Westheim points out, was already given by the Renaissance creation of the old bishop. Another guide line was given by the configuration of the ground—lawns and tree-dotted glades rhythmically undulant. One feels the movement, the freedom and the music in both sets of

Poelzig's preliminary designs. The plan of the theatre itself determines its developed form as in all true architecture. The conglomerate stone from quarries in the neighborhood is admirably suited to give the impression of weather-beaten antiquity or homogeneity to the mass —all part of the air or texture for which Poelzig strives. The whole project, as it has crystallized on paper, after its precipitations from Poelzig's hand and brain, is subject to that endless, tireless remodelling and recasting which characterize his work.

In all this there is a core of immense vitality, the glamor of the creative, the fascination of the fanciful. We have to deal here with new architectural harmonies evolved out of the intuition of a great expressionistic artist, a revolutionist, a transvaluer of values occidental and oriental, one who is working to make a petrified art become fluid once more. His association with Reinhardt is of great significance and may become very fruitful. It follows that if the theatre is to be liberated, its architecture must also be liberated. In Germany today we are witnessing the clash of social orders and of new ideas transferred to the realm of the theatre—the battle between the Rang-Theater and the Ring-Theater—the aristocratic theatre of the tier, and the democratic theatre of the circle.

The Festspielhaus at Salzburg, even though as yet its corner-stone alone is laid, will be a milestone in the progress of the modern theatre and modern theatre architecture. If Reinhardt has exhausted one environment, he has found another. In this, aided by some of the dominant creative spirits of our time, and inspired by an atmosphere of adoration, beauty and noble tradition, he

[198]

may build up something which will be another and greater Oberammergau, a place of pilgrimages which will draw its swarms, not every ten years, but season by season.

The Passion Plays produced here will be born of music, song and beauty, not of agony and renunciation. Religious masterpieces and music will find expression here, yet the spirit of the Festspielhaus will be pagan with the paganism of the mellow and radiant Mozart.

The enterprise must also be considered as the flight of a panic-stricken art—blighted by the mordant gases of the war, by the drift towards the abyss of nations sundered like ice-floes, by hunger, hate, by the paper tyranny of bureaucracy and the tribute-taking state—back to nature. A happy Abbey of Theleme, such as Rabelais dreamed of, is to be reared here for the children of Shakespeare, Mozart, Molière, Goethe, Beethoven, Grieg, Strauss, for the great Elizabethans, for the modern Irish drama. A monastery and a caravansary for the priests and pilgrims that make the flight from Actuality into Art. A kind of fortress, I feel, in which beauty and clarified joy may defend themselves against a world that seems bent upon converting itself into a hospital.

III

THE REPERTORY OF FESTIVAL

BY HUGO VON HOFMANNSTHAL

The festival is the true idea of art in the minds of the Austro-Bavarian people. The foundation of a festival

[199]

house on the very border between Austria and Bavaria is the symbolic expression of deeply rooted tendencies, which are half a thousand years old and bespeak an inherent cultural union extending from Basle to Oedenburg and Eisenstadt, and down to Meran. The powerful underlying basis of these tendencies is medieval. Gluck was their forerunner, Mozart their peak and centre. According to them, dramatic and musical life are one; exalted drama and opera, different only in name, were already united and inseparable in the baroque theatre of the seventeenth century. Here Weimar approaches Salzburg: the real dramatic element in Goethe, for all its power, is, as the Salzburg festivals will show, a grand unified structure of all the forms of theatrical expression which sprang from the South German soil: from the Mystery and Morality plays, by way of the marionette theatre and the Jesuit school drama, to the court opera with chorus, mechanism and pageants. And what is Schiller's work—not the youthful but the mature Schiller's, from "The Maid of Orleans" to "The Bride of Messina"—except a desire for an opera without music?

That is how Weimar and Salzburg join hands. South German characteristics stand out strikingly, and at the same time a kindred spirit unites them. In no other form can the innermost polarized instincts of the German soul find their unified expression. And at the centre between these two poles stands Mozart. This is no imaginary conception, it is a natural truth. The Romantic element in Mozart's life is not accidental, not the mere fashion of the day; it is of all times, a necessity, one link in the chain. With Mozart's triad—"Idomeneo," "Don Juan," "Zauber-

flöte" ("The Magic Flute")—at the centre, Gluck must
be included, and with him the antique drama, as far back
as our theatrical instinct can imagine it. For Gluck was
only a struggling desire of the German spirit toward the
antique, just as Racine had been the longing urge of the
French spirit toward it. Gluck's drama was the renaissance of the antique tragedy through music.

By way of "Don Juan" and other Mozart comedies,
contact may be established, too, with Calderon's profane
as well as his religious drama. This highest activity of
the dramatic baroque spirit comprises the religious as
well as the profane play—when good taste can approve
of the latter. The sound German naiveté of "The Magic
Flute" and the whole emotional world of Mozart's comedies, lead naturally to Weber's works and finally to Ferdinand Raimund's fairy world, imbued with delicate music.
Shakespeare was represented in this dramatic structure
from the earliest moment—above all, the Shakespeare
of "The Tempest" and "A Midsummer Night's Dream."
The repertory of the festival plays is endless. In review,
it gives the appearance of diversity, though of intrinsic
organic unity. And thereby, I repeat, the conventional
antithesis of opera and drama seems to fade away to
nothing. Let us survey a few groups which come readily
to mind:

"Faust, I and II," the *fantastic* element, the German
Walpurgis night or witches' Sabbath; "A Midsummer
Night's Dream"; "Der Alpenkönig" ("The King of the
Alps"); "Le Misanthrope"; Weber's "Oberon" and
"Der Freischütz."

"Faust," the *antique* element, the classical Walpurgis

night; the fairy plays of Euripides; Grillparzer's "Hero and Leander."

"Faust," the marionette plays as a symbolic tragedy of most *exalted* style; Aeschylus' "Prometheus Bound"; the Hindu drama; Calderon's "Life Is a Dream"; and, as an echo, Grillparzer's "Der Traum, ein Leben" ("Dream, a Life").

In this third group belong the first two productions made under the auspices of the Salzburg Festspielhaus Committee, "Jedermann" ("Everyman") and "Das Salzburger Grosse Welttheater" ("The Great World-Theatre"), both in versions of my own. The latter borrowed its entire basic metaphor from Calderon.

The six characters by which mankind is represented are: the king, the rich man, the peasant, the beggar, wisdom, and beauty. Wisdom is a nun, beauty a court lady. As is evident, such naïve restraint as this goes back much farther than the seventeenth century of Calderon. These figures, each in its own niche surrounded by intricate Gothic tracery, belong to the world which we meet in the Flemish and northern-French tapestries of the fifteenth century. The World-Theatre is a miracle play, or a theatrical allegory. This is a very old dramatic form which has had its great epoch in all European literatures: in England of pre-Shakespearean times, and also in France before she surrendered her literature to the imitation of the Ancients. But with us, at least, this old form has never quite died out. Up to the end of the eighteenth century, Catholic South Germany and Austria possessed its folk-theatre, the subjects for which were drawn indiscriminately from the Bible or from the old treasures of allegory and the Miracles. And Oberammergau with its Passion Plays is simply a survival of this naïve theatrical world, the last protruding point, so to speak, of a sunken island-continent. With the spirit of rationalism which spread over Europe at the time of the French Revolution, these old art customs were finally swept away. In my present work, and in the earlier one—a dramatic reworking of the primitively and universally European "Everyman" material—I have quite deliberately taken up the torch which with us still lay glowing on the ground; and believe that in this—as always happens to the seemingly quite instinctive processes of the artist—my hand has been guided by a concealed plurality. The new element which I have added to the traditional material is to be found in the figure of the beggar. In my work he stands as the chief character of the play, and is brought out as an individual against all others. The beggar of the old miracle plays was passive and resigned, the poor man of the gospels who is chosen for blessedness by the mere nature of his fate; while in this life, however, he is simply an object whereby other people can be tested. But I have presented the active beggar, the excluded, the disinherited, eager for a place among those who have inherited—a figure, consequently, such as could be seen in these proportions probably only at the present moment: the threat of chaos to the world of order.

I can not say that the public had any difficulty in reacting to this religious or allegorical play, or that the play had any difficulty in carrying the minds of these people along with it. Everything happened without any one having to think of the process itself. Yet it was the most mixed public conceivable: not only because we, for the first time since the war, had assembled a completely international audience at a spot in Central Europe, but also because those elements belonging to our own nation—I refer to the Germans and to the Austrians—were a very mixed audience socially. Alongside of the *nouveaux-riches* there sat many plain people, peasants with their wives and daughters, the petty bourgeoisie of our little country towns in the Alps, priests and nuns, and among them Americans, Scandinavians, Frenchmen, and residents of Berlin. The credit for having amalgamated this extraordinary jumble of incoherent individuals and viewpoints into an audience, yes, into a completely unified and truly naïve public which let itself "be taken in" in an almost childlike fashion, the credit for this lies entirely with Reinhardt's settings. His *mise-en-scène* was the complete expression of the ripeness which this leading stage-manager of Europe has arrived at in recent years. It laid few stresses; but where it did stress, the result was extraordinarily powerful. And by means of the great rhythmic art with which these stresses were weighed against one another and distributed throughout the length of the play, it knitted together the entire action, lasting over two hours without pause. As a result, there was no suspicion of drag, and the entire production was followed really breathlessly. A strong rhythmic faculty forms the essential effectiveness in this great stage-manager's poetics; his unusual sense of space is the natural correlate to this: for the rhythmic is the attempt to grasp and organize time like space. In the twenty-five years that Reinhardt has been working as a stage-manager the analysis of space has formed the real centre of his activity. And in this tendency to conquer space as a new medium of expression, he is the appropriate dramatic director, leader, and representative of his entire generation. For the modern European actors—and I am certain, the Americans also, in so far as they are representative actors of our epoch— are interpreters of our new spiritual relationship to space. Consequently, what is essential to them, the mimic element—of which the spoken word is only an ingredient —manifests a mysterious affinity to the tendencies of modern painters. (The actor of the earlier generation— I will name it, roughly, the Wagner generation—stood in the same relationship to music.) If we observe a European painting of this generation, as a canvas of Kokoschka, the figures stand out in space in such a manner as we never see them arranged in any picture of an earlier generation. Heavy with hate, or love; as if charged by electricity; in what one would call a rarefied atmosphere; a man sinks like a phantom into the depths of the picture; another, breathless, swollen with scorn, comes out at us like a straw-colored tongue of lightning. This is completely identical with the compressed and violent juxtaposition and opposition of figures which Reinhardt conceived for an interior of Strindberg, peopled with men who hate one another, fear one another, standing, so to speak, with their faces in a dull reality, and their backs in a dream.

Reinhardt's *mise-en-scène* was extremely simple. The church in which we played is the work of a great architect of the eighteenth century. It is built in the style of the Palladio, a palace both solemn and festal in which

God's altar has been placed. The inside is splendid, gorgeous. Although it is decorated with brightly colored stuffs and with marble figures in its niches, it takes its tone, which is that of a Haydn symphony, from the harmony of its form, the spiritual beauty of the proportions of an immense and graceful cupola. Many of the churches that the Spaniards built in Mexico in the century following the conquest are reminiscent of this building. The high altar was draped by Reinhardt, and a drapery of the same color, scarlet—the ecclesiastical color for martyrs—ran about the church at a height of from five to six yards. The simple structure Reinhardt had designed for the play was covered with the same stuff. It was nothing but a platform across the entire width of the church in front of the high altar. Just before and beside the altar it was higher, a sort of upper stage, from which one climbed down five steps in order to reach the lower front stage. All the other altars were draped.

The scarlet of the drapery and the marble of the walls were the only colors that Reinhardt had allowed to remain. But the effect he achieved by using so simply the solemn awe of the height of the church was remarkable. The words, whether stern or merciful and consoling, to which the angels give utterance at various points in the play, floated down from little loges ranged by the architect about the cupola. It really seemed most likely that the white-winged figures whose voices came so suddenly from above had flown down from heaven; not at all that they had climbed up from below out of so prosaic a spot as an actor's dressing room.

One particular scene in this play was among the most

impressive ever accomplished by Reinhardt. It was so impressive that a shudder, half sigh, half audible moan, ran through the audience crowded together in the twilight of the church, and for a moment it seemed as though the effect might be too much for their nerves. It was the moment when Death comes to fetch, one after another, the various persons who together compose the World Theatre —the King and the Beggar, the Rich Man and the Farmer, Beauty and the Nun—in order to lead them off the stage.

Reinhardt had worked out his scene as a Danse Macabre performed by Death with each of his victims. As for other incidents in the play he had used to such astonishing advantage the spaciousness of the church, so in this scene he made similar use of the bodily formation of his actors. The actor who played Death was very slender, with most expressive features, and a thorough athlete. During the play he had stood motionless as a statue on a high column covered with scarlet cloth. He and the angel who stood at a similar height opposite him might readily have been taken for part of the church's architecture.

At the moment when God gave him permission to take up his part in the action, he left his lofty perch and climbed soundlessly down by means of an invisible ladder concealed in the scarlet stuff. As he came, he beat with two long bone drumsticks upon a tiny drum fixed to the girdle of his costume. His costume was that of a Spanish cavalier, all black, and he walked with a strange, slim grace. The fearful rhythm of his drumming sounded from gongs and kettle drums hidden in the organ loft.

He came so to the first figure he had to summon, the King. Striding backward, his cavernous sockets fixed on the King, he compelled him by the power in his drum-beat to come down from his throne and to follow him step by step. But the power of the drum was such that the King was attracted and repelled by it at the same time. He walked no longer like a living being to the beat of an instrument. He walked as though his soul were no longer in his body, but in those drum-beats. Like a puppet hanging by strings, the King followed the Drummer and jerked out mechanically the lines he had to say. So Death led him toward the audience; then, by the very strength in his drum, jerked him back and forth, and finally forced him into his place again.

Then Death took the next person—the Rich Man or Beauty—and did the same thing, forward and backward; and so, one after another, with all six figures. And during the sixfold repetition of his gruesome dance, the audience sat as though hypnotized and rooted to their seats.

Great is the power of a director who can find the thing that will plunge through the senses deep into the heart and who knows just when to use it.

DISTILLING THE ATMOSPHERE OF THE ORIENT BY SIMPLE MEANS

A Sketch by Ernst Stern for a Setting for the Pantomime, "Sumurûn," Using Drop Curtains for Background to the Action

TWO SCENES FROM THE PANTOMIME, "SUMURÛN"

Sketches by Ernst Stern

Chapter XVII

THE GENIUS OF MAX REINHARDT

BY MAXIMILIAN HARDEN

[For many years, even antedating the war, Americans looked to the independent and provocative pen of Maximilian Harden for an astringent picture of Central European men and movements, whereby to check and correct the routine rumors and reports of newspaper, magazine, and Prime Minister. Harden's mouthpiece, the tiny pamphlet *Die Zukunft*, has been an obstreperous megaphone, broadcasting castigation and praise without heed for tradition and reputation. Castigation nine times out of ten. Praise from Harden, therefore, is to be treasured, and this tribute to Reinhardt's genius, ruthlessly qualified by occasional disagreement, is fitting finale to this survey of Reinhardt and his Theatre.—THE EDITOR.]

"Ye elves of hills, brooks, standing lakes, and groves;
And ye that on the sands with printless foot
Do chase the ebbing Neptune and do fly him
When he comes back; . . . all ye, by whose aid—
Weak masters though ye be—I have bedimm'd
The noontide sun, call'd forth the mutinous winds,
And 'twixt the green sea and the azured vault
Set roaring war; . . . graves at my command
Have waked their sleepers, oped, and let 'em forth . . .
By my so potent art. But this rough magic
I here abjure, . . . I'll break my staff,
Bury it certain fathoms in the earth,
And deeper than did ever plummet sound
I'll drown my book."

[209]

MAX REINHARDT AND HIS THEATRE

PROSPERO, magician and duke of Milan utters these words. And with his tongue, according to a beautiful tradition that grows old in wisdom, of which no philologist can ever deprive us again, speaks a poet, who, at the threshold of his fiftieth year, in full possession of his imaginative force, releases himself of his own free will from the strong compulsion of his own art of enchantment and abjures his magic at the cloud-darkened parting of the ways, in order to stride into the cramped life of a mere earthly being. Nevermore will mighty Caesar and glowing Cleopatra, the hero of Corioli with his winsome silence, the weary worldling Antony and the Johns, Henrys, and Richards of England, come forth at his summons from their graves to breathe again. Never again will he recall to life the dusky general and the gray Jew of Venice, shake mighty forests as if they were a single bough, waken the swallow on Duncan's castle-wall, smash masts and yards in tempest on the sea, and then when the winds in their rage have fully worked his will, beckon forth the sun that shall soothe to smiles the roaring, foaming maws of the sea. Not for one hour, does he yield to the all-too-human deception, that action in the realm of reality could raise him higher, make him happier than did the decades when from an inert mass, he created breathing life. Like Prospero's Ariel, it is "in the elements" that he longs to be. Not for the sake of wild or aimless play, but, modest in his mastery, he would return to learn from Nature what she unveils to her faithful pupils. Nature's stage is ever new, since she creates an audience ever new. Life is the masterpiece of her invention; and Death, her medium to enhance that life. Man she swathes in dullness and eternally spurs him on to light. She ties him to the earth, indolent and slothful, and then shakes him up again and again. He who, on a frail pillar, had been exposed to all the winds, even to those he masters, whose eyes and ears have tired of lightning and of thunder, feels drawn toward earth's constricted atmosphere. On his home soil, he longs gently to glow away until the earth, which he had helped to make fertile, becomes his pillow and his cover, and from his cold body, claims what—though the meanest part of him—is of use to her. "Methinks, indeed, it were a happy life a humble shepherd just to be, to sit, like here, upon a hill and cut sundials, gracefully. Thus, minutes, hours, days and months and years, reaching their destined aim, would lead the white head to its peaceful grave."

The country gentleman's day, however, does not flow past in gloom and humble apprehensive readiness for death. He sows and he will harvest. His hand pats the plough horse's neck and the soft skin of the cows in the stable. Out in the pasture, with knowing touch he strokes the fleece of the sheep, and playfully twists the purring tomcat's whiskers. He watches the mulberry tree, which his youthful hand planted, to see whether it thrives; protects the oak from the choking grip of the ivy; prunes a young fruit-tree; and makes sure that the grain and the clover are planted in good season. A simple yet active life, with the universe as a restful background, and he, an orderly member of an unpretentious community. No longer exposed to curiosity, no longer the knob on the top of a steeple with noisy crows proclaiming its presence.

MAX REINHARDT AND HIS THEATRE

"And, like the baseless fabric of this vision,
The cloud-capp'd towers, the gorgeous palaces,
The solemn temples, the great globe itself,
Yea, all which it inherit, shall dissolve,
And like this insubstantial pageant faded,
Leave not a rack behind. We are such stuff
As dreams are made on; and our little life
Is rounded with a sleep."

Away from the noise and whirl of London, to the peaceful island, to Stratford-on-Avon. And always as in the inconceivably great poet, whose mightiest works, "Hamlet," "Lear," "Macbeth," "Othello," hardly need the spoken word to live, so also it is on his last journey, on which the eye can follow him to far off distances. The earth rejoices under the hoofs of his horse, bearing him far from the recruiting centres of the Puritan spirit, through the mist that still hides them. The rider drinks in the breath of the meadow, sees the stag on the edge of the forest, thinks of the numerous deer his shots have felled and still will fell, leads his horse from the dusty village road to the brook. And the stage behind him burns down, and leaves his world all in ashes. And to this perishable playhouse, all through his ripening years, he has dedicated his thought and his strength; had thriftily saved up his funds; and every beautiful piece for the house he had viewed with the bridegroom's expectant joy. There in the attic lay his manuscripts and his plans. Everything reduced to mere smoke. Dreams will be life: in the autumn.

Such was the denouement, brilliant, yet tragic, in the sense of supreme injustice, that I had wished for Max Reinhardt. Thus, a radiant passage from the narrowness

SKETCH FOR A SCENE IN THE GHETTO, DESIGNED BY ERNST STERN

SETTING OF A STREET SCENE, FROM A DESIGN BY EMIL ORLIK

TWO PRODUCTIONS OF "THE MERCHANT OF VENICE"

IN THE PARK AT BELMONT

A STREET SCENE IN VENICE

"THE MERCHANT OF VENICE"

AT THE DEUTSCHES THEATER, NOVEMBER, 1905

of the mere actor (though one without equal) into the wide plain of life, at his own self-chosen hour, and with a will-bound creative spirit like that of the director of the Globe, who steps into the narrow life of the land-owner, with neighbors closing in around him. My wish was not that fire should destroy three theatres, one acquired and two built according to his own plans, but it was that, in our spiritually dull time, garbed in dark material of mixed coloring, a unique experience should not vanish in the sand, and take its course like Tom, Dick and Harry's managements, "which (so it is written) will never, in spite of errors in aim and direction, be forgotten in the history of the stage." After what I consider an act of greatest daring, which carries Fortuna's favorite into the roaring current, and drops him—not against his will— far off from everything that pleases, he arises on the shore with the laughter of Coriolanus. He does not wait for the wreath, nor for the praise of senile stage officials, nor for the stammered thanks of admiring youth. He breaks his wand, turns off the large and small light in the heavens, and, on a young horse, canters into a world without footlights. "The festival is at its end. Our players, I told you, were ghosts, and have dissolved into air and vapor." Then, there is silence (because with numerous progeny assured, no material harm has been done, no crown estate is at stake); and out of this grows the legend. Like Ariel, who can be bird and harpy, chantecler and watchdog, flame and source of dew; who can skip on the pearly foam of the ocean, ride the storm, run along the zig-zag of the lightning, delve through the frozen surface into the bowels of the earth, chuckle in the murmur of a cataract, sing with the voice of a harp-playing nymph—like this airy creature, with the breath of the muses, this mysterious alluring unison of the most delicate youthful charms of both sexes, who for years was held prisoner in the narrow cleft of a fir-tree by Sycorax, the withered mistress of Satan—thus dramatic art, a creature of the imagination borne on light wings, had languished in the bare and sunless confinement of reality—and a make-believe reality, at that. Henceforth, it would not be the only aim of that art to be a copy of chance reality, a copy faithful to the hair on the wart and the pimple on the nose, to the exclusion once and for all of the "unnatural." With the same right, we might insist that chamber music should be made up of everyday noises. A young Austrian actor gradually grew sick of his duty of serving as vent for the emanations of miserable, puny souls and—night after night—of stuffing cabbage from an earthen pot into his mouth. Through the mist shimmers the gaily colored magnificence of the Burg Theater, which had charmed this youth. It would be much more beautiful, young Roscius Reinhardt thinks, to carry more spirit and yet more youth into it all. With a few cheerful comrades, who hear his call, his first choice falls on "Schall und Rauch" ("Sound and Smoke"), circling like mists around the heavenly spark. Then—to free Ariel from his fir-tree—he rents a building large enough to stage the entire Globe Theatre inside it, and from there sallies forth into the brilliant light of the Deutsches Theater. What happened to him then, an old sheet of paper bears witness:

[214]

"Though you are now in the position to which Goethe's theatre director aspired, I do not suppose your mind is cheerful just because you can watch how they 'squeeze onward through the narrow gate of grace; by daylight, even, they push and shove to reach the seller's box, a fighting host; and, as for bread before a baker's door in famine, to get a ticket almost break their necks.' I do not think your mind is cheerful. You can not exist without the public; but you wish to owe your success to its noble instincts, not to its lesser ones. To this day, we have no reason to believe that you aim only at making money. Against this speak the unprecedented expenditures with which you burden your small realm so that all be 'fresh and new and pleasing and alive with meaning.' The throng at the 'gate of grace' would not be less—perhaps even still more—if you dispensed with the help of Humperdinck and Pfitzner, and bought the properties for your stage from well-known firms, instead of hiring artists to work them out in the most minute detail. The crowds you attract could not be larger, even if you remodelled your shabby theatre, still decorated in the style of Lindau, either into a comfortable modern playhouse with nothing to annoy the most exacting tastes, or into a dream of elegance such as we have not had in Berlin since Schinkel's noble creation in the Schillerplatz was ruined by restoration.

"From what I have said, you need not fear that I take you for the egregious idealist who desires to play the part of Immermann, and who, after a few false starts, must flee from Thalia's domain in the guise of a beggar. No; I see you as a fanatic, outwardly calm, but with soul aglow; as one prepossessed, for whom there is no rest until his aim is attained, his vision materialized, whether his goal be a kingdom or a wooden scaffold. There is no need for him to be impractical; the frail lieutenant Bonaparte, the greatest of the pale-faced crowd, was not impractical. Your ambition aims not at robbing kings of their crowns or at winning the love of the daughter of an apostolic majesty. Your India is at closer range. Yet, you wish to be more than a thespian peddler who merely fills his pockets. What the papers call a propagator of culture, is that it? You are eager to win back for the stage—which Nietzsche was not the first to despise and which he taught us also to abjure—the interest and loving care of the finest and freest spirits. To create the best theatrical art attainable today and to place this combined art of poet, stage director, painter, musician and actor—like the statue of a serene goddess with a festive wreath, a palladion, visible to the most profane eye—inside the empty building where German culture shall make its home tomorrow. To leave the realm you chose for your work better than you found it: a thing of more importance, of greater repute. To work, is your desire—not to pocket money. And yet, you are compelled to read, day in, day out, that you attract the crowd with common bait because you give it greater opportunities to 'share and wonder' than the others. You are condemned to read that your success is due to a motley display of tinseled ornaments. And that is why your mind is far from cheerful, despite crowds at the box-office.

"At first, when a clever mind in your entourage gave out the catch-phrase, I laughed about it and thought: this

BEFORE THE REVOLUTIONARY TRIBUNAL

A Sketch by Ernst Stern for a Setting in "Danton's Death" by Georg Büchner

time the wise man, who scented danger in the wind, was, contrary to expectation, only wise enough not to be wise. You had made us a present of 'A Midsummer Night's Dream,' really made us a present of it. For the wonders of that poem had never fully lived on any stage in Berlin nor in the rest of Germany. That was the beginning. Everyone had to concede that in the Neues and the Kleines Theaters you had played Ibsen, Lessing, Wilde, von Hofmannsthal, Maeterlinck, Strindberg, Wedekind, Shaw, Beer-Hofmann, Gorky, Schmidtbonn, Bahr, Rüderer and many another, with the finest artistic feeling. At that time, your playhouses were still *des théâtres à côté* (theatres in the side streets), as the Parisian calls them: something for the gourmet, but harmless from the standpoint of competition. The avalanche began, swelling from day to day. 'Of course, he makes a pompous show of Shakespeare's comedy. That always draws.' Really, the bluff was too stupid. Never had 'A Midsummer Night's Dream' been staged less pompously. At the Hof Theater, the huge orchestra and the *corps de ballet* are called into action; stage properties and costumes are much more luxuriously pompous than on your stage; Theseus lives in the style of a real opera potentate. You even spared us the closing effect of the gorgeous festive hall, and permitted a corner of the starlit sky to look down upon the simple scene of wedding bliss and elfin pretense. Because you felt that this interplay of elemental spirits must not be mewed up, locking Nature out; that Nature here is paramount, rollicking actress and frolicking Amazon, fate and God; that those who embraced each other here in passionate dances, must remain within the realm of Na-

[217]

ture and must not be separated from her by solid walls; and finally, because you had grasped the poem's spirit in which the will apes the mind, and instinct apes reason— therefore you devoted all your efforts to summoning Nature to life on your boards. Stage decoration? Your forest is very beautiful. But the famous much-mocked moss-carpet could have been seen with Beerbohm Tree years ago after his last dandy had crossed the stage, and even in our Hof Theater before your time. Never in the past had it called forth either enthusiasm or indignation. Your ceremonies at Hippolyta's court are meager. Titania's bridal party might disclose greater fancy. And your wedding march sounded weak, not to Amazons only. Not to these things was your success due; it would have come even without make-believe trees. But was any one permitted to say it? Could a humble actor accomplish what the whole literary tribe had failed to do, the tribe which, since Dingelstedt's successful years, had invaded the theatrical business? Could he plumb the deepest meaning of a great poem and, from that depth, irradiate the work with a light strong enough to make it appear something new, something never seen before, so that it attracted the crowd to a 'mere show' of yesterday? To admit that, would have meant advertising their own impotence. That is why they said: 'Gorgeous decorations!'

"When I went to see your 'Midsummer Night's Dream,' an old State secretary sat opposite me; and I could see how this tired, care-worn man was transformed by the charm of your production, how he grew young and joyful beneath his gray beard. Do you think he admired your moss, the roots of your trees, your glow worms? I doubt whether he even noticed that your stage looked a little different from the ordinary stage. And what were my impressions? I, who have seen so much excellent scenic art in almost every country in Europe that I am hardened against theatrical effect? What I saw were childish things with a child's laughing joy, with that drunkenness of joy which would be the poet's if he could see again such daring and yet wise reconstruction of his work. And after that experience, I read that you had expelled Shakespeare's spirit, and had hung motley rags in the void. And all I could do was to laugh at the pitiful stupidity of such comments.

"I laugh no longer. You have moved into the Deutsches Theater, which, after having been for years a splendid specialty playhouse, had become the home of a homeless man. From now on, you will transform it once more into a first class theatre—a German theatre—knowing the obligations which its name implies. In no metropolis can two stages with universal literary ambitions exist side by side for any length of time. Irving had to make his home in the provinces, after Beerbohm Tree, tired of Polish Jews, planned with the painter, Alma Tadema, to appear as Caesar. And that happened in London, which itself has the population of a province. Since Dr. Brahm at the Emil Lessing Theater (Sudermann's abode can not well take its name from the great Gotthold Ephraim Lessing, and, besides, that building emanates more of the spirit of its stage manager, Emil Lessing, than of Brahm) ventured into the fantastic with Calderon, Schiller and von Hofmannsthal, it was evident that he would not limit himself to that special form of art, but would compete with you for the first place. That meant no easy struggle for you. Aside from the elemental Lehmann, he has no actress worthy of mention; but he has excellent actors. And, what is still more important, he knows how to handle the critics. *'Nourri dans le sérail, il en connaît les détours.'* I do not rate his theatrical achievement very high. He discovered no new poet, not even a new actor, except you. But by means of high salaries, he acquired the most popular players and thus gradually built an ensemble suited to his genre, the easiest genre for the manager, as you remember from 'The Lower Depths.' He is no stage manager, is unable himself to direct his company, but he paralyses them to such a degree that every play foreign to his tastes is a failure. The old story: A man succeeds only with that in which he has faith. This very same old-fashioned truth was ignored also by Lindau, your predecessor at the Deutsches Theater. He would still be in clover, if he had built on Augier, Bauernfeld, Blumenthal, Fulda, Lindau and Kadelburg, instead of on Wilde, Shaw, Heijermans. He did not break down, as foolish scribblers thought, because he was not modern enough; on the contrary, because he wished to be too modern and gave plays which were repulsive to his very soul. Dr. Brahm is of a different nature—educated, intelligent, diligent, tenacious. When he wished to return to the Deutsches Theater (which, at the time, was already yours), I advised him secretly to combine the two enterprises. I referred to your colleague, Goethe, who said in 1826: 'I see the time coming when a clever man, a master of affairs, will take over four theatres at once and, by alternating the guest rôles, will be better off with those

A SCENE IN "THE GOD OF VENGEANCE" BY SHOLOM ASH

Produced at the Deutsches Theater, March, 1907, with Rudolf Schildkraut
and Hedwig Wangel

A SCENE FROM SCHMIDTBONN'S "DER VERLORENE SOHN"

("The Prodigal Son" or "The Wanderer")

(Left to right) Joseph Schildkraut, as the Son; Rosa Bertens, as Elisa; Max
Nemetz, as Korah; Rudolf Schildkraut, as the Father

"THE BLUE BIRD"

At the Deutsches Theater, November, 1912

Ernst Stern's Costume Sketch for the Rôle of Bread

four than if had only one.' In the present case, two clever heads would have managed four playhouses and would have had such human material as Berlin had never seen before. No more jealousy as to plays and actors. All the associate would have had to do would be to look after his pets, kindred to him in spirit, on whom he could rely in the realm of imagination. Nothing came of it. You moved to Schumannstrasse and announced that your first night would bring us Kleist's grandiose historic play of the days of knighthood, 'Das Käthchen von Heilbronn.'

"When I heard that news, I sent you warning. This drama presents to the manager about the hardest and most ungrateful task imaginable. It suffers from a serious defect of fundamental structure and becomes so weak and confusing toward the end that a strong, harmonious effect is impossible. Whether it was just that difficulty which challenged your youthful daring, or whether it had become too late for 'The Merchant of Venice,' which I had proposed as a safe first play, you stuck to Kleist and his 'Käthchen.' And they cut you up ruthlessly, so that hardly a smooth hair remained on your head. Not everywhere, to be sure. And yet, even in the leading papers, the praise they bestow on you always sounds as if you just had a possible chance to stand beside Messrs. Hülsen, Grube & Co. Pompous stage outfit, nothing but outfit! And the greatest of your crimes: you left out the scene at the trout brook.

"Would you like to have a good laugh after all these weeks of labor? I open the famous Kleist biography by Otto Brahm, the very doctor at whose pulpit they wish to slaughter you. After I read that the 'Käthchen' was

written for the Theater an der Wien, I find the following
sentences: 'At the theatre, a well-defined tendency toward
the supernatural play prevailed. Kleist himself follows
this tradition. He aims at effective staging, at gaily
colored, gorgeous pictures: the knights appear on horseback, the cherub presents himself with wings bathed in
light, and Moors and satellites contribute to the pomp
of the closing apotheosis. Yet all these expedients could
not cover up the inner defect of the play.' Thus, the most
gorgeous staging was what the poet himself desired. Do
not take it as an offense, but your production was more
meager than any I have ever seen in a performance of
this play—almost too meager. Kunigund's chamber in the
Strahlburg might be cosier; the imperial demonstration
at Worms, the bridal procession in the castle square,
might be more brilliant. Think of all the money the Duke
of Meiningen spent on this drama! And no one ever had
a word of censure for him. Also our Hof Theater presents much to the eye. Förster, the first *regisseur* at the
old Deutsches Theater, offered still more. And the scene
at the trout brook? On the same page, Brahm says: 'His
fond interest in his heroine leads Kleist cheerfully to introduce scenes like the one at the trout brook which the
timid child dares not cross—scenes that charm the reader
but confuse the playgoer, for they mean nothing to the
development of the story, hardly anything to that of the
character.' Every intelligent stage manager, therefore,
will cut them out, because they confuse and take up time.
The indispensable parts of the play alone require a long
evening. I am sure you never expected to be able to call

[222]

"TURONDOT" BY GOZZI-VOLLMOELLER

Deutsches Theater, October, 1911

Costume Plates Designed by Ernst Stern

this witness against your opponents and to see him so effectively disperse their accusations.

"Your 'Käthchen' kept us under her charming spell for almost five hours. We went home exhilarated. In Utopia, Lessing grumbled, you may find the stage on which every lantern-snuffer is a Garrick. Your ensemble, of course, has weak moments. You know that you can not grow Mounets and Matkowskys out of the earth. And yet, it seems to me, you have given good proof, in the meantime, of your talent at discovering genius by placing on your boards five women of strong individuality and mature art, of whom four were unknown or had passed unnoticed. Your Friedrich Wetter (Kayssler) lacks radiance; as a boy, he did not learn to laugh, and, as a man, he never yielded to fun and mischief. He is a strong, clean, typically German knight, however, genuine in all his gestures, stern and honest, like Kleist himself in every feature of his character. The little daughter of your armorer (Lucie Höflich), is young, clean, lovable, sheerly charming under the elderberry bush. Still she is too hesitant. She is no imperial descendent, no nursling of the cherubim, too much the child of lowly parents in carriage and behavior. Old Theobald, whom you played yourself, I did not like at all—pardon my saying so—although it was praised on every hand.

"On the whole, the performance was certainly the best that our drama had seen for decades; much more refined than the Meiningen company's had been, much more in the poet's own spirit than that of the L'Arronge theatre, even considering Sorma's participation. Of the text of the poem, you retained as much as one evening permitted. You were able to do this only because the revolving stage saved much precious time in changing the scenes. The first act was convincingly impressive: the judges of the Vehmic court in the gloom of night, through which their voices sound and the steel glints when they move about in their armor. Kunigund's scenes were in quite a new style which would have intoxicated the author of 'Zaches' and 'Princess Brambilla,' even without champagne. German people in a German landscape. Garments and stage properties selected by the artist's hand. A beautiful festive night. I know not what I should praise in the sad state of our present stage, if I should find fault with your achievement. Once more, the spirit of the poem was grasped correctly. For the first time, the story of Käthchen and her knight was a German fairy tale; for the first time, the realm of the legend was purposely hedged off against the very breath of the commonplace—Thurneck, a fabulous monster! the Rheingraf, a drunkard and fighter of old time legends; the Emperor, somewhat stiff and exaggerated in conscious majesty, such as children like to dream him; and the ecstatic lovers between them. That is why we remained alert and in receptive mood for five full hours; not because your sky and your trees were different from those we are accustomed to see behind the footlights. One feature only, I think, you missed. Käthchen must stride through the play radiant with confidence, almost triumphant; and she must know, not only in her dreams but also awake, that the Count is madly in love with her, and that he is going to marry her a year from Easter. Tell her and give her three days to think it over; and your jewel will beam in unparalleled splendor. Not one of the critics discovered this shortcoming.

"After 'The Merchant,' which followed, there was much talk again of too great scenic pomp. This, although you had made less ado than your predecessors. Your Venice was really genuine; the park at Belmont, the most beautiful picture I ever saw on a stage. Just think how this play was overburdened with gondolas, princely retainers on horseback, carnival processions and carnival uproar when played by the Meiningen company, by Barnay and by Hochberg's Hof Theater. With you nothing of the kind, nothing. What you show us are the temperament and the quick-tongued gentry of ancient Venice. And the mood of your court scene is far from gentle and mild, as if the judges were merely watching a quarrel over the head of a sheep. With a smile, one must realize that this entire little community—Christians and Jews and heathen—is of small consequence, pursues the glimmer of gold, lies and forges unscrupulously, perverts the meaning of the laws, lives in rank lust beside its suffering neighbor; yet, in spite of its degradation, engenders new life and, in joy and savagery, prepares the ground for a new era of culture. In spite of defects, the spirit of the poem confronts us full stature. This time the crowd comes to you.

"But now, I laugh no more. For the catch-word has broken through. From all sides comes the cry: 'Effective stage decoration! That is how that man Reinhardt succeeds; it must be evident; and the art of the theatre, of course, goes to the devil.' Such success, I should think, gives you scant pleasure. If your contribution were limited to mere pomp, I would be against you more bitterly than anyone. I will bear emphatic witness to the fact that it is not so and never was so. Let him who wishes to see silly pomp, the most disgusting display of it, go to the Hülsen Haus, which was never censured on that score. Whenever you did spare neither scenery nor machinery, and showered a profusion of stars, it was always necessary, always controlled by the sense of artistic refinement. Yet it was not your pomp that taught us to embrace the stage once more, the stage which had long disappointed us. It was your intent spirit, your sense for the essential, you fanatic love for the idea itself. Because you never gave us anything worthless; because you staged every poem and every farce in its own atmosphere; because you brought out clearly the structure and individual note of every drama, in harmony with the visual and acoustic conditions of the playhouse; because you never misinterpreted a poet nor falsified his meaning to please the mob; because you handled Wilde's plays differently from Strindberg's, Kleist's from Shakespeare's; because, instead of imposing your will on the actors, you always took pains to develop their individual gifts; because you saw the classic with eyes young and undimmed by tradition and indifference, just as Rossi saw Lear, Othello and Romeo, or as Ristori conceived the consort of Macbeth; because you never scattered substitutes on the market, nor cheap bazaar bargains; because you never were bent on pleasing the many, but always were moved with the spirit to stand faithfully by the poet's work; because every evening spent in your playhouse, without exception, brought refined, festive joy; because you are an artist, and

"SUMURÛN"

THE SCENE BEFORE THE HAREM

Designed by Ernst Stern

"THE MARRIAGE OF FIGARO"

THE BALLROOM

Designed by Ernst Stern

modestly and reverently, yet with iron zeal and with all the vigor at your command, you put yourself at the service of other artists: therefore, however distant from your final goal you may still be, we love you and would hate to see you discouraged. But what must discourage you and might in the end destroy your enthusiasm, is that foolish talk about stage setting for effect. Since we of today wish to see man characterized by the surroundings which contribute to his making, we have no further use for Shakespeare's bare stage. Why not profit, then, by the achievements of a highly developed technique? Why let rags shut out the celestial vault and the clouds that scurry across it? Symbolized forms, stylization, will come in their day. Meanwhile, your stage decorations are no more pompous than those of other Berlin theatres; they are simpler, as a rule, produced by artists only, not turned out by rote from the factory. No, it is not with gaily colored trash that you have won us, but with the unbounded imagination of your wisely creative spirit. And that is why we hope you may stoutly pursue your chosen course.

"For it is an extremely serious and important question, whether the stage will again mean something to us, will again become a means of new hope in our desire to fuse into one great unit the finest elements of different cultures. Almost as important as the price of pork, the revolts of the Reds, the latest murder story out of Russia's tragi-comical hot-house adolescence. Because it seems so important to me, and because I see in you the man, who, if he keep strong and cheerful, has it in him to found that German theatre of our dreams, I am writing you this letter, while hardly any other voice is raised in your behalf. 'He who creates must be cheerful,' exclaimed the aging Fontane, who realized how worry and rancor devour human strength. Keep your mind cheerful for your difficult task! It is of no consequence that the most blatant part of the press is against you; it would be unnatural if it were otherwise. I look forward to more festive nights; I am positive, too, that a cherub will finally guide your abused Käthchen through the flames of the woodpulp fire."

That was eighteen years ago. Since then came earthquake, deluge, the end of a world. And still the sweetsour criticisms written about Reinhardt are an echo of the old story. An echo, I say. The principality—that is what the "covered wagon," that primitive form of theatrical life, was called in the days of Eckhof, Schröder and Ackerman—had become an extensive enterprise with honorary diplomas from various countries. A cautious person dares approach such precious material only with a silk brush. Yet, the tenor of criticism scattered a spray of destruction over barren, almost flowerless banks: "Your outer form of expression often was pompous, sometimes beautiful; the inner defects, we who are always indulgent prefer to ignore at this hour of parting." Then, as certain as the soup follows the *hors d'oeuvre*, the thought turned in devout admiration to dear old master Brahm whose fame unswervingly reigns over Berlin's newspaper land. How strange! This industrious German Doctor of Philosophy, Otto Brahm, was not lured toward the theatre by the summons of his heart. His connection with

[228]

it was never blessed by Eros. He had written, with sound rationalistic ability, a Kleist biography; with greater enthusiasm, he had started a Schiller biography on a rather superficial foundation. By the wide trail of Brandes and Passarge, he had approached Ibsen, whose "The Vikings at Helgeland" and "The Pillars of Society" were known at that time only to Germany's advance guard. As a dramatic critic, he had done work of medicore quality, attempting at one time to prove that the wizard Sardou was not "a modern poet"—Sardou who created Rabagas and Cyprienne, but never for an hour in his life posed as or considered himself a poet. After that, this literary historian, his salary raised, felt the urge of the hero within himself, like Percy. Through rather wearisome efforts, I succeeded in winning him over to the plan for the Freie Bühne (Free Stage). He became its director, and from quiet beer and wine backrooms, he stepped into the limelight of the Berlin salons. He proved well qualified for bringing together disorganized forces, and also for guiding them. He was still better qualified to make propaganda for anything which he considered important. He was able to start a journal, and, as agent for his westeastern patrons, found money enough between Voss- and Drakestrasse to lease the Deutsches Theater from old L'Arronge. And he who left the Schiller biography unfinished in his desk, who called theatrical criticism "a miserable trade," proved a sensible employer and an honorable merchant in his management of that playhouse. His first aim was to minimize the importance of the theatrical form as such.

"Why the hard work of dramatic composition, why

[229]

build theatres, why dress up men and women and torture their memories, and why invite the whole town to one place, if my work and its performance have no other purpose than to awaken a few sensations which any good story, read at home in a quiet corner, is likely to arouse in any of us?" On putting this academic question of Lessing's, the little newspaper philologist, who always had a cold, shrugged his shoulders benevolently. He could chat so pleasantly and, when listening to you, would roguishly search his brain for some sarcastic phrase, while the bridge-work in his mouth kept moving up and down. His luke-warm little soul preferred the novel with attenuated dialogue, especially a story from the gloomiest depths of misery which he himself had never known. This trustee and business manager for a capitalistic group brought out plays whose chief merit was the scourging of the capitalistic social order and of the demoralizing abuses it carries daily in its wake. Because this policy filled their purses, his backers did not object. Dependable actors, thorough preparation, only one playhouse—and therefore no inconvenient shifting of parts resulting in unfortunate relaxations of contact among a group always playing together in familiar surroundings—neither star engagements during the winter, nor ever a new venture: these positive and negative qualities led to clean, sometimes successful performances. Of course, this, is true only of such plays as stood within the range of Brahm's realm of "reality," which—as countless nights, even in dusty royal theatres, have since proved—can easily be played with success by any group of dependable actors. All his attempts at reaching higher, up to Shakespeare, Goethe,

[230]

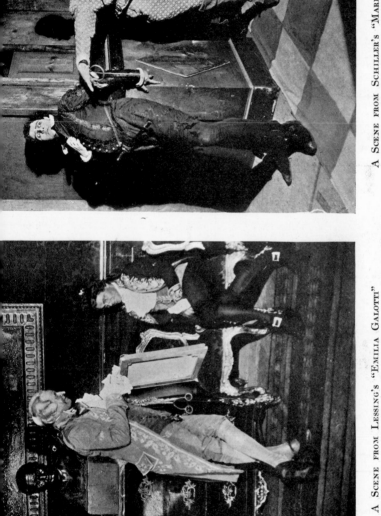

A Scene from Lessing's "Emilia Galotti"
Albert Bassermann as Marinelli and Alexander Moissi as the Prince

A Scene from Schiller's "Maria Stuart"
Fritz Delius as Mortimer and Ferdinand Bonn as Leicester

GERMAN CLASSICS AT THE DEUTSCHES THEATER

THE SETTING FOR THE GARDEN SCENE

Alexander Moissi as Tasso and Alfred Abel as Antonio

SETTING AND SCENE FROM GOETHE'S "TORQUATO TASSO"

AT THE DEUTSCHES THEATER

Calderon and Schiller, were miserable failures. All dramas, born in the realm of the imagination, such as those of Hauptmann, von Hofmannsthal, Eulenberg and Schnitzler, were murdered, died in and of his sober dullness, which barred as unnatural all things of beauty, any rising flame, anything aglow with the fire of youth, with festive joy or with wrath. In "The Wild Duck," to begin with, the imagination was actually lamer than the wounded bird in Ekdal's attic. The poet's mystical idea was not materialized—only his attempt "to pull his own ear," and, in an unpleasant *rencontre,* to confront his exponent of exacting idealism with the necessity of having to live a lie. The true Ibsen in Brahm's hands sank into a sphere of commonplace reason just because he was determined to make of him a "naturalist," in order to introduce him as John the Baptist to the author of "The Weavers." For at that time, Hauptmann had not found his way home to romanticism. Of course, Ibsen might be resurrected into long life with Rosmer, Solness, Borkman and Rubek, if he only had the atmosphere which he requires. A set of plays which omitted "Brand," "Peer Gynt," "The Pretenders" and Julian the Apostate in "Emperor and Galilean," those powerful regal dramas, went by the name of "Ibsen cycle." Could we accept a Schiller cycle which excluded everything before "Don Carlos?" Annually, there came new plays by Sudermann, Fulda, Hirschfeld. The door to fame was opened also to the trash of Skowronnek, Lubliner and Vacano, never to the best and most vital that the times brought forth. Dr. Brahm never played Strindberg, Wilde, Wedekind, the genuine Maeterlinck, Shaw, the best of

Tolstoy. And that stands as a crime never to be forgiven. What an inspiration it would have been to Strindberg if he could have lived to see on the German stage the full force of his powerful dramas, banished by relentless hatred from his native country! What might have become of Wedekind, if want and the mocking about him had not compelled him to force his way to public notice by shrill shouts and over-spiced viands! That these two appeared on the stage only after their death in that "living form" without which the dramatist fails to carry his mission into wider circles, is the fault of the theatrical manager Brahm.

Brahm himself never discovered a poet, never an actor of superior powers. His own theatre harbored the two ablest men in constructive theatrical work, Max Reinhardt and Gordon Craig. He failed to visualize the possibilities latent in them, so he let them go. Not because, like Director Laube, a man equally overestimated, he despised all scenic art and puritanically clung to the text. Later, at the Lessing Theater, Brahm, fearing Reinhardt's competition, also kept painters and upholsterers busy, sparing neither settings nor machinery, and trying to imitate and to surpass the outer form of his neighbor's work. That neighbor honored him, only to be hated by him. The result of these attempts was many a contribution to Famulus Wagner's museum. He persuaded his friends and in the end himself, too, that a man and a scholar had a dignified purpose in life, when he used such trash as Sudermann's "Stein unter Steinen" ("Stone among Stones"), "Die Zwillingschwester" ("The Twin Sisters") and "Das Blumenboot" ("The Flower Boat"), to

BANQUET SCENE IN "MACBETH"

Deutsches Theater, February, 1916

Design for a Setting by Ernst Stern

bring him fat financial returns. He was no stage manager. He could never be more to his actors than just an intelligent audience. Nor could he prove of any use to those writers he loved; and this, despite his considerable knowledge of modern philology and his experience as a critic. He had less the fiber of a powerful artist than Egmont had of a Spanish grandee. In his monotonous dullness, he had no comprehension of cheerfulness, passion, imaginative fancy, all those beautiful springlike qualities of the human soul, which has a rhythm of its own. The actors left this robust disciplinarian in peace, and attuned themselves to their own harmonious chorus. With sound and gesture, they endeavored to create for their imaginative world an atmosphere of which their responsible head, devoid of all instinct, lacked the faintest conception. They only sighed when the Doctor admonished them to stand rooted like trees on the ground of reality, after scenes which rent the clouds of the northern sky with lightning or breathed morning wind on the awakening violets in the garden. Yet, he was kindly, punctual, reliable in all his business transactions, superior without being haughty. Therefore, he was popular; though the drab sobriety of his pedantry, easing up a little only in the vein of irony, fell like mildew on all creative verve, like rose mold on the longing for summer's radiant splendors. Some of his old colleagues of the guild were of the opinion that the manager of a playhouse should be more than a mere office clerk; but he jollied them along diplomatically, grouping them between the reliable and the unreliable, as Jacob separated Laban's sheep. And the "unreliables" who had grumbled because Brahm gave bad plays too often and good ones not well enough, were just the ones who glorified him without end, only to throw Reinhardt under a still deeper shadow.

Compare the two? Dullness or malice would do so. Where the realm of the elder ceased, there on the stage the younger one began. If you insist on comparison, select Max's brother, the equally remarkable Edmund Reinhardt, the perfect "director," who, holding his real self deeply veiled in the background, embodies the new type of the theatrical business man. (This intricate phrase is certainly in its right place here.) He lacks philology and *universitas litterarum*. Yet the achievement of the two Reinhardts presents a parallel. The promoters of the *"Grands Magasins du Louvre"* and *"Au Bon Marché"* are likewise comparable to those merchants who have a thorough knowledge of a well-restricted field —viz., form and method of production, recruiting of help, possibilities of the market—and who, therefore, became department heads in those all-embracing enterprises. The day has come, as prophesied by Goethe, when one mind, well-equipped for the task will take over four theatres at a time and fare better with them than with only one. Though the difference may be as wide and as deep as that between the department store itself and the specialized shop (read Zola's romantically glowing description and Matajas' soberly scientific analysis!), the two forms of management and the two managers themselves—the Brothers Reinhardt—may well be compared. It is impossible, on the other hand, to compare that "art-dealer" with his modern philological training, who from his study tries to bedim the stage's glare, unbearable to his spec-

(Left to Right) Albert Bassermann as Percy; Wilhelm Diegelmann as Falstaff; and
Alexander Moissi as Prince Hal

(Left to Right) Wilhelm Diegelmann as Falstaff; Friedrich Kühne as Bardolph, and
Sophie Pagay as Mistress Quickly

TWO SCENES FROM "KING HENRY IV," PART I

AT THE DEUTSCHES THEATER, OCTOBER, 1912

"HENRY IV," PART I

AT THE DEUTSCHES THEATER, OCTOBER, 1912

Wilhelm Diegelmann as Falstaff

tacled eye—and our theatrical genius who sprang from that very same glare and who, in order to give of his best, requires its very atmosphere. Brahm, unlike his ideal, the Parisian stage official, Antoine, neither found his writers and players himself, nor trained them to self-created style. In business only, never in dramatic composition, was he of assistance to his friend Hauptmann, who is gifted more with poetic feeling and mastery of language than with creative power. At Brahm's playhouse, a strictly limited kind of play, "the realistic, descriptive play," was performed very ably. Productions like Brahm's interpretation of Hauptmann's "Der Arme Heinrich" ("Henry of Aue"), still more that of Hauptmann's "Kaiser Karl's Geisel" ("Charlemagne's Hostage"), "Und Pippa tanzt" ("And Pippa Dances") and "Griselda," of Schnitzler's "Der Schleier der Beatrice" ("The Veil of Beatrice"), of von Hofmannsthal's "Das Gerettete Venedig" ("Venice Preserved"), of Eulenberg's "Blaubart" ("Bluebeard") would have been impossible in Berlin after Reinhardt came. To this day, I believe that the partnership, which in answer to his question I advised Dr. Brahm to enter, would have ripened exquisite fruit. To Brahm's eyes, however, such an alliance seemed a joyless prospect. In his own way, he gently tapped with his index-finger on his pale cheek, and his high-pitched voice flashed the short sentence: "You, of course, would like Reinhardt to eat me alive."

I wonder whether the little philologist's ghost did actually bite a savory piece out of young Reinhardt? Reinhardt did not think like Zarathustra: "Ye are my faithful ones: but what are all faithful ones worth?" That is the voice of him who is mild and defiant, above whom the sky can not be quiet and high and solitary enough, of him who desires no disciples because they are obtrusive and clumsy like puppies, and who shakes them off his cloak and admonishes them that they must learn to doubt him with all the rest. "Not until all of you have disowned me, shall I return unto you." It would be asking too much to expect such aversion to applause from one who makes his bows in a world of make-believe. Such a one needs your faith in him; he requires trustful approval of what he has created, and of that for which he strives. He is not immodest, not conceited and vain. He, too, is aloof from the illusion which he enthrones in everlasting glory. Never did he deny a mistake, never the insufficiency of his achievement. But he is wounded to think that, from the ranks of those who do creative work, he is shoved into the company of those who beat their pound into money. He feels hurt to realize that often when praised he has to taste as well the bitter drop of their anger; that they are the ones who spend that money; that his way is obscured by the shadow of the candles which light the altar of Brahm and his cult. He is the demonic artist, who can fall in love with the most alien object, who will live for the child of another's mind, give it more care, and clothe it better than its own father did. Yet this man of a sturdy, stocky body like Bonaparte, somewhat flabby, perhaps, from too much sitting, is also an epicurean, a Medici (from Baden near Vienna) for whom the *Casa Buonarrotti* would be too bare and too close to breathe in. He loves to dream the atmosphere of the great world. And when abroad in it, he takes pleasure

MEDIEVAL BRITISH POMP AT THE DEUTSCHES THEATER

Prince Hal at the Head of His Army in the Production of "King Henry IV," Part II, in October, 1912

THREE COSTUME DESIGNS BY ERNST STERN

A DESIGN BY ERNST STERN FOR A SETTING BY THE SHORE

"TWELFTH NIGHT"

AT THE DEUTSCHES THEATER, OCTOBER, 1907

in watching the gait and manners of those men and women of rank whom he had seen before only in the carnival procession of his soul, in the costumes of Southampton and Elizabeth. And there he feels the prickling, irritating joy of him who is admitted but who "does not belong." "Canst thou with rich enjoyment fool me, let that day be the last for me." He who looks for enjoyment in life, does not wish to go through this world homeless, without peace and without rest, eternally unsatisfied like Faustus. He longs to break away from the current of life, from the storm of activity and from its everyday worries and difficulties, from the blame which, batters him like a hailstorm. He longs to be in the sun, and almost unconsciously tones down the rhythm of his will to the measure which the world-old Faust calls "wise and deliberate." His youthful joy in gay and uproarious plays dwindles. His house of art, not yet uniform in style, not yet pure in its expression, opens wide and admits discursive novels tainted with dialect and illogical monster tales, which will throw him off his course and gradually destroy his very soul. "If he does not do so, the others will give these things to the public. And the press calls for Brahm's repertory!" Amongst these was one monument, highly admired by Wilhelm's fine artistic judgment: "Glaube und Heimat" ("Faith and Home"). That period also brought "Der Weibsteufel" ("The Demon in Woman"), hysterical rubbish, to which this door should never have opened. Four Kings knock at the door, John, Richard the Second, Richard the Third, Henry the Fifth; Cleopatra and Cressida, Coriolanus and Timon, Götz and Hagen, Klärchen and Marianne, Egmont and Alceste,

[237]

MAX REINHARDT AND HIS THEATRE

Angelo ("Measure for Measure") and Tartuffe, Crespo from "Zalamea," Rubek's Irene—all these look longingly through the bars, and the host of those who between twenty and forty think that they must write plays, rattle the gate violently. But the key only squeaks, the door opens only to those whom their contemporaries had pronounced "modern" yesterday. Since the incessant yell of "Stage effect which destroys the spirit" has robbed him of the pleasure he had taken in creating with color and scenery; since, too, at every corner a novice in the art of magic bluntly apes his outer forms,—the master, all out of humor, looks for compensation by exploring new heights and depths. For a while, the play is lifeless; heavy curtains hide the stage. Then, the rays from the light-reflector become the sculptor, who out of shadow forms polychromatic reliefs, with some of the figures in the foreground standing out fully illuminated. Then, he devotes all his efforts to reconstructing the scenery, always with finest artistic taste. Turrets on the sides, movable partitions, an adjustable proscenium. In a huge stone circus, the action proceeds over a steep flight of stairs down into the orchestra, the place whence the voices of the chorus rose in the open temples of the Greeks, those centres of religious and national art. What ever-changing, ever-glowing life! But the shadow of that old philologist falls on his stoutest efforts and over his brightest joys. And—who knows?—in the end philology itself, dry and dusty, may even approach that field from which the magician and his art have been banished.

In 1887, among the posthumous papers of Luise von Göchhausen—who was a physically deformed but highly

GOETHE'S "URFAUST" AT THE DEUTSCHES THEATER, OCTOBER, 1920

A Design by Ernst Stern for the Appearance of the Earth Spirit

GOETHE'S "URFAUST" AT THE DEUTSCHES THEATER, OCTOBER, 1920

A Design by Ernst Stern for a Street Scene

intellectual lady-in-waiting at the court of the Dowager Duchess Anna Amelia, and whom court gossip called "Thuselchen"—a copy of the Faust sketch, unknown till then, was found. Goethe had brought it to Weimar. Carl August jokingly remarked: "A fragment of a play, which, I am afraid, will always remain a fragment." A skeleton, yet a heart beating in it. Written soon after the Sesenheim episode, the Gretchen theme is not worked out in detail, although the broad outlines and characteristic features are all there. Of the Faust spirit only that is present which had been gathered from the incense fumes and magic vapors of the old legend. Those wise scholars, deeply concerned with Goethe's papers, resisted the temptation to bring their discovery to the stage, even though it was only a philologists' meeting in Weimar. Not one of those playhouse managers, so anxious to get into print, could overcome the feeling of reverence toward an artist's heartblood creation. But just that well-nigh insurmountable problem fascinated Reinhardt. From the announcement on the bulletin board to the final clatter of the prison bars, one maze of words and stage properties. "Urfaust" (original Faust) is an academic word, easily coined and grasped; but he who uses it for announcing a play which shall be real life to us, is like that stupid sergeant who lets Fritz (Frederick the Great) exclaim: "And now, boys, into the Seven Years' War!" Title? "Gretchen." "That Affair with Gretchen." There is hardly more to it. Gretchen in a sleeping compartment, so narrow is her room and cell. Faust's den, Auerbach's pothouse, a square in front of the Cathedral, a garden, a prison, a church aisle. One is reminded of a sleeping car, with its wide open doors brightly lit against the dark background of the station, when, between the high pillars, the pictures of Gretchen's chamber appear. In the sleeper, much pottering about from washstand to trunk and couch; in the play, from desk to furniture, trees and fountain. The light-cone of the reflector roves until it finds the desired persons and objects. One step further, the famulus stands before the doctor; two steps more, Gretchen kneels before the image of the *mater Dolorosa*. This is not Gothic, it is early rococo. The desired impression, however, is to be the lofty pillars of a Gothic portal. I can not see what the boisterous behavior of Leipzig drunkards and Rhenish lovers has to do with that. That is eighteenth century, without any trace of metaphysics. Goethe himself refused the proposition to stage his own times in Gothic style. "It is always a masquerade which, in the long run, can hardly have any good effect; it does not correspond to the reality in which we are living; it is the result of a shallow and superficial way of looking at things and only enhances that frame of mind." If any special style is desired, do it only in the black and white manner of a drawing book. Action, however, proper lay-out of the land, wide and free motion of the actors, must be present in every-day scenes. The Gothic hobby is disastrous. At first, Faust resembles that haughty magician of Rembrandt, so foreign to Goethe's world as well as to all demons; later, without the rejuvenating drink, he resembles a lyric, melancholic scholar. The Spirit of the Earth possesses a head which lacks nothing but rolling eyes and flaming nostrils to make it a bow-wow. In the scene where Mephisto roasts the

[240]

GOETHE'S "URFAUST" AT THE DEUTSCHES THEATER, OCTOBER, 1920

A Design by Ernst Stern for the Scene at the Well

GOETHE'S "URFAUST" AT THE DEUTSCHES THEATER, OCTOBER, 1920

A Design by Ernst Stern for the Scene Before the Mater Dolorosa

student, his book, full of the sour wisdom of Merck, glows in a genuine eighteenth century fire. Gretchen wears the long flowing dress of Memling's virgins. Who would believe that her hands are rough from the stove and the washtub, that she rejoices in the possession of earrings and gold chains, that she trembles with joy when a stranger greets her, or, finally, that her bosom longs for a lover? Even before she enters the church, she becomes repentant. She disrobes like a penitent sinner who wishes to suppress guilty desires by an attitude, unesthetic and commonplace. Frau Thimig should never appear as Claire or Gretchen, though she might enact Viola, Ariel, Luise Miller, Hedvig Ekdal, Irene, even Princess Leonore or Queen Rhodope. In Sorge's drama "Der Bettler" ("The Beggar"), she was superb as a radiant girl with a naked hellenic soul; also as Marie Beaumarchais, without leaning toward the French conception, a humble receptacle overflowing with sentiment; also as Rosalind, not with supercilious mockery, not impatient for a word duel, more of Mozartian than of Shakespearean loveliness; also as Stella, with her many shades of spiritualized, bashful sensuality. This sensitive artist, with her almost too easy, yet masterly, art of mingling tears with laughter, can hardly see Gretchen as a walking wooden Madonna, holding her head on one side, more as a tired girl-scout. She is asked, however, to adapt herself to a Gothic atmosphere. Thus, she plays a withered, pale, stiff woman so that even the most daring would lack the slightest desire "to act boldly with a harlot of that type." Bridal yearning, a woman's awe, which should move the hangman to pity, melt away like the wax of a thin candle

[241]

when the wick is too long. This sickly, anemic Gretchen feels most at ease at her neighbor's house. The latter, at the stage manager's command, appears distorted to a tippling, shameless Jan Steen harlot, free to every visitor. And, do you believe it, the Evil Spirit, Gretchen's bad conscience, later on speaks through this very woman's voice! A serious artist, who, if properly guided, might become David, Mahomet, Herodes (Hebbel), who could try his strength on Posa and Hamlet, struts about, very un-Satanic, more like an amateur at a house-party; and flops himself on the writing desk, so that even the youngest freshman can not mistake him for a professor. In the professorial scene with its demonic humor, there are still remnants of flat pedantic wit. Why does the devil come to the Magister's house? Why do he and Faust suddenly enter Auerbach's cellar (one eighth of the entire playing time)? Why does Valentin stammer a few verses and then disappear again? The profiteer probably understands, he who paid exorbitantly for seats for himself and his sealskin-clad wife. If only the play would move like young wine in fermentation! But it is lame. It hastens only, when it should slow down and take a deep breath. After the first kiss: "I can not think what he finds in me!" Lights out! Ten seconds later (which embrace the whole trembling happiness of Margaret's girlhood), new contact: "My bosom yearns for him alone." Goths are fast horsemen! And every time when the hoof strikes the ground, your memory searches for the accompanying text. "A golden cup, they say, his mistress gave him on her deathbed." Was that it? Memory again and again beats upon you, like a disturbing noise,

[242]

GOETHE'S "URFAUST" AT THE DEUTSCHES THEATER, OCTOBER, 1920

A Design by Ernst Stern for the Scene in Field and Forest

GOETHE'S "URFAUST" AT THE DEUTSCHES THEATER, OCTOBER, 1920

A Design by Ernst Stern for the Prison Scene

and blocks the passage through which the sound of pure
art tries to reach you. A torture, that evening. Instead
of the noblest crown jewel, an unwashed piece of pegma-
tite with a diamond vein in it.

> "A speculative wight . . .
> Is like a beast on moorland lean, that round
> And round some fiend misleads to evil plight—
> While all about lie pastures fresh and green."

During the three weeks devoted to rehearsals, Faust's
immortal vein might have been freed from the accompanying flaws and resurrected to a fresh and pure life.

Why—in the spirit of sarcastic empiricists—does
that "wight" speculate? Because they mistook the
abundance of Reinhardt's visions for the result of specu-
lative greed, and uprooted him from a happy, ingenious
simplicity. Because in eight cases out of ten the blame
was unjust, and in six out of ten, praise, blind and deaf,
has stumbled over the very finest. Also, because in hours
of disappointed hope the epicurean in him mastered the
over-sensitive artist and induced him to surround himself with flatterers who approved of all his proposals and
admired him as Gretchen did her great Heinrich. His
attempt to bring the second part of "Faust" to the stage,
thereby reducing the pious Gretchen theme to the mere
episode it was, had slight success, although he placed at
its service the full power of pure and glowing imagination. It was condemned much more severely than the
failure he made of his hurriedly improvised "Urfaust."
Like Saint Sebastian facing the shower of the arrows of
the Mauretanians, he stood firm then and after every en-

[243]

terprise ungraciously received. Long ago, he turned his back on the younger artists, from whom the critics imperiously demand plays only to disgust the public after their performance by pointing out nothing but their imperfections. That was a mistake; for, as he was able to give more to the young than anyone else, their genuine warmth would always have warmed him, would have fed his strength at the very fountain of life, and would have called him back home from expensive excursions to the realm of the past.

During recent years, "Der Bettler" ("The Beggar") was the ripest fruit of his art. Perfect in atmosphere and individual flavor, too, like "Salome" and "Mésilande" of old, were "The Taming of the Shrew," a picture conceived under the influence of champagne and lovingly carried out in hilarious mood; Sternheim's "Bürger Schippel"; Strindberg's "The Thunderstorm" (by far superior to "The Spook Sonata"); Molière's comedy of the doctor; Tolstoy's "The Living Corpse" ("Redemption"). They all passed almost unnoticed. Often before, less genuine art received louder praise. It was said that the gentle trio—Viola, Orsino, Olivia—in "Twelfth Night" was drowned in boisterous, noisy scenes; that in "As You Like It" the fool and Jacques (the Ur-Hamlet) broke up the symphony of the spirits; that graceful feminine legs in tights mischievously danced away large portions of both poems. Not all the arrows hit you, Sebastian; the eye of the keenest marksman sometimes misses the vulnerable spot. But let his skin be merely scratched and the pain will shoot right through his sensitive body from head to toe. Since wrath and irony blow around the Grosses Schauspielhaus—the object of his ambition for the last ten years—he would like to flee into solitude, taking along the leper's rattle. His esthetic friends try to comfort him.

Also in Salzburg, the Great Spirit speaks, not in forest and cavern alone. This earth still has some pleasures in store: to give a new halo to that rubbish, the "Mysterium," in front of the marble Cathedral; to rattle the money bags under the muffled church bells in the presence of Christians from Ischl and other cottage ascetics.

It is true, this smacks somewhat of Bayreuth and of salvation. But the mountain air prevents it from penetrating into your clothes, and tomorrow heavy rains will wash away the sweetish scent. Today is ours. Hellas, Nazareth, von Hofmannsthal: Julian's dream of the third empire opens a view into the distance. Which way is Berlin? Not even from the belfry, where the telephone wires meet, can you see it. Here Reinhardt as a boy had been a starving "character actor" who held his breath in awe in the realm of the spirit of Mozart, of Solari, the architect of the Cathedral, and of Schwanthaler. With foolhardy hope, he clung to the far-famed actor of the Burg Theater, Ferdinand Bonn. A quarter of a century passed. Salzburg is a centre for his festival plays, the summer abode of world-wide fame such as no manager ever enjoyed before, the goal of American star-seekers. And this owner of a princely palace, this self-supporting landed proprietor and theatre Khalif, who is just fifty and in splendid health—should he be worried by remembering that hostile winds sometimes blow over the Spree; that the well-covered Panke river sometimes exhales offensive odors; that at times a few sharp-shooting critics lie in ambush for him; that the operating cost of the three theatres rises, while the tax collector snatches a large slice of the enormous box office receipts; that the ridiculously overpaid film stars stay away from rehearsals and appear on his horizon only when they choose? Sebastian needs no Irene; he can change into the Magnifico of the Medici. Inside, outside, there is plenty of space for the artist, for the epicurean. By his lake, the owner of Leopoldskron is invulnerable, even to a pinprick. Did the large number of pictures irritate you? Do the sparrows still pick up seeds in the Circus? Come and see simplest things in a simple frame. Goethe truly Gothic! Even the "Urfaust" may arise here. That was a mistake (it seems to me, not to him). What does it matter? Since we resented that poor "Sketch" as an offense against the holy majesty of genius, the only one which commands veneration, we should not muffle our criticism, as they muffled the Cathedral bells for a market-fair. After he had reconstructed Lenz's tragedy of soldier life and Schiller's tragedy of civilian existence, from cellar foundations to the roof, after he had called all the spirits from Duncan's Castle to the hypochondriac Argan's sickroom to a new dance of life; at the height of his creative powers, he became the poet of another man's poem. And he has won the right, for once, to create for his self-enjoyment what we can not enjoy with him. At last he has found himself, so he dares to play with his faculties. As a result of much stupid gossip, farewell testimonials were written far too soon.

True, Reinhardt refuses to stand in the limelight any

longer, merely as a theatre director. He refuses to be the target for every arrow of criticism. Yet, as an artist, he remains faithful to his art. His most daring enterprise carried him, Fortuna's favorite, into wilder currents than he or any one else had ever known before, and—not against his will—lands him far from what the crowd adores. He burns all bridges behind him, turns out every lamp, and on a fresh young horse canters into a world which knows no footlights. He still owes his talent, however, to his work. Almost everything powerful and effective on the contemporary European stage—even in opera, ballet and the film—grew from seeds he sowed. It is chiefly his merit that Germany today has more good theatres than ever before, and that everywhere the best plays reach the masses. The host of actors (who, after all, know more about their craft than we do) besiege him, long for him; and the most mature among them do not deny that no one else can replace him. At last, freed from all business responsibilities, Reinhardt will have to give them, both masters and apprentices, more serious, more kindly assistance than he has been able to do since before the war. The authors, too, need him; there is many a poet whom he alone can help, whose star only he can lead to success. Never must he weigh a drama only from the standpoint of whether it will give the stage manager an opportunity for finer or coarser effects. In "Stella," for instance, the many could not discern him, although the select few felt the presence of an all-powerful creator. You must not flatter and fawn upon him; but venerate him with the grateful love he deserves, he who made Germany's stage the model for all others, even for Stanislavsky,

[247]

Gémier, and Forbes-Robertson. If the circus drama and the arena-play are, as seems to me, not only an imperfect beginning, but an actual mistake, then, instead of keeping the highly profitable steam-roller going, let him start out for his India, through fog and through storm, taking his possessions and his reputation along in his ship. And let him discover a new America on his adventurous voyage to the East. He whom earnest admirers love for his merits, need fear neither hostile rivalry nor the poisoned arrows of criticism. He need not protect himself against peevish gossip at a "royal" court, in which no mortal ever survived for long. Versailles, Potsdam, Bayreuth! All that he who is tied to this earth needs is peace and space and solitude above him. "Face to face with thee, Nature would make life worth while." He is one to whom enjoyment means a moment of rest between two battles, and who finds inspiration only in active creation.

"THE MIR

The Century Theatre as the Cathedral into Which It Has Been Trans

ORK, 1924

Gest by the Young American Scenic Designer, Norman-Bel Geddes

APPENDIX I

"THE MIRACLE"

[The *Regie* Book or production manuscript of Reinhardt has long
been a tradition in the theatre throughout central Europe. Mention
of its voluminous detail regarding scenic settings, lighting, movements of the characters, gesture, intonations, and all the other details
of an interpretative nature, has been made in more than one chapter
of this volume. Several hundred such expanded manuscripts are
filed in the libraries of the various Reinhardt theatres and in his
castle home in Salzburg. This is the first time, however, so far as
is known, that one of these manuscripts has reached public print.
The publication of the *Regie* Book of "The Miracle" therefore, is
interesting not only for a glimpse behind the scenes of the production of this wordless play by Karl Vollmoeller with score by Engelbert
Humperdinck, revised and extended by Friedrich Schirmer, which
Reinhardt has made at the Century Theatre in New York for F. Ray
Comstock and Morris Gest, but also for its intrinsic merit as a first-
hand revelation of the wheels within wheels which go to make up a
Reinhardt production. The copy of the *Regie* Book which is presented
here is that which has been annotated, in close collaboration with Reinhardt, by Norman-Bel Geddes, the young American artist who designed
the production of "The Miracle."—THE EDITOR]

COLOR KEY AND LEADING MOTIVES

(All Colors are Against Black and Gold.)

SCENE 1—CATHEDRAL

Statues, Nuns, Priests, Populace, Knight.
(Dark, Musty Stone.)
[249]

APPENDIX I

Scene 2—Summer Forest

Incense, Mist, Elves, Knight, Count, Hunters, Bushes.
(Tapestry.)
Green, blue-green, blue.

Scene 3—Banquet

Count, Banqueters, Gypsies, Prince, Servants.
(Stained Glass.)
Blue-violet, violet, red-violet.

Scene 4—Wedding

Bed, Lanterns, Witches, Prince, Companions, Emperor,
Conspirators.
(Enamel.)
Vermilion, yellow, ivory, gold.

Scene 5—Coronation

Candles, Cymbals, Bells, Palanquins, Emperor, Empress,
Courtiers, Revolutionists.
(Gold Treasure Objects.)
Gold, ivory, crimson.

Scene 6—Inquisition

Confusion, Storm, Torches, Mob, Street, Soldiers, Judges,
Executioners.
(Puppets.)
Crimson, brown.

Scene 7—Manger

Soldiers, Wenches, Star.
(Tryptic.)
Brown, ivory.

[250]

"THE MIRACLE"

SCENE 8—WINTER FOREST

Stars, Snow, Shadows, Dead Lovers.
(Skeleton of Church.)
White, gray.

SCENE 9—CATHEDRAL

Christmas Evening, Choir.
Gray.

SYNOPSIS

(Stage directions read "RIGHT" and "LEFT" from the
point of view of the audience.)

SCENE 1—CATHEDRAL

CHARACTERS

THE NUN	THE LAME PIPER
THE ABBESS	THE KNIGHT
THE OLD SACRISTAN	THE MADONNA

*Nuns and Novices. Peasants, Townsfolk and Children.
Bishops, Priests, Monks and Pilgrims. Cripples, Blind,
Lame and Lepers. Patricians of the Town, Knights and
Troups of Soldiers.*

1. The interior of an early Gothic Church.
2. High, massive columns rise into mystic darkness.
3. Gothic arches, stone ornaments representing tendrils and
   lace work, a richly decorated iron grating, entangled
   scrolls and figures.
4. Narrow, high church windows in deep, rich coloring.
5. Aisles, corridors, doors, an unsymmetrical arrangement
   of mysterious openings, windows, stairways.

6. Votive statues on columns, small statues with candles and flowers before them, crucifixes, offerings brought by grateful people, wax flowers, embroideries, jewels, a child's doll, decoratively painted candles.
7. In the background a richly carved altar, with a golden shrine and candles seen through a grilled screen.
8. The eternal lamp burns before it.
9. A Cardinal's hat hangs above.
10. Altar, with table, to divide and open, with steps through it.
11. The floor is of large gray stones, some of which are tomb stones.   In the centre of the floor the stones are to be glass with lamps below, so wired as to spread the light from the middle outwards.
12. Flickering light from behind columns as from invisible candles throws fantastic shadows.
13. Shafts of sunlight, coming through the high windows at the right, projects patterns on the floor.
14. At left and right of auditorium, cloisters with vaulted ceilings and stone-floors.
15. Chandeliers of various sizes in the auditorium to cast light downwards only, adding depth and mystery to the ceiling.
16. Several poles for flags and lanterns fastened to the seat ends in aisles of auditorium.
17. Panelling of balcony rail to show here and there between flags.
18. A clock above pulpit.   This clock is to strike at various times during the dream parts, to suggest the existence of the church.   Remember the sound before the clock strikes.
19. On top of the clock two figures to mark the hours, by striking a large bell between them.   One of these figures symbolizes life; the other death.
20. Clerestory windows around upper part of auditorium. Choir stands and triforium openings below windows.

21. All doors have heavy bolts, locks and knockers to create business and noise.
22. Large keys on rings for various doors.
23. The doors immediately behind proscenium lead to sacristy.
24. The doors below the lodges lead to exterior.
25. Small midnight mass bell, near top of tower, to be rung from rope on stage floor.
26. Wind machines, thunder drums and voices also to be there.
27. When audience takes their seats, everything is dark.
28. The sound of a storm far away.
29. Soft candle-light in the auditorium, only where it is absolutely necessary, and flickering behind the columns around the altar screen.
30. Clusters of candle-lights in distant places in the auditorium and stage, high up in the tower to produce an effect of tremendous size and of incredible distance.
31. There are to be candles around the altar screen and on the altar itself. The candles should be of various lengths and the bulbs of very low voltage and of various pale colors.
32. In chapels tiny candles suggest side-altars against darkness. Prominent clusters of them unsymmetrically chosen. Flickering candles on the columns in the apse and cloisters throwing shadows.
33. Candles on altar, altar screen and in chapels to be wired individually and lighted or extinguished by nuns. Candle bulbs to be no larger than one-half inch in diameter. The bulb must not show.
34. Candle extinguishers and wax tapers.
35. The large altar is dark.
36. One recognizes gradually among the towering columns several dark figures huddled together absorbed in prayer.
37. From a distant tower a bell sounds.

38. Large bells are located in ventilating shaft over auditorium and controlled from orchestra gallery.
39. A praying voice from behind the triforium windows is indistinctly heard; now and then a Latin word is audible.
40. Chairs are pushed about, some one blows his nose, others cough. The echo resounds through the church.
41. After that, silence.
42. An old sexton appears carrying a lantern.
43. His stick taps the pavement, and his steps drag over the stone floor.
44. He pulls back the green curtain over the Madonna statue.
45. He goes to the tower. Up the winding staircase the lantern shows through little windows and finally at the top.
46. He crosses a bridge and disappears through a door way in the wall.
47. The organ starts and bells ring high above the church.
48. Nuns in pairs march through the cloisters toward the altar in two long columns, to take part in the coming ceremony.
49. The windows of the church become more brilliant from sunlight without.
50. Outside a young bright spring morning has awakened.
51. Sixty nuns dressed in ivory colored garments trimmed with black. They all wear ropes. The black nuns' costumes appear like shadows passing in the dark and must be cut in such a way that the white undergarments show conspicuously when the nuns flutter like white doves in their excitement at the loss of the Madonna.
52. The chin cloths must be drawn very tightly, so that they never look slovenly. In fact they are to be made so that they can not be worn otherwise.
53. One column is headed by the Abbess.
54. The Abbess may be dressed either in white or in black,

A CHOIR BOY
COSTUME PLATE BY NORMAN-BEL GEDDES

wears a crown and carries a silver staff, like the Bishop's, but smaller.

55. In this column the aged feeble Sacristan of the convent is carried in on a chair by four nuns.

56. In the other column a young nun, still but a child, is led in. She takes a tearful farewell of her mother, father, and grandmother who are seated at the right.

57. In an impressive ceremony the young Nun is dressed in an over-garment similar to that of the old Sacristan and receives the keys and office.

58. The Abbess sits in a special chair during the ceremony. She sings while one nun holds a music book for her and another holds a lighted candle.

59. This is accompanied by responses without music from the choir gallery.

60. In front are the holy pictures and the statue of the Madonna which stands on a column. It is a stone statue, painted in blue tempera and gold-leaf and wearing a crown set with precious stones.

61. The statue is to look as stone-like as possible and heavy, even if clumsy.

62. She must wear the white muslin nun's garb, as an under-garment.

63. The white head-cloth always has to remain on and be drawn as tightly as possible.

64. The Madonna holds the child in her arms.

65. The pedestal is decorated with many flowers, and large and small candles.

66. Crutches stacked around the base.

67. This pedestal altar conceals steps, covered with soft rubber. There must be supports for the Madonna under her arm-pits, at her waist, a seat, and recesses cut in floor for her feet. Her shoes are rubber-soled.

68. There are five statues of saints at other positions.

69. Large bells in the distance begin to sound as the Convent Church is revealed in its full glow of light.

70. The Nun, for the first time as the new sacristan, opens all the doors with her keys.
71. A great commotion and the hum of voices comes from without.
72. The sound of music grows nearer, the organ starts with massive tones.
73. A great procession pours into the church through all the doors. Men and women who are making the pilgrimage to the celebrated miracle-working statue of the Madonna.
74. First come the visiting orders of Nuns in white.
75. Then peasants with banners.
76. Women in vivid colored clothes, some bare-footed.
77. Towns-people following, carrying banners with coats-of-arms of towns.
78. Tradesmen carrying the various emblems of their trade on poles.
79. A group of peasants bring in an enormous cross.
80. A great crowd of children with a may-pole.
81. Priests carrying church banners.
82. Acolytes swinging incense.
83. Choirboys with their large books.
84. The Archbishop carries his staff and walks beneath a canopy carried by four men.
85. Under another canopy is carried the monstrance. Church dignitaries follow.
86. Then monks carrying wooden statues of saints on poles.
87. A great mass of cripples on primitive crutches and stretchers, wearing dirty ragged clothes.
88. Blind people, who are led.
89. Widows in mourning.
90. Mothers carrying sick children on their backs, in their arms, and with others clinging to their skirts.
91. Lepers with clappers.
92. Pilgrims with broad-brimmed hats, staves, bundles and flasks.

93. Finally the knights in vivid color.
94. Followed by heralds, squires, men-at-arms, in full dress.
95. No one comes empty-handed. All who have nothing else to carry bring full-leafed birch-branches.
96. The procession fills the whole stage and all the aisles in the auditorium.
97. There is much singing and waving of the yellow green branches. It looks almost like a green forest, waving to and fro.
98. The voice of a priest, whom no one sees, is heard.
99. The music stops.
100. A bell rings at the altar.
101. A white vapor begins to rise from the vessels containing the incense.
102. The crowd falls on its knees.
103. The sick crowd up to the statue of the Madonna and pray without halt. The Archbishop leads the prayers from the pulpit.
104. The tension grows. A breathless silence.
105. Finally there arises in the audience a completely lamed man, who had been carried in on a stretcher. He gets heavily to his feet, with convulsive twitchings, and raising his arms high in ecstasy strides to the figure of the Mother of God, where he dances with joy.
106. A cry, the organ, rejoicing of the crowd. A miracle has come to pass.
107. The pilgrims leave the church singing.
108. The candles are extinguished and the nuns slowly pass out.
109. The young Sacristan goes about her duties of locking the doors.
110. In the last doorway there stands the healed fellow blowing harmlessly upon a flute. This demoniac figure, who runs through the play and has an evil influence upon the fate of the young Nun, is the lure of sensual life. At this moment his appearance resembles that

of the Pied Piper. He wears a broad-brimmed hat over his faun-like ears.

111. Children surround him in their curiosity and listen to his music.
112. The Nun stands still as if under a spell and hears his tunes with the same astonishment and naïve joy as the children.
113. The children, unable to resist longer, fall into the rhythm, crowd into the church and force the Nun, who resists, into their ranks.
114. An unconscious yearning for the spring without causes her momentarily to forget her new office.
115. In her childishness, the Nun lets herself be forced into the dance.
116. She lets her keys fall and dances joyfully.
117. In the meantime, the Piper's tune has attracted a young Knight, who quietly enters and is fascinated by the graceful dancing of the Nun.
118. Suddenly, on seeing him, she becomes frightened and rooted to the spot as they exchange glances.
119. The Nun hears nothing as the bell rings for vespers.
120. Nuns approach in a column, the Abbess at their head.
121. They become enraged on seeing this pair in the church.
122. The children and the Piper slyly escape through the open door.
123. The Abbess rebukes the young Sacristan who stares about her, dazed.
124. At a nod from the angry Abbess the keys are taken away from her and the heavy bolts locked behind the Knight who has slowly gone out.
125. She is sentenced to spend the night in prayer before the statue of the Madonna.
126. The nuns again depart and the church sinks gradually into night and silence.
127. The Nun prays fervently before the statue of the Holy Virgin.

"THE MIRACLE"

128. In her confusion she scarcely knows what is happening to her.
129. Her thoughts, which she seeks vainly to discipline, escape through the stone walls and wander tirelessly into the night in the direction of the young Knight.
130. The poor child returns again and again to her prayers, seeking peace and comfort there.
131. Her youth, awakened for the first time, struggles against the cold discipline offered her.
132. She runs to the font and sprinkles herself madly with holy water.
133. Her heart beats wildly, she throws herself about on the steps leading to the miracle statue.
134. She wrings her hands and plunges desperately into passionate prayer.
135. At this moment something happens that can just as well be a raving dream of fever as a fantastic reality. With the rapid pace of dreams, one experience chases after another and drives the Nun back into the church after a moment of actual happiness through a martyrdom of indescribable suffering. Dream, or reality, it is intense, terrible, vital, as endlessly long as an intense dream, as horribly short as a full life.
136. Suddenly there is a light but insistent knocking at the gate. The Nun grows tense.
137. The knock is repeated. Is it her own heart-beat? She tries not to hear and prays aloud.
138. The knocking continues, always louder, and finally sounds from all sides and from all doors. Each door should have a heavy knocker.
139. She springs up involuntarily, takes several steps toward the door.
140. She stands still in fright, throws herself on her knees, wrings her hands, is torn back and forth.
141. Finally like an excited but caged bird, she flutters anx-

iously to and fro, beating her head against the cold walls.

142. The knocking grows wilder, her yearning more uncontrollable.

143. She shakes the locked doors with all her strength.

144. Throwing herself on her knees, she begs the Mother of God to set her free.

145. The moon shines through the windows.

146. As if mad, she dashes toward the Holy Virgin and points fiercely at the child in her arms. She is yearning for the child, for everything out there.

147. Completely out of her mind she finally takes the holy child from the arms of the Madonna and holds it high.

148. A warm glow radiates from it and then suddenly the child disappears in a flash of light.

149. Everything grows dark. A sound like thunder resounds through the high church.

150. When it is again light Mary has heard the passionate pleadings and has performed a miracle.

151. The high altar glittering with candles, slowly opens, forming a Gothic arch, with a knight in silver armor and a blue mantle, visible through the high candles on the altar tables.

152. The Knight and the Nun stand regarding each other.

153. The Nun shrinks back frightened and flees to the foot of the Madonna.

154. The Mother of God smiles as graciously as ever. Her will is plain.

155. The altar table, with the candles on it, opens slowly, exposing a flight of steps.

156. The Knight slowly approaches the Nun. She rises shyly.

157. He offers her his hand to lead her forth. She looks at her clothing and hesitates to go out in her holy costume.

158. She removes the black nun's veil, the white cape, the rosary with its large cross, the belt and finally her dark

WIDOW IN MOURNING
COSTUME PLATE BY NORMAN·BEL GEDDES

dress and lays them all tenderly on the steps of the miracle statue.

159. Rising, she shudders at the sight of her underdress, feeling that she is without clothes.
160. The Piper who was behind the Knight brings in the blue cloak of the Knight and covers the young Nun with the dress of life.
161. Again she kneels, and the Knight with her, at the foot of the Virgin.
162. Then he catches her in his arms and runs off with her into the world.
163. The church is deserted.
164. A sigh comes from somewhere within the walls.
165. The Madonna statue begins to glow with an unearthly light.
166. It seems as if she were opening her lips and smiling. The figure moves.
167. The light on her face changes from unearthly to the pink of life.
168. She opens her eyes.
169. She smiles.
170. She turns her head.
171. She drops her robe.
172. She descends.
173. She lifts her arm.
174. She removes her crown.
175. She holds it up high.
176. She lays it on the pedestal.
177. Then she gives a sign for the altar to close, and it becomes as before.
178. The Virgin bends low, and in sweet humility puts on the simple costume of the Nun.
179. She goes to the tower and rings the bell.
180. Voices of singing nuns. The Virgin kneels and prays in front of her pedestal.
181. The nuns come into the church for mass.

182. The Abbess glances at the supposed Nun, sunk in prayer, and chuckles fondly at the repentance of her favorite.

183. By accident her glance falls on the spot where the miracle statue has stood, but now where only her cloak and crown lie. She does not trust her eyes, stares, consults the sister.

184. A terrible fear seizes all the nuns.

185. They scream, run around enraged, cry out, weep, threaten their supposed sister, fetch the priest and ring the alarm bell.

186. With clenched fist and swinging cords, all rush at the poor Nun, who has obviously permitted the theft of the precious treasure in her impious sin.

187. The Nun's head remains humbly bowed.

188. Whenever the threatening sisters surround her in a wild rush, she gently floats a short distance into the air without changing her position. This is done on a trap on the right.

189. In silent awe they draw back from her; staring at this miracle speechlessly, they recognize that a higher power is obviously at work here, and that the young Nun is the chosen agent.

190. Returning to the earth, she goes about her duties like an ordinary nun, taking a jar of oil to fill the eternal lamp.

191. The nuns form open rows and follow their holy sister spreading their arms wide and singing in ecstasy.

192. The scene grows dark.

Scene II—Summer Forest

CHARACTERS

THE NUN.	THE ROBBER COUNT.
THE KNIGHT.	THE SHADOW OF DEATH.
THE PIPER.	HUNTSMEN AND FOLLOWERS OF THE COUNT.

1. The bells on high ring and the narrow lacy church windows light up in their dark, varied colors.

2. Thirty men in costumes, suggestive of green bushes, stand at the foot of the altar replacing branches that had been placed there.

3. The organ peals softly and one hears an old Gregorian chorus in the pure high voices of girls in the choir gallery.

4. Soon the interior of the church becomes visible. In the flickering candle light one sees the dark figures of people praying.

5. With a wax taper a church servant lights the candles on the altar and between the piers there moves a shadowy column of nuns.

6. Then while the choir is still singing, everything sinks again into darkness.

7. In the vague darkness comes a procession to the altar. A priest, acolytes swinging incense, and nuns following.

8. The priest reads a quiet prayer and rings the little bell at intervals.

9. Incense floats upwards. The stage has to be piped for smoke behind the columns and around the edge of the glass floor. It finally fills the stage and becomes a fog, while it is still dark.

10. At the elevation of the Host, through the mist glows a light as though in it, which rises slowly, appearing like the moon.

11. The lights in the windows die out, the nuns come downstage and the fog thickens.

12. In the ensuing forest scene and in all following changes the Cathedral remains standing with its columns and walks, galleries and lacy figures, and only through separate decorations, drops and lighting does it receive the necessary changes, whereas the all enclosing church remains in the darkness and is more felt than seen.

[263]

13. Through the mist one can still dimly see the candles on the altar which now seem like glowworms in a mist.
14. Some rise very slowly while others fall. The windows have disappeared.
15. The nuns begin to dance. Their clothes become but a film and they appear like nude elves. Their hair-dresses have vanished and in their stead is green hair.
16. These fine-limbed elves form rings about the trees and twist and turn in the wind. They float about noise-lessly and dance the joy of a young spring night.
17. During the dance, the fireflies have all gradually risen in the mist and now appear like stars in the sky.
18. Moonlight comes as if through dancing foliage from the centre left of the balcony.
19. The altar looks like a group of young trees in spring.
20. Out of the mist has risen a great tall forest.
21. The Knight and the Nun come into view through the trees.
22. The Piper as a faun precedes them, jumping about mer-rily playing on his Pan-pipes as he drives away the dancing elves.
23. The Nun and the Knight come slowly into the foreground closely embraced.
24. The Nun throws aside her cloak and turns around in overwhelming happiness.
25. The Knight puts his arm around her, draws her close, and tries to kiss her.
26. She escapes and runs away laughing. He follows her.
27. She dances and plays around the trees as the elves did before.
28. Finally he catches her, carries her to the centre and they embrace passionately, as she lies in his arms.
29. The Piper summons the green bushes, worn by invisible men, to circle around the lovers.
30. The circle gradually grows smaller as they are sur-rounded and finally completely hidden by the thick foliage.

[264]

THE DOORS OF THE CATHEDRAL IN "THE MIRACLE"

As Produced in London at Olympia, December 23, 1911

Designed by Ernst Stern

31. The Piper then tiptoes to the front and calls as if up into the hills with a moose-like cry.
32. The answer is heard coming from the upper gallery, then the middle one, and soon from the lower one.
33. The blowing of horns, the barking of hounds and the crack of whips.
34. Then he hides behind two of the bushes which he had called aside.
35. A merry hunting party appears, as if from over a hill, coming down both centre aisles through the audience, suggesting something of the religious procession.
36. Instead of sacred relics, they carry trophies of the chase. Porters carry deer down one aisle and game down the other.
37. The hunters have spears with glowing points like candles.
38. Trumpeters and retainers carry spears, axes, knives, bows and arrows.
39. Ladies carrying falcons on their gloved hands.
40. Men with lanterns light the way.
41. In their midst is the master of the chase, a Count, an unusually large powerful man with Mongol features. He has a hunting knife in his belt and a whip curled around his hand.
42. The party turns to the left and discovers the Piper who has purposely put himself in the way.
43. They regard him with merry curiosity.
44. He plays on his pipes and runs away. They follow him in a wild chase, as if he were an animal.
45. He runs down to the front again at the right, the hunting party at his heels.
46. Arrived in front, he looks about quickly and finally hides himself in the foliage where the lovers are sheltered. The hunters dash into the bushes and discover the lovers there.

[265]

APPENDIX I

47. The Nun rushes out and covers her face with her hands
    in shame. The Knight follows.
48. The company surrounds the two and the Count approaches
    the Nun to look at her.
49. The Knight steps in front of the Nun to protect her, and
    confronts the Count.
50. The Count pushes the Knight aside. The Knight draws
    his sword, but is seized by the other men.
51. He resists, is conquered after a brief struggle and is
    tied to a tree, just where the Madonna stood.
52. Lanterns are placed on the ground around the prisoner.
53. He is now obliged to observe how the Count forces his
    attentions upon the Nun.
54. She at first stands as if in a trance and then watches with
    horror how her lover is bound. She wrings her hands
    in despair, pleading with the Count for mercy for the
    Knight. The Count laughs cynically.
55. The Piper approaches the Count, whispers in his ear,
    points to the Nun and indicates the movements of
    dancing. The Count understands and commands the
    Nun to dance for him. The company applauds.
56. The Nun draws back in fright and hides her face.
57. The Count stamps his foot impatiently and repeats his
    command. The Nun merely shakes her head. The
    Count orders the Knight to be killed, if she refuses to
    conform to his wishes. The hunters draw their knives
    and point them at the Knight's breast.
58. The Nun cries out in horror, falls at the Count's feet and
    begs for the life of her lover.
59. The Count insists that she dance. She has no choice.
60. The company forms a circle about her and she dances
    with anguish but believing that she is saving the
    Knight.
61. As the Piper starts to play, the hunters constantly draw
    closer to the dancing girl.
62. The Knight struggles painfully in his bonds.

63. Then the Piper creeps over to the Knight and secretly unties his bonds.
64. The Knight rushes at the Count, who is making love to the Nun and is again thrown back by the hunters, severely wounded.
65. The Shadow of Death suddenly appears behind the dying man and remains by him until he collapses, dead.
66. The Counts leads away the Nun, who resists violently. The company follows him boisterously.
67. The Knight's crumpled body with the knives sticking in it suggests the figure of a martyr.
68. Clouds pass over the moon.
69. Only the Piper is lighted. He stands beside the body of the Knight and blows on his pipes held aloft in a satanic manner, playing for his first victim the always recurring tones of a song of death.
70. Suddenly he jumps into the blackness.
71. The Shadow of Death shines in the dark beside the body of the Knight.

SCENE III—THE BANQUET

THE NUN.	THE PRINCE
THE PIPER	THE SHADOW.
THE COUNT.	

Friends and Guests of the Count, Followers of the Prince, Servants and Gypsies.

1. The elves come out of the trees again dancing around the Knight, as the fog descends.
2. The organ and drums play a funeral march in the same tempo as when the Knight appeared.
3. The elves return to their former state as nuns and lay the Knight on a stretcher of pine boughs.

[267]

4. Merely his face is illumined in the dark.
5. They carry the Knight's body through the right side around behind the altar where his body is covered with a pall.
6. They continue round the other side. The procession is ghostly in the dim light. The Shadow of Death follows behind. Nuns carry candles in front of and behind the bier. Other nuns carry his sword and gauntlets.
7. Steps have been brought in and the bier is placed on this platform.
8. It seems as if the nuns were weeping at the bier.
9. Nuns carrying candles kneel by the bier.
10. Great silence.
11. Responses of other nuns in the choir.
12. A voice from the pulpit.
13. The nuns step back as the young Sacristan approaches the bier.
14. She lifts the pall and pulls it back to see her dead lover, dropping the cloth in horror at the sight.
15. A light glows below it.
16. The Nun draws it back revealing a table of irridescent fruit instead of the body.
17. In the auditorium the rose windows light up.
18. Then those in the proscenium side arches.
19. Finally the great middle arch.
20. These proscenium windows have invisibly been lowered into position in the dark. The windows are to hang where the proscenium-curtain would hang. One recognizes a frieze of small figures along the bottom of the proscenium windows, which are guests at a banquet standing at transulcent tables.
21. The tables which are on top of steps were pushed into position on a line with the transverse axis of the arches.
22. The light comes on very slowly, first from the rear, behind

A GYPSY WOMAN
COSTUME PLATE BY NORMAN-BEL GEDDES

56. The Piper jumps back to the table and points to the Prince.
57. The Count, who has drunk too much, rises, the Piper supporting him.
58. The guests salute and bow to the Prince.
59. Then the Prince bows and his friends likewise and the Count invites the Prince to sit at his table.
60. The Count desires to give the seat of honor to the Prince, but he wishes the Nun to sit there, too. So the Nun sits in the middle, the Prince to the right of her, the Count to the left.
61. Then a girl, a man, and a girl on either side.
62. The Prince throws money to the gypsies.
63. Servants bring more wine in cups like chalices and wine jugs like religious oil vessels.
64. Drink. Flourish. The Nun sits like a statue.
65. The Piper plays to the Prince.
66. Prince and Count kiss the Nun's hand.
67. They wish to kiss her lips, and ragingly stare at each other.
68. Suddenly, all give a piercing cry and daggers appear everywhere.
69. There is almost a battle when the Piper produces a deck of playing cards.
70. He points to the Prince, to the Count, deals them cards and suggests that they play for the Nun.
71. The daggers drop. The Piper deals the cards, and the Prince and Count play.
72. Again and again, always faster, more excitedly. Finally the Piper deals the Prince the high cards. The guests look on excitedly.
73. They play. The Prince by his stroke of luck, wins.
74. Consternation! The Piper plays his violin madly. The banquet breaks up.
75. The Prince drags the terrified Nun through the auditorium,

[271]

out the way he came. All guests follow to a march, played by the gypsies.

76. And finally the Piper follows.
77. The Count, alone, abandoned by everyone, tries to follow the Prince, but falls back in a drunken stupor.
78. The lights die away with the music.
79. The Count stares about desperately, takes a jug from the musician, drains it, laughs, but breaks off, his head sinks down on his chest, the jug drops.
80. The Shadow of Death appears through the steps and presses a dagger into the Count's hand.
81. The Count takes it mechanically, starts in the direction of the Prince, stops, plunges it into his own heart and falls heavily to the ground, dead, the Shadow of Death behind him.
82. Red light in the floor and from above.
83. The Piper plays the tune of death.

Scene IV—Mock Wedding

CHARACTERS

The Nun.
The Prince.
The Emperor.
The Companions of the Prince.
The Piper.
The Shadow.

1. Deep-toned bells ring.
2. The voices of a nun and monk praying.
3. In the cloisters, a priest passes by, carrying the last sacrament.
4. Two acolytes in front, carrying lanterns.
5. They walk hurriedly and depart on the other side.

"THE MIRACLE" IN BERLIN, 1914

The Crowd Hails the Wonder-Working Statue of the Madonna in the Cathedral.
A Drawing by the Artist, R. Leonard

"THE MIRACLE" IN BERLIN, 1914

The Madonna's Resumption of the Crown as Depicted by the Brush of the Artist,
R. Leonard

6. The funeral music from the choir goes over into a satirical wedding march.

7. The bells sound like cow-bells.

8. There is a suggestion of light in the stained glass windows in the auditorium which just as quickly vanishes again.

9. The sound of a wedding procession coming down the aisles.

10. In each aisle, a majordomo in exaggerated religious robes and a foolscap with bells.

11. Instead of crosses they carry poles, with fauns on them.

12. Then come acolytes dressed, carrying, instead of candles, Hallowe'en lanterns.

13. Girl pages shake flowers from trays which they carry on their shoulders, their head sticking through a hole.

14. This whole scene is sensuous and decadent.

15. On one side come bridesmaids in the guise of witches on broomsticks. They are really young men and wear masks of beautiful nuns.

16. On the other side the groom's gentlemen, riding on hobby horses. These are girls, masked.

17. Two caricature incense carriers burning something, which sputters, evil smelling.

18. Then on one side enters the bride wearing a wreath of myrtle, under a canopy. Two little girls carry her long veil. An old witch leads the bride.

19. The Piper dressed as a caricature Bishop comes last, a tremendous mitre on his head, with bells on it and donkey's ears. His mantle is very stiff, exaggerated high collar standing away from his neck, a donkey painted on the back of his costume. He rings a cow bell.

20. Down the other aisle comes the groom under another canopy. Two boys carry his train.

21. Priests follow, dressed in grotesque, painted costumes,

[273]

with starched and exaggerated collars. One carries a miniature bed as he might a relic, on a cushion. Another two rings; another, an exaggerated goblet; another, a gigantic book.

22. During the procession, nuns appear in the shadows of the cloisters, weeping.

23. The bride struggles, but is dragged on to the stage, where the two processions meet. At the top of a high flight of black steps between the centre columns is a bed. It seems to float in mid-air and appears like a vision.

24. Nuns appear in the shadow of the cloisters weeping in their soft kerchiefs.

25. The flower girls shower their flowers over the steps and bed.

26. The bride's and groom's canopies are placed over the bed forming a single large canopy illuminated from within. The bed covers are irridescent.

27. All the guests group themselves in a semi-circle about the steps. The Piper as Bishop holds a devil's mass.

28. Black magic. Acolytes, jumping about like goats, hand the Bishop his staff with the ram's head on it.

29. On the right stands the groom, with his back to the audience. The bride on the other side.

30. The witch who presented the groom gives large horn-rimmed spectacles, with orange peels instead of glass in them, to the Bishop, while another holds a large book upside down for him to read from.

31. The Bishop reads in Latin.

32. The goblet is handed to him and he drinks.

33. The organ plays a cheap street tune.

34. Some sit on the bed playing cards.

35. The Bishop asks questions of the bride and groom. The Nun is horrified.

36. The Bishop takes the exaggerated rings, large enough for thumbs and joins their hands.

37. A witch dance follows to the organ music.

38. The bride breaks down.
39. The companions whisper to the Prince, pointing to the Nun.
40. The clock strikes.
41. All the companions bow satirically and put out the lights. Only the bed remains lighted. They disappear in the dark.
42. The Prince tries to make love to the Nun. She tries to free herself.
43. Whispering comes from all parts of the church. High cackling laughter. The bride tries to escape. Rushing to all doors she rattles them but only laughter greets her behind each door.
44. The Prince laughs at first, but then grows angry and chases her up the steps to the bed, dragging her.
45. She tears her veil from her head and she pleads at his feet.
46. Right and left in the misty darkness, nuns kneel in prayer. The nuns in this vision are the conspirators in disguise, his friends.
47. Women voices in the choir.
48. The Prince is lifting the Nun on to the bed when the loge-door is opened by the Piper, as a court jester, followed by the Prince's father, the Emperor.
49. His robes are of gold.
50. The door slams behind him. Its echo resounds through the whole church. The Prince drops the girl.
51. The Emperor comes between the two and demands that she be set free. The son is wild at his father's interruption.
52. The Emperor looks at the Nun, himself fascinated. The son sees this and laughs.
53. The Father, furious, points to the door.
54. The son refuses to leave, but finally does go out into the darkness.

55. Where the nuns were, are the son's conspirators. The Piper is also there, dressed like the others.

56. The Emperor turns to the Nun to take her away. But she, weary and exhausted from suffering, draws back.

57. The Emperor, however, quiets her. He is a calm and dignified man. So she takes his hand and looks at him.

58. Far away the nuns are heard, quite pianissimo. Is she sleeping or is she awake?

59. The Emperor and the girl descend, and start toward the exit at the left.

60. She sees moving figures in the dark and feels that some misfortune is about to occur.

61. Suddenly, a vivid red hand comes out of the black. The Nun stares.

62. She would hold the Emperor back. The Emperor thinks it is only a fancy and goes to the left.

63. She sees an apparition of the Madonna as she passes the column, which disappears as suddenly as it came.

64. Tension.

65. Suddenly the son jumps at the Emperor, the other assassins behind him. The Nun shrieks, but only makes the formation with her mouth; the sound comes from the gallery.

66. The father does not recognize the son. There is a fight in which the Piper, as conspirator and wearing the other red gauntlet, hands a knife to the father through the canopy of the bed. The Shadow of Death appears.

67. The Emperor stabs his assailant, not aware of his identity. The girl is petrified.

68. The Emperor turns to her; she instinctively knows who it is.

69. The Emperor is utterly bewildered.

70. The red hand lifts the corpse's cloak and removes the mask.

71. The Emperor despairingly stares at his son, lifts up the

head in his arms and the corpse falls back, dead. The Black Shadow is there.

72. The Emperor tries to shriek, but can not. He kneels down by his son's body, kisses his face, and wishes to stab himself.
73. The girl, at a sign from the Piper, stops him, pleading for him to kill her.
74. The Emperor drops the knife. They start off together.
75. At the place where the murder took place, he is suddenly seized by convulsive terror, holds on to a column, rushes terrified to the other side and goes insane.
76. He begins to live through the episode.
77. The Piper warns the Nun not to leave him, so they depart together.
78. The Piper plays his tune of death, beside the body of the dead prince. The red light appears.
79. The Piper jumps into the darkness.

Scene V—The Coronation

CHARACTERS

The Nun.
The Emperor.
The Piper.
The Grandee of the Emperor's Court.
The Revolutionary Masses.
The Shadow.

1. Choir: "De Profundis." Death Mass.
2. A procession of black figures passes across the front of the stage.
3. They carry lighted candles and behind them is the Black Shadow with his unmasked face of death.
4. He plays with bones on an invisible drum.

5. Hundreds and hundreds of candles are lit by the black figures against the dark background.
6. Large heavy golden candelabra are arranged in two rows, and gradually become recognisable as stiffly dressed court servants.
7. These footmen hold candles in both hands and wear them on their head.
8. These candles are also lit by the black figures.
9. A procession comes through the opened high altar, down the steps.
10. Hollow bells ring.
11. The Piper, as Master of Ceremonies, carries two golden staves.
12. Then, cymbal boys.
13. Pages carry the crown and insignia on pillows.
14. Noble gentleman whose dress suggests a goblet.
15. Court ladies, among them the ladies of the Emperor.
16. Ecclesiastics, in stiff golden clerical vestments.
17. The chancellor.
18. The treasurer, the keeper of the great seal, and cup-bearer.
19. At last the Emperor and Empress on two palanquins carried by gold armored knights.
20. All costumes are of gold—stiff and rigid, without life.
21. The master of ceremonies, the chancellor, the treasurer, the keeper of the great seal, the court cup-bearer and other courtiers have glittering stars and crosses of orders on their breasts, on their side, and on ribbons.
22. The court ladies have diadems in their hair and wear much jewelry, glittering and sparkling in the soft candle light.
23. Fan carriers stand behind the palanquins.
24. Three banner bearers immediately follow each palanquin.
25. The train moves with heavy steps slowly towards the front. It is as if the holy relics of the treasure room were exhibited. A stiff, rigid magnificence.

26. The Emperor, who is in a frenzy, wears his state dress of stiff gold, a crown on his head. He carries tenderly a puppet. It is the son.
27. The procession divides into the following groupings:
28. The priests walk to the altar and take their positions at the right and left.
29. The chancellor in front of them in the centre.
30. On his right and left the treasure-bearers.
31. The pages with the insignia go also to the altar, in the centre.
32. The footmen who are dressed as candelabras form a trellis that reaches in all directions.
33. The palanquins are placed in front of the columns opposite each other and facing inward.
34. The Emperor at the left. The Empress at the right.
35. About the Emperor in strict order, the courtiers, knights and his banner-bearer.
36. Behind the Empress, the chief ladies of the court and about her in corresponding order, knights, and her banner-bearer.
37. A strict arrangement according to rank which the master of ceremonies directs.
38. Left and right, in the corners, the cymbal boys.
39. In front on the steps, with his back to the auditorium, the master of ceremonies.
40. On his left and right, two youths, dressed as bells, who at the sign from the master of ceremonies ring by moving themselves. The tone of this ringing reminds one of the numerous tones of the clear bells that are used at the altar for mass.
41. The coronation march is played until the whole court company has taken its position.
42. Then occurs a rigid, solemnly oppressive pause. No one moves.
43. In the following ceremony, which is accompanied by soft organ music, the master of ceremonies retains the

direction which guides the official life on this highest step of worldly might, and forces in these phantom forms a rigid etiquette.

44. Everything human must subordinate itself to this court compulsion. Whether it be the frenzy of the Emperor, his ceaseless pain and his grief over his lost son, whether it is the unspeakable suffering of the martyred Nun, nothing may outwardly disturb the fast-laid and consecrated rules of this life. The original contents of these forms evaporated long ago. Only the ceremony has remained for this ready-to-be-destroyed world. The Piper celebrates them, dark, fanatically rigid, pedantic, but without any internal participation.
45. The Emperor heaves a sigh.
46. The ceremony begins.
47. Processions forward.
48. Processions back.
49. Oaths.
50. Solemn, silent walking, with ringing before each step.
51. Without music.
52. The treasure-bearers step forth with robes, the crown, the sceptre, the cup, the cross.
53. The Nun must take an oath on a cross.
54. A solemn marching to and fro, constantly forming new groups. The clock strikes eleven.
55. The crown is placed on the Nun.
56. The master of ceremonies raises his staff.
57. The living bells, on his right and left, ring. Mass bells.
58. The organ begins.
59. Short pause.
60. The master of ceremonies strides to the Emperor, bends a knee, awaits the signal to begin.
61. The Emperor caresses the puppet, tenderly strokes its forehead and hair, but does not look at the master of ceremonies.

A NOBLE GENTLEMAN

COSTUME PLATE BY NORMAN-BEL GEDDES

62. The master of ceremonies strikes with his staff.
63. The two courtiers behind the Emperor approach and reverently call his attention to the master of ceremonies.
64. The Emperor starts, stares at first, absent-mindedly, nods and indifferently lifts his hand as the sign to begin.
65. Immediately, thereupon, he turns again to the puppet, converses with it and raises the hand of the puppet, also, as a signal.
66. The master of ceremonies and treasure-bearers emit a soft but energetic ssssssst at the behavior of the Emperor which is not in accordance with etiquette.
67. The Emperor, frightened, becomes silent and stares sadly.
68. The master of ceremonies strides to his place.
69. Short pause.
70. Again he raises his staff.
71. The two bells ring.
72. The master of ceremonies goes toward the altar. In passing, he makes a slight customary genuflection in front of the Emperor.
73. At the same time, at the altar, there is a movement among the stiff priests and treasure-bearers.
74. Two treasure-bearers place themselves at the right and left of the master of ceremonies with their backs to the auditorium, page in back of them.
75. Then, accompanied by two treasure-bearers followed by the page, he goes to the Emperor with the orb.
76. There, all four kneel in their relative positions.
77. The Emperor takes no notice of it but busies himself exclusively with the puppet.
78. He arranges its clothes, smoothes them tenderly, listens to its heart beat and nods happy and satisfied.
79. The master of ceremonies, while kneeling, hands the orb to the Emperor.
80. The Emperor holds it in his hand mechanically while fixedly gazing at the puppet.

APPENDIX I

81. The master of ceremonies strikes the ground with his staff.
82. A general sssssssst of the treasure-bearers interrupts the Emperor.
83. He glances about him uneasily.
84. The courtiers point to the kneeling group in front of the Emperor.
85. The Emperor looks sadly and inconsolably toward the master of ceremonies and his companions. These bow their heads low.
86. The group withdraws, in the same formation in which it advanced, stepping backward impressively without turning its back to the Emperor.
87. The master of ceremonies leaves the altar and resumes his position in front—bending his knee slightly when passing the Emperor.
88. Again, all stand immovable and in fixed solemn calm, except for the Emperor whispering in the ear of his puppet.
89. He points to his consort and to the crown on his head.
90. The Nun sits as if lifeless, while she dreams all these happenings.
91. The master of ceremonies again raises his staff.
92. The altar boys, at both sides, ring.
93. The master of ceremonies goes again to the altar, this time, however, followed by the two altar boys.
94. In pairs the knights leave the groups of the Emperor and Empress.
95. The entire group, well arranged, steps backward to the altar. When passing the Emperor, all kneel abruptly.
96. At the altar the treasurer hands the chancellor the crown placed on a cushion. It is a three-fold crown, the sign of the power of the church which the Emperor unites with worldly power. It reminds one of the tiara of the pope without really resembling it.

97. From the altar toward the Emperor's throne, strides the master of ceremonies with the staff.
98. At his side the altar boys.
99. Back of them the first priest with the crown.
100. Then follows the chancellor with the crown for the Empress.
101. Next to him the treasurer with the sceptre and the imperial globe on a cushion.
102. Now come two other priests, one with a gold bowl over which a cloth is spread, the second with a gold goblet.
103. They place themselves in the same order, in front of the Emperor.
104. The two courtiers, next to the Emperor, step forward.
105. The Emperor looks at the approaching group, fervently grasping his son's puppet, suspicious and fearful as if they wished to take the puppet from him.
106. The group kneels in front of the Emperor.
107. The master of ceremonies rises first, places himself at the Emperor's right, and strikes the floor solemnly with his staff.
108. The altar boys ring.
109. The courtiers take the wordly crown of the Emperor and with outstretched arms hold it high over the Emperor.
110. Second signal of the master of ceremonies.
111. The first priest rises, places the churchly crown on the head of the Emperor.
112. The Emperor permits it. He now wears the three-tiered crown, and the courtiers hold the worldly crown over this.
113. The cymbal boys strike the cymbals gently.
114. All bow their foreheads toward the floor.
115. At a third signal of the master of ceremonies, the second priest steps forward and holds the bowl toward the Emperor.
116. The first priest removes the cloth.

117. The Emperor, after a slight hesitation, places the puppet of his son on his knee, tenderly and carefully.
118. Then he dips his hands into the empty bowl and pretends to wash them.
119. The first priest hands him the cloth.
120. The Emperor dries his hands.
121. The priests step back.
122. At a fourth signal of the master of ceremonies, the chancellor steps forward with the crown for the Empress.
123. The Emperor takes it with both hands.
124. The cymbal boys again strike the cymbals.
125. The chancellor holds the cushion.
126. The Emperor replaces the crown of the Empress on the cushion.
127. The third priest advances, hands the Emperor the goblet.
128. The Emperor places it to his lips, without drinking and then sprinkles the crown from the goblet.
129. A fifth signal of the master of ceremonies.
130. Ringing of bells.
131. The Emperor returns the goblet to the third priest.
132. The treasurer hands the Emperor the sceptre and imperial globe.
133. The Emperor sits crowned with the globe and sceptre in each hand.
134. The puppet of the son glides from his knees to the floor.
135. The Emperor becomes greatly alarmed and wishes to pick up the puppet.
136. A universal, respectful but decided sssssst makes him desist.
137. He struggles with himself, is greatly excited, complies, however, and remains seated.
138. The tears roll down his cheeks and heart-rending yet silent sobs shatter him. He gazes sadly at the puppet.
139. The courtiers and priests kneel in front of him.
140. They rise and return solemnly to the altar, backwards, always facing the Emperor.

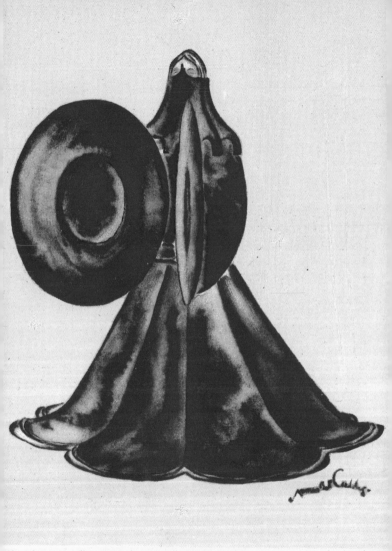

A CYMBAL BEARER
COSTUME PLATE BY NORMAN-BEL GEDDES

141. The master of ceremonies with his altar boys leave the altar and go forward to their places; while passing the Emperor they bend the knee slightly.

142. All are again motionless.

143. After a short pause the master of ceremonies again raises his staff.

144. The altar boys at both sides ring.

145. All at once the courtiers of the Emperor, the court-ladies of the Empress, knights from both sides, even the master of ceremonies and the altar boys, begin to stride forward to the altar—slightly bending the knee when passing the Emperor.

146. At the same time there is a stir at the altar.

147. At each meeting of the treasure-bearers at the altar, the master of ceremonies, chancellor and all the rest bow to one another—stiff, formal bows.

148. With the assistance of all the priests and treasure-bearers at the altar, a procession forms and strides with the crown from the altar toward the Empress.

149. In front is the master of ceremonies with staff and back of him the two altar boys.

150. Then the chancellor with a roll of parchment.

151. Back of him, the treasurer who carries the crown for the Empress on a cushion with upraised hands.

152. At his side two court-ladies.

153. Then two treasure-bearers.

154. Two courtiers of the Emperor.

155. The entire priesthood follows. In front, the first priest with a tall gold cross.

156. At the side of the first priest, two candelabras with gold candles.

157. The rear is made up of pages and knights. In their midst one golden knight carries a banner.

158. All of this group bow first one knee in front of the Emperor and then kneel in front of the Empress.

159. The master of ceremonies strikes with his staff.
160. The two court-ladies, next to the Empress, step forward and whisper something to her.
161. She raises her hand as if in a dream.
162. The kneeling group rises.
163. The master of ceremonies places himself next to the Empress.
164. The altar boys near him.
165. The others stay in their groups and place themselves near the throne of the Empress.
166. The Emperor does not take part in this ceremony but continues to stare at his puppet and hold the sceptre and imperial globe in his hands.
167. He leans forward and whispers apologizingly to the puppet at his feet.
168. The master of ceremonies raises the staff.
169. The altar boys ring.
170. The candelabras walk beside the chancellor, who unrolls the parchment, moves his lips, reads inaudibly and finally raises the coronation document with the imperial seal toward the Empress.
171. She sits motionless.
172. He rolls the parchment up again.
173. The keeper of the big seal steps forward, receives the paper from the chancellor, covers it and steps back.
174. The master of ceremonies raises the staff.
175. Ringing by the altar boys.
176. Two ladies of the court, who were walking back of the treasure-bearers, bring a gorgeous mantle, with a long train.
177. They place it over the shoulder of the Empress.
178. Again the signal of the master of ceremonies, and ringing of altar boys.
179. The Empress sits motionless, her eyes closed, like a doll, permitting everything to be done to her.

180. The chancellor lowers the pillow with the sparkling jeweled crown for the Empress. It is strikingly like the halo of the image of the Virgin.
181. The chancellor places the crown, with the help of the ladies of the court, on the head of the Empress.
182. The master of ceremonies strikes with his staff.
183. The Empress slowly rises.
184. The cymbal boys strike louder on the cymbals.
185. All sink on their knees, touching the ground with their foreheads.
186. The Empress standing as in a dream.
187. The two treasure-bearers step forward. One delivers the sceptre.
188. The master of ceremonies raises her arm as if she were a lay figure.
189. The chancellor presses the sceptre into her hand.
190. Two of the Emperor's courtiers step forward, receive a ring from the second treasure-bearer and place the ring on the Empress.
191. All step back into their places.
192. A signal from the master of ceremonies.
193. Ringing of altar boys.
194. The priests step forward, the first one with the cross.
195. He inclines it a little towards the Empress.
196. She, always supported by her court ladies, supposedly unseen but really very visible and guided by the master of ceremonies, lays her fingers on the cross in taking the oath.
197. Signal of the master of ceremonies. Ringing of the altar boys.
198. All rise and with a jerk the hands of all those present fly up, the fingers raised, in a pledge of faith.
199. The cymbals strike.
200. The golden banner is swung on high.
201. The whole group stiffens as if a living vision.

202. From the tower the hour strikes slowly and far away, twelve o'clock.

203. After a pause, the master of ceremonies raises his staff. Altar boys ring sharply.

204. All start up as if out of a sleep.

205. The treasure-bearers step back reverently, with the master of ceremonies leading and followed at a distance by the altar boys.

206. The Empress steps down from the throne, led by her two court ladies and followed by the two courtiers of the Emperor.

207. The rest arrange themselves in the same order in which they came, and the whole procession moves toward the Emperor.

208. The Emperor, his attention called by his courtiers, stares frightened at the procession coming toward him. He holds the sceptre and globe in an ostentatious manner as he was told.

209. The group kneels down, with a jerk, at a sign from the master of ceremonies and the altar boys.

210. The train of the Empress, carried by two pages, is now spread out its full length. The Empress bends her head deeply and painfully.

211. The master of ceremonies gets up, goes to the side and strikes hard with his staff. The altar boys ring.

212. The Emperor stands up, at the whispering of the courtiers, looks around anxiously, then throws a frightened look at the inexorable master of ceremonies.

213. The latter indicates to him with his eyes and with a sharp, hardly noticeable movement of the head, to come down from the throne and extend his hand to the Empress.

214. The Emperor understands, wishes to go, sees his puppet on the floor in front of him, and can not bring himself to stride over his son. He stands irresolute—looks pitifully at the master of ceremonies with his repeated command to come down.

PEASANTS CARRYING THE CROSS IN "THE MIRACLE"

A Sketch by Ernst Stern from the Berlin Production at the Zirkus Schumann,
April, 1914

THE PIPER IN THREE OF HIS GUISES IN "THE MIRACLE"

Costume Plates Designed by Ernst Stern for the Berlin Production, April, 1914

215. The master of ceremonies strikes again with his staff for a vehement reminder and throws an angry glance at the Emperor's two courtiers.

216. The treasure-bearers raise their heads astonished.

217. The Empress stares shocked at the spectacle. The altar boys ring shrilly.

218. The Emperor, greatly frightened, lifts his foot, tries to walk over his son. He can not do it.

219. At a commanding wink from the master of ceremonies the two courtiers bend over to lift the puppet out of the way.

220. The Emperor, with a sudden movement, lets the globe and sceptre fall and throws himself with a gurging sound on the two courtiers.

221. In his mute wild frenzy, he tears the puppet away from them and clasps it tightly to himself. He looks around, wild and threatening, and breathes deeply.

222. The master of ceremonies turns his head away angrily. All likewise turn their heads to the opposite side and close their eyes.

223. Only the Empress stares with wide open eyes at the calamity. Tears run down her face. She suffers greatly.

224. The Emperor, who assures himself that no more danger threatens his son, carries him cautiously and tenderly to the throne and carefully prepares a bed for him.

225. Suddenly, in a fright, he throws himself over the puppet, shakes its head, as in the preceding act, covers its face with kisses in an effort to reawaken its life.

226. Disconsolate, he lets it fall back and, sobbing, strikes his chest and forehead, and draws a knife to kill himself.

227. At a stamp of the master of ceremonies, the Empress gets up and stretches out her arms toward the Emperor. He pauses. The knife falls to the floor.

228. He removes his crown, places it on the puppet and steps

down, swaying and trembling, to the Empress to whom he gives his hand.

229. A sign from the master of ceremonies and the loud ringing of the altar boys.

230. All the people stand up and the ceremony continues.

231. The Emperor and Empress follow the master of ceremonies toward the altar.

232. There they are followed by the treasure-bearers, priests, courtiers, court ladies, knights and pages.

233. The Emperor and Empress ascend the altar backwards as if on a throne.

234. The worldly crown is placed on the Emperor.

235. The congratulatory procession starts, to solemn, pompous music.

236. In front, on the Emperor's throne, leans the crowned puppet of the prince.

237. The Emperor and Empress ascend the throne and remain standing, stiff and rigid.

238. The entire assemblage forms a wide arc around the throne. While facing their Majesties, they recede with their backs to the auditorium.

239. A procession is formed of treasure-bearers, courtiers, and court ladies who file in pairs in front of Their Majesties. When they reach the throne, they bend their knees, walk backwards, and take their places at both sides of the throne.

240. Their Majesties accept homage—nod like pagodas.

241. At the approach of the master of ceremonies, Their Majesties step down from the throne, walk stiff and unhappy through the espalier, nod graciously with frozen smiles.

242. The court assemblage kneels, raises its arms in homage and seems to shout a silent hurrah.

243. When reaching the front, the Emperor suddenly kneels in front of the puppet of his son.

244. The master of ceremonies is already at his side and forces him with his inexorable look to arise and place himself at the head of the group on the left, by his side.

245. Meanwhile, the Empress places herself opposite him on the other side.

246. While the Emperor was kneeling, some astonished courtiers hurried to him and they do not leave him.

247. The court ladies direct the Empress who also gives expression to her unhappiness.

248. To the sound of pompous music, a solemn dance begins. It is directed by the master of ceremonies. He opens his mouth, seems to call out; but the voice sounds from far off. It gives orders in Latin for a sort of Quadrille. (Salve.)

249. The two rows, led by the Emperor and Empress, walk toward one another, bow, and then go back to their places.

250. The two rows go toward one another and change places. The ladies change with stiff bowing on all sides.

251. Emperor and Empress go alone toward one another and bow.

252. The Emperor, unhappy and helpless, wishes to go to the puppet but is held back by the master of ceremonies.

253. The Emperor opens the dance with the Empress. Both dance stiffly and solemnly without really touching one another.

254. They cry silently and ceaselessly like children who have been forced against their will. They turn towards the front.

255. The master of ceremonies frisks about from one pair to another, giving the sign for the dance in strict order of rank, so that a stiff, silent, ghostly, court-ball ensues.

256. When the Emperor and Empress have reached the front, the Emperor, escaping the eyes of the master of ceremonies, quickly goes over to the puppet and dances with it tenderly.

257. The Empress remains alone in the front.

258. Seeking to arouse her pity, the Emperor places the lifeless puppet in the arms of the Empress, imploring her to dance with it.

259. The Empress dances with the puppet. The Emperor claps his hands.

260. Bejeweled and crowned architectural figures loose themselves from the columns and altars. They resemble stone saints. They mix with the others, turn around in the circle, seem to grow in height and rise and sink with the rhythm of the dance.

261. Light shining on the vaulting of the Gothic arch makes them appear like fountains.

262. The master of ceremonies disappears (in order to change his costume) and in his place frisks a Black Shadow with a mask. It swings the golden ceremonial staff.

263. Circles and stars are formed and all the figures finally group themselves into a high Gothic structure that resembles a tabernacle. The whole thing suddenly lights up and the Empress seems to float over it.

264. The puppet lies in the arms of the Empress. And the Emperor dances, in front, as if possessed. It reminds one of the dance of the cripples in the first scene.

265. There is a strong menacing knock on one of the doors of the auditorium.

266. The dance music breaks off shrilly.

267. All the golden figures stiffen as if in deadly fright.

268. The knocking is repeated in always shorter intervals with increasing vehemence.

269. Finally it resounds from all the doors round about and ends at last in a mighty, growing, threatening thunder.

270. In between, one hears warlike fanfares. At first dull in the distance, then nearer and louder, from all sides.

271. A wind-storm whistles through the windows and hurls in scraps of revolutionary writings.

272. A dull gradually swelling murmur of people is heard from all sides.

273. Shrill whistles, menacing blows on the doors from the outside.

274. Inside, in the room, eveything is petrified. Nothing stirs.

275. Outside the noise increases, the roar of a wild mob.

276. Rebellious songs are sung and accompanied by hoarse laughter.

277. The fountains of light become blood-red.

278. The storm bells ring in a wild medley.

279. The whole house seems to shake to its foundations.

280. Axe blows.

281. A breaking of doors, a clatter of windowpanes from the throwing of stones.

282. Ragged, wild forms enter from everywhere. They come first singly from all sides and then climb in wild haste from the windows of the balcony and the galleries into the room.

283. They are black from head to foot. They swing black axes, clubs, and flags.

284. They crowd in ever growing numbers.

285. The savage noise suddenly ceases. Vehement cries, soft whistles, suppressed wild laughter, spooky whispering.

286. A black flood comes in and grows to a gigantic shadow that threatens to darken everything.

287. The heavy tombstone tablets are broken open with axes and lifted up.

288. Black forms crawl out in clanging chains like prisoners. They are freed and armed.

289. The black mass stumbles and falls over one another, spills out of the tower—from above, from below, from all sides. There seems to be no end.

290. In front is the Piper as leader of the revolution. Jumping all around, appearing now here now there, distributing winks and orders. He gives signals with his

shrill, gurgling flute, instigating all of them to rebellion.

291. The mob fills the room without being distinguishable from the black background.

292. They encircle the golden figures who stand completely petrified. They press in on them.

293. A noiseless, wild struggle ensues. A wrestling with occasional suppressed screams. The golden figures have difficulty in protecting themselves. They surrender to the greater force.

294. All lights are blown out and butchered by black hands.

295. The golden figures are finally overthrown like towers, and lie on the floor in a jumble—gasping and groaning.

296. The Piper swings himself onto the chancel.

297. He gesticulates vehemently, seems to deliver a speech in which he attacks the Empress. The talk is inaudible and is accompanied by noiseless applause.

298. The black forms dance a dance of joy.

299. It seems as if the whole church is being demolished and vanishes in darkness.

300. Heavy iron chains are fastened on the Emperor. He is led away in triumph.

301. The Nun flees again, as in the first act and in the wedding scene, from one door to the other, breathless, groaning, tortured.

302. Everywhere black shadows step in front of her, black hands grab at her.

303. Finally the Piper grasps her, drags her through the auditorium, as he pipes his melody of death.

304. His shadow, with the unmasked death-head, dances around between the golden figures strewn on the ground.

305. It becomes totally dark.

"THE MIRACLE"

SCENE VI—THE INQUISITION

CHARACTERS

THE NUN
THE EMPEROR
THE PIPER

THE EXECUTIONER
THE TWELVE INQUISITORS
THE CROWD

1. In the darkness, an angry voice is heard praying in the chancel.
2. A large congregation responds vehemently, fervently and as if pursued.
3. Bells ring confusedly.
4. The wind whistles and storms.
5. Fanfares and marches, confused as before.
6. On the stage one hears the erecting of a scaffolding. Boards fall. Hammer blows.
7. A drum rolls. Thunder overhead. Clappers.
8. A wild mob runs about in disorder. A thousand hurrying steps. Something terrible seems to be preparing.
9. Whispering of many voices.
10. One sees nothing in the darkness except numberless, horrible, pale, drawn faces crowding one another, staring out from above and below, hanging from balconies— the awfully frightening vision of a horrible dream.
11. The clock in the tower strikes.
12. A trombone.
13. The light is gloomy.
14. A densely thronging multitude fills all passages clear to the gates, excitedly crowding and running about in confusion.
15. People hang from the windows, columns and balconies.
16. Others stand on their shoulders, gesticulating wildly.
17. Torches fly from hand to hand over the heads of the raging mob.

[295]

18. Thunder; storm bells strike; the roar of the organ; confusion of excited voices.
19. The blowing wind sweeps in from all sides.
20. Excited pealing of fanfares, revolutionary marches and in the distance long drawn out shrieks of those who are being persecuted.
21. In the centre, the inquisition stand, with the executioner's block.
22. Judges' seats. Benches for criminals. Behind it, three rough-hewn crosses.
23. Smoking torches. Fog.
24. Several limp golden figures, hanging high in the air like a vision and from lanterns and gallows, sway in the wind.
25. Absolute stylization, nothing human left.
26. An instigator appears suddenly, brilliantly illuminated, in the chancel. It is the Piper.
27. He swings a flag.
28. All crowd toward him.
29. He delivers a speech of which not a word is understood on account of the raging noise. One sees only the big mouth and the vehement gestures of a foaming, furious demagog.
30. He appears to say: "Brothers, Sisters, Friends—"
31. He bends down deeply from the chancel and addresses the Revolutionists personally.
32. They crowd around. All wish to hear and excitedly call the others to order—without success.
33. He swings a bell.
34. "Your day has come. You are free."
35. He stretches his arms out wide. There is a movement in the crowd.
36. "The black night of your slavery has given way. Your chains are broken." He fetches broken pieces of heavy iron chains from the chancel and throws them among the multitude.

A GUARDSMAN
COSTUME PLATE BY NORMAN-BEL GEDDES

37. Loud rejoicing among the people. The iron chains are thrown from hand to hand.

38. The people jump around and dance.

39. The instigator tries to procure quiet and attention again.

40. "Your tyrants" (he points with wild gestures at the golden figures which hang from the gallows and balconies), "whose clothes were of gold" (gestures), "whose hearts were of stone" (he beats his heart), "whose heads were empty" (he beats his brow), "are no more" (vehement gestures of destruction).

41. The people rejoice and dance.

42. "They did not stand high enough over us," he laughs diabolically. "We have lifted them as high as they deserve. We have placed their trusted ones in the right light. See, there is the place that belongs to them," he points with wild laughter up at the balcony.

43. Stormy laughter among the people. All point up to the gallows and lanterns. Some push the hanging figures so that they sway to and fro.

44. "We, we have done it." He beats his breast wildly. "They are dead so that you can live." Eloquent gestures. "We, we are the living!" He stretches his arms out. Stormy applause.

45. The revolutionists embrace each other.

46. "We had to work" (he shows brawny fists), "so that they could dance." He parodies grotesquely the festive dance motions of the Golden Epoch.

47. These motions are imitated with mocking laughter by the people.

48. "We had to hunger" (he strikes his stomach furiously), "so that they" (he points with his thumb at the hanging figures), "could gorge themselves." He makes the motions of eating and wildly shakes his fist at the golden figures.

49. All shake their fists.

50. "Our brothers" (he becomes sentimental and points at

the people), "our wives, our children" (he is stopped by his emotion), "had to die so that they could live."

51. A universal movement. Many women sob loudly.
52. "But all of that is at an end." (He strikes triumphantly with his fist on the chancel.) "Brothers swear by this flag" (he waves it), "that no golden one shall ever again rule over us."
53. All lift their hands for the oath.
54. "We will now dress in gold." He clothes himself with gold.
55. Several of the people do likewise and don golden headgear.
56. "We wish to dance."
57. Noise. Applause. The speaker is embraced and congratulated.
58. The instigator takes a golden flute, plays, turns himself and dances.
59. All the people jump, dance, and turn.
60. Again and again there develops out of the noise, cries, rejoicing and song, a wild revolutionary dance, a sort of carmagnole that is danced by the people in wooden shoes and flares up, now here, now there, like a flame.
61. Drums. Guardsmen enter in pairs drumming strenuously.
62. Crowding.
63. The guardsmen form a lane.
64. The instigator calls to the crowd from the chancel, "Fear nothing. They are our brothers."
65. He opens his arms wide, as a welcome, jumps down from the chancel and embraces the guardsmen.
66. The entire multitude is intimidated at first, then also embraces the guards.
67. Jubilation and general fraternizing.
68. The instigator hurries to the centre, points to the auditorium entrances, shakes his fist threateningly at the oncomers.

69. All turn toward the entrances, shake their fists likewise and point outward.

70. A menacing murmur increases gradually.

71. The instigator speaks again, scolds and screams. His words remain inaudible, but his expression, his gestures seem to say: "Look, look there, oh look! There come our oppressors, the tyrants, the murderers, who have drawn the blood out of our veins" (he strikes the vein in his pulse), "who have made money out of our misery."

72. His mouth foaming, he points to the captured booty of golden costumes. "Down with them, hang them!" He makes the unambiguous motion of hanging.

73. A crowding of the populace.

74. Increasing noise.

75. Whips. Screams from outside, increasing buzzing of the oncoming masses.

76. Through the line of guardsmen come four of five of the golden figures, leashed together like animals and escorted by the executioners' assistants.

77. They are deathly pale, and as if paralyzed by fear and horror.

78. They are driven forward like cattle with clubs. Cracking of whips and shouts.

79. The guards have trouble holding back the cursing multitude which throngs to the centre.

80. Behind comes the Emperor, preceded and followed by two soldiers.

81. The prisoners are driven to the right, up the steps.

82. The Emperor, received with menaces and curses, greeted by clenched fists, pays no attention to the roaring noise.

83. He walks along slowly, drags long chains after him. His crown is crookedly set upon his head, his beard is unkempt, his hair hangs in wiry strands. His wandering, rolling eyes seek everywhere and unceasingly for the puppet of his son.

[299]

84. He stares madly at the multitude, and whines softly, raises his crown despondently and lets it fall heavily.
85. The instigator blows on his flute.
86. The Emperor dances to it automatically.
87. General laughter.
88. When he reaches the stairs, the Emperor discovers a man with a mask. It is one of the hangman's assistants who came with the golden prisoners.
89. The Emperor throws himself upon him, opens his mantle and raises his mask with increasing hope.
90. A dull face stares at him.
91. He shakes his head, sadly disappointed, raises his arms again despairingly, lets them fall helplessly.
92. Astonishment, laughter among the people.
93. He ascends the steps. A fellow steps on the chains which the Emperor trains after him. The Emperor stumbles and falls down. The crown rolls off his head.
94. Hoarse laughter.
95. The crown is thrown to and fro like a ball by the black revolutionists.
96. Finally the instigator replaces the crown on the Emperor.
97. He presses a short broom in the Emperor's hand for a sceptre. The Emperor apathetically lets them do anything with him.
98. Laughter.
99. Spurred on by the approving laughter, a young fellow with a hood over his eyes and ears, advances toward him and strikes his chest with a club.
100. Several continue to laugh. The others become strangely quiet.
101. The Emperor totters several times, threatens to fall over, cries out unexpectedly and joyously, however, throws himself with wide open arms upon the puzzled youth, embraces him vehemently and covers him with tender kisses.

THE INQUISITION MOB IN SCENE VI
. A SKETCH BY NORMAN-BEL GEDDES

102. It becomes very quiet. No one stirs. All stare at the Emperor.
103. He raises the hood of the youth with trembling hopefulness, gazes into his rough visage, shakes his head again, painfully disappointed, raises his arms again in desperation and lets them fall helplessly.
104. He weeps silently and convulsed and sinks upon the condemned bench.
105. The general feeling of the people, who have followed these happenings silently, threatens to turn in favor of the Emperor.
106. Trombones and drums resound.
107. The instigator, standing in the centre points with wild and joyously excited gestures, out to the auditorium, toward the entrances, claps his hands fanatically, swings his red cap enthusiastically and seems to call Hurrah with wide open mouth.
108. All of the people turn toward the front and swing their caps, raise their arms and roar Hurrah.
109. The instigator together with several others turns toward the oncomers.
110. With fantastic jubilation, swinging of caps, cries of approval, with resounding trombones, drums, organ tumult, shrill clanging of bells, the judges advance from the auditorium, marching solemnly.
111. In the midst, the chief judge is borne in on the hands of the revolutionists.
112. He and the other judges wear the caps worn by the medieval criminal tribunals, that cover the entire face, leaving only the eyes free.
113. The procession moves over the steps on to the stage.
114. The chief judge stands in the midst of the other judges facing the people.
115. All clap their hands and pelt the chief judge with flowers.
116. The Emperor jumps up from his seat in great excite-

[301]

ment, stares tremblingly, throws himself upon the chief judge and lifts his mask.

117. The face of the diabolical, smiling Piper, who has just rushed off as instigator, is visible, brilliantly illuminated.

118. The Emperor is once again painfully disappointed and frantic.

119. He is laughingly pushed to one side and sinks back into his seat, apathetic and melancholy.

120. The judges, amidst reiterated trombone sounds, ascend their tribune, and take their places, headed by the chief judge.

121. The chief judge strikes a metal plate with a hammer.

122. The trial begins.   Silence prevails.

123. The figure of the public accuser dressed in red vestments appears in the chancel.

124. The hangman's assistants free one of the golden prisoners from the group and lead him forward to the centre.

125. The chief judge leans far forward, stretches his right arm toward him, seems to ask something.

126. The prisoner nods.

127. The judge raps again.

128. The public accuser throws his hood back, shows once again, strange to say, the face of the Piper.

129. He takes a parchment, reads a short Latin accusation, dry, sharp, short.   His voice seems to come from far off.

130. He points with sharp, stinging movements at the accused.

131. When he has finished, there is acquiescence from the people and the galleries.

132. The entire auditorium now takes part with signs of approval and other outcries, in the proceedings which are carried on with gruesome haste.

133. The judge bows toward the other judges.

134. These throw wildly, one after the other, black balls into a bowl that stands before the judge.
135. The judge agrees, takes a staff and breaks it in two in sign of condemnation.
136. Applause of approval from the entire house.
137. The condemned one is seized.
138. One of the slabs of the graves in the floor of the church is raised.
139. The condemned is pushed down.
140. Laughter. Cries from above. The slab is replaced.
141. Repeated sign from the judge.
142. The second, third, fourth prisoners are led forward, likewise accused, judged and condemned.
143. The crowd acquiesces, calls here and there, laughs and applauds.
144. The slab of the grave is raised. The condemned are thrown in.
145. The public accuser drops his hood when he has finished his accusation.
146. The golden figures disappear in the subterranean vault.
147. The chief judge gives a renewed sign of the head.
148. Trombones.
149. The public accuser goes to the judges' table, receives a parchment with a seal, goes to the left of the Emperor.
150. He reads the abdication document to him. His voice comes from a distance.
151. Murmur of approval. The Emperor nods apathetically.
152. Challenging calls from all parts of the house.
153. The Emperor rises, looks to all sides, also to the galleries from which calls came, nods slowly, takes his crown in both hands, holds it for a moment, smiles sadly, thoughtfully, and hands it to the public attorney.
154. General approbation from all sides.
155. The accuser carries the crown to the judges' table and retires.
156. The Emperor strokes his forehead and hair, breathes

[303]

deeply, looks around the room tremblingly and searchingly, raises and drops his arms as if in desperation, sits down brooding sadly.

157. The judge strikes the plate again with the hammer.
158. Trombones, louder.
159. All turn suddenly to the entrances, point outward.
160. Growing excitement. General talking and confused cries.
161. Organ roar. Cracking of whips, increasing thunder.
162. The penetrating bell of one condemned.
163. The executioner comes in with hangman's assistants from the front through the auditorium.
164. In their midst, the Empress, stript of all splendor, clad in the shirt of one condemned.
165. The rigid puppet of the son, with stiff outstretched arms, is bound on her back, resembling a cross.
166. She is bound with chains and is pulled and driven by them.
167. The hangman's assistants have scourges in their hands, knotted ropes which resemble those worn by the nuns.
168. The assistants look rough, brutal and gruesome.
169. A one-eyed man has the Nun on a cord and scourges her on. Again it is the Piper.
170. She drags herself painfully forward.
171. A priest, with a book, walks behind her, murmuring a litany.
172. A frightful crowding.
173. Storm wind.
174. The executioner is a big, strong young fellow and carries the axe on his shoulder.
175. The Empress is received with clenched fists, threats, curses and many cries from all sides.
176. The guards have difficulty in holding back the mob.
177. Mocking songs are sung which compete with the Miserere which intervenes mightily from above.
178. Once, the Empress seems to break down.

THE INTERIOR OF THE CATHEDRAL IN "THE MIRACLE"

In the London Production at Olympia, December 23, 1911

"THE MIRACLE" ON TRIAL

A Caricature by Olaf Gulbransson of a Hypothetical Interview Between the Pope
and Reinhardt, Producer of "The Miracle," and Karl Vollmoeller, Its Author

179. She is pulled up by the chains and scourged onward by the one-eyed hangman's assistant.

180. When she reaches the steps, black stones are thrown at her from all sides. They fall to the ground noiselessly.

181. She breaks down silently under this stone throwing.

182. Sudden quiet.

183. A crowding around her.

184. The priest hurries to her.

185. They lift her up slowly.

186. She is led, amid muffled murmuring, to the Madonna column.

187. The noise ebbs.

188. Only the condemned one's bell keeps ringing stubbornly.

189. The Empress looks around, sickened.

190. On all sides, eyes stare at her.

191. She closes her eyes.

192. The one-eyed man wishes to bind her to the column where the Madonna stood.

193. Trombones.

194. The Emperor looks up suddenly, does not trust his eyes, rises trembling, points with wide outstretched arms at the puppet which he recognises.

195. With a dreadful cry, he rushes to the Empress, unfetters the puppet, and presses it tenderly to himself with wild sobbing.

196. He rocks the puppet in his arm, sings to it and is prepared to defend it against everyone.

197. The Empress stares, frightfully shocked at this spectacle.

198. Suddenly the shadow appears next to the Emperor.

199. The one-eyed man goes toward the Emperor to take the puppet from him.

200. The Emperor snatches the one-eyed man's short knife from him, lifts it high, shows it to the puppet and hastily whispers something in its ear. He points to his breast, nods to the puppet as if he wished to quiet

a remonstrance.   He speaks at first sharply, then imploringly.

201. He presses the knife in the hand of the puppet, guides this hand with the knife against himself and stabs himself.

202. He distorts his face in pain, then smiles released and sinks heavily to the ground, the puppet clasped tightly to him.

203. The shadow bends over him.

204. Still in his death struggle, the Emperor raises himself up, snatches at the shadow's mask and lifts it automatically.

205. The death head becomes visible.

206. The shadow disappears.

207. All look on, petrified without stirring.

208. The girl stands rigid with horror.

209. Her countenance becomes troubled.   She longs to cry out, in her unspeakable torture, but is unable to utter a sound.   She longs to throw herself upon the unhappy Emperor but her feet are as if rooted to the spot.   She looks upward with sick eyes as if she wished to ask whether the measure of her suffering were not yet filled.

210. She suddenly lifts her arms, snatches at the air as if to hold herself up, then breaks down suddenly and noiselessly.

211. A sympathetic whispering passes through the room.

212. The one-eyed man and his companions laugh coarsely, push and shake her, pull her up, fainting, with the chains.

213. She sways, leans against the column and stares with bright eyes at the one-eyed man.

214. The disposition of the people seems to be changing into sympathy for the martyred Nun.

215. Cries from above, from the ranks, to the hangman, to the judges, make a manifold echo.

216. The one-eyed man binds the Nun to the Madonna column.

217. Hands are lifted from the crowd, bidding him to desist.

218. A man throws himself upon the one-eyed man, pushes him forcibly to one side, rushes to the Nun full of pity and unconsciously falls on his knees before her.

219. Murmurs. A quarrel of several voices.

220. The head judge strikes loudly with the hammer on the plate.

221. Quiet.

222. The public accuser stands between her and the dead Emperor. He points to him, then to her; shakes his fist at the Nun. He seems to say:

223. "You are the cause of all the unhappiness in the land. On your account the son lost his life." He lifts the puppet toward her. "Because of you the Emperor went insane and died." His voice seems to come from far away and naturally remains unintelligible.

224. He turns toward the judges, points to the executioner's block and the executioner.

225. The Nun, bound to the column like a martyr, stares at the accuser and evokes general pity.

226. Voices are again raised from the galleries, at first singly then in increasing numbers. They protest on behalf of the Nun and do not permit the accuser to finish speaking.

227. He gesticulates mightily but is grabbed by some of the people who rush on to the place of execution.

228. He tries to defend himself.

229. They tear the mask from his face. It is the Piper.

230. A close fight follows.

231. The judges jump up from their seats.

232. The head judge strikes the plate.

233. Trombones. Hard beating of the drums.

234. The soldiers push the people back with force.

235. Suppressed cries.

236. Several of the black revolutionists fall down injured.

237. The head judge points to those who have fallen and lifts his hand, as a threat and warning, toward the crowd and the galleries.
238. Everything becomes very quiet.
239. The accuser has disappeared in the crowd.
240. The soldiers guard the place and, with transversely held lances, push the people back.
241. The first judge rises, with the shadow standing behind him. He begins to read, stutters, stares at the Nun, tries to read on, stammers, stares at the Nun again; his hands begin to shake visibly.
242. He lets the paper sink, sways, and suddenly he rushes down from the judges' table to the Nun, sinks on his knees in front of her, lifts his arms in adoration and finally fervently kisses the seam of her poor dress.
243. The judges have jumped up again.
244. Among the people arises greatly excited but suppressed conversation.
245. At a sign from the chief judge, the rebellious judge is seized and killed at the feet of the Nun.
246. Silence.
247. The head judge gives the document to the judge who is standing on his left.
248. The latter rises slowly, with the shadow still behind him. He takes the paper, stares at the Nun, tears it in bits, rushes like the others to the Nun, lifts his arms eagerly toward her; turns toward the front to the people in order to speak for her. At a signal he is likewise seized by the soldiers. They hold his mouth closed.
249. He gesticulates vehemently but is also killed at the feet of the Nun.
250. The Nun lifts her eyes upwards in unspeakable despair.
251. Louder but still muffled grumblings are heard from all sides and from all ranks.
252. The head judge jumps up, takes the Emperor's crown,

THE ASSISTANT EXECUTIONER
COSTUME PLATE BY NORMAN-BEL GEDDES

which lies on the table in front of him, and sets it with bold and grand gestures on his head.

253. He throws back his hood and reveals the face of the Piper.
254. Deadly silence.
255. He signals energetically to the executioner who stands to the left, then points to the Nun, lifts his staff on high and breaks it violently.
256. Trombones.
257. He lets his hood sink again and seats himself.
258. The bell for the condemned rings.
259. Drums.
260. The hangman's assistants unfetter the Nun.
261. The priest steps forward, reads in a whisper some words from his book, gives her absolution and makes the sign of the cross over her.
262. She bends her head low, and is led by the executioner's assistants to the block.
263. The executioner stands at the block and bares the Nun's neck.
264. A muffled but increasing murmuring is heard from all sides.
265. The Nun lays her head on the block.
266. Stillness.
267. The chief executioner seizes the Nun's hair and throws it towards the front in order to free her neck.
268. He takes a deep breath, lifts the axe but refrains and lets it sink.
269. He falls on his knees.
270. At this moment, a mighty shriek is uttered as if from a single throat by hundreds of people.
271. The general excitement and indignation waxes to a hurricane.
272. The crowd storms and rolls from all sides onto the place of execution. One sees suddenly bobbing up here

and there in the crowd the face of the Piper who henceforth spurs them on to liberate the Nun.

273. The wildly excited people forcibly push the soldiers back
toward the centre, break the barrier of lances; rush
in the middle. They snatch the axe from the executioner, free the Nun, storm upon the judges' table
and tear the chief judge (now a dummy) literally into
pieces.

274. A struggle between soldiers and people ensues. Many
fall.

275. Thunder, lightning, organ roar, storm bells.

276. The Nun is carried away.

277. The Piper appears in the chancel erect and blows his
death melody.

278. The floor is covered with those who have fallen.

279. Obscurity.

280. The masked shadow dances in the darkness.

SCENE VII—THE MANGER

CHARACTERS

The Nun   The Women
The Piper   The Soldiers

1. The noise breaks off suddenly in the darkness.

2. After a silence, the choirs start from above. Lamenta-
tions.

3. A child's voice alternates with women's and men's
choruses.

4. Between the centre columns, a sparsely lighted half-hut,
half-stable.

5. The roof has partly fallen in. A low opening leads to
the winter without.

6. It is snowing.

7. Stars shine in from above.
8. To the left a rudely constructed partition of wood, through which one discerns in the darkness the head of an ass at a fodder crib.
9. Soldiers sit around an old keg, drinking in silence.
10. They are dressed and prepared to mount at any moment.
11. At the right, resting and cowering in front of a glimmering fire are several painted women.
12. They are partly enveloped in covers and are sleeping.
13. A light on the keg illuminates the carousing soldiers.
14. They whistle, hum softly and play at dice.
15. The wind blows out of doors.
16. The Piper, as a soldier, enters from the outside, covered with snow.
17. Clinging to him is the Nun, run down, neglected and enveloped in wretched wet rags.
18. She clings to him, her life, in passionate and tender devotedness.
19. She is exhausted from the long tramp.
20. Her movements are tired and trailing.
21. The Piper throws himself on a stool near the keg and hurls his knapsack in the corner.
22. The Nun takes off his coat, carries it to the flickering fire to dry it.
23. The wenches at the fires, awakened and furious at the disturbance, scold and push.
24. The Nun groans heavily and holds her bosom as in pain.
25. With forethought she takes a cloth and puts it around the Piper's shoulders.
26. The Piper, who in the meanwhile has taken part in the game of dice, ignores her.
27. She gently strokes his hair.
28. He pushes her angrily from him, so that she almost falls to the ground.

29. He takes a pitcher from the keg and whistles to her to fill it.
30. Full of gratitude that he asks a favor of her, she runs with the jug into a dark corner where the knapsack lies, in order to fill it and bring it to him.
31. He stamps the ground with his feet; they are cold and wet.
32. He empties the jug.
33. Meanwhile she takes off his shoes with great effort, dries his feet with her hair and warms them with her hands.
34. Meanwhile, he throws dice and drinks.
35. She crouches at his feet like a faithful dog.
36. He rises, steps over her, visibly feeling better, goes to the other women at the fire and embraces them.
37. The women laugh and screech.
38. The Nun crouches on the floor looking at him sadly.
39. The Piper whistles again, shows with his fingers that he wishes to play.
40. She arises at once, although with difficulty, runs to the corner again and brings a bag pipe.
41. The Piper, while in the arms of the women at the hearth, begins to play a dance, jumps up, hands the bag pipe to one of the soldiers and wishes to dance with the Nun.
42. She shakes her head silently.
43. The Piper, beside himself with rage at her refusal, approaches her threateningly; raises his fist to strike her.
44. She embraces the threatening fist tenderly and whispers something in his ear, shamefacedly.
45. He listens unwillingly at first, then laughs roughly, frees himself from her, staggers to the soldiers and wenches. He whispers to them as a joke the secret confided to him.
46. In vain the Nun, in shame, tries to prevent him.
47. He thrusts her away brutally and all break into a mocking laugh.

48. The Piper grasps a wench, who clings to him fresh and coquettish, and starts a common dance with her. He is visibly intoxicated.

49. The soldiers accompany the dance with bagpipe, drums and whistles.

50. The Nun sinks down, weeping quietly, and stares painfully at her loved one.

51. At the end of the dance, the Piper staggers, threatening to fall.

52. The Nun catches him and kisses him.

53. She wastes all her tenderness on this rough unworthy remainder of what is left to her of her strongly coveted life.

54. The soldiers play a second dance.

55. The wenches crowd up to the Piper.

56. The Nun, unable to witness this, forces herself amid bodily and spiritual pain to dance with him.

57. She is obliged to stop several times while the others laugh at her faintness.

58. The Piper takes no notice of her pleading and forces her to continue to dance with him, until she falls to the ground exhausted.

59. In exasperation, he thrusts her to one of the other soldiers.

60. The crowd breaks up, extinguishes the lights, except the hearth fire, and dances out wildly.

61. The Nun remains foresaken in her unspeakable misery.

62. The soldiers are heard going off to the tune of a jolly march.

63. The hearth fire slowly dies out.

64. In the darkness a cry of agony. Up in the choir the singing of a child and a gloria.

65. A star shines above the hut.

66. It gradually become light again and there appears a tryptich as a gold background.

67. The Nun sits by a lighted cradle.

68. A child is born.

[313]

69. People come from the audience.
70. The three kings from the East appear from the three sides.
71. The black king from the Orient, the yellow king from Syria and the white king from Byzantium, followed by shadows, who do not reach the stage but remain on the steps.
72. The Piper appears in the guise of the servant of Herod. He wishes to kill the child, but the Nun flees with the baby.
73. An old cradle song is sung.

Scene VIII—The Winter Forest

CHARACTERS

The Nun
The Soldiers
The Piper

The Dead Lovers
The Shadow of Death

1. In total darkness, a short time after the soldiers' march has died away, the stillness is rent by the cry of a woman in agony.
2. A clear soft child's cry follows.
3. Then a mighty radiant Gloria from above.
4. In the darkness a star sinks over the hut.
5. In the semi-darkness the stable becomes a three part gold tryptich.
6. On the left are seen again as before, behind a partition, the heads of animals at a feeding crib.
7. The Nun sits pale and exhausted before a small crib in which a light shines.
8. The Nun's eyes are closed and she scarcely moves her lips.
9. A clear soft voice sings an old cradle song.

[314]

THE INQUISITION—SCENE VI
A SKETCH OF THE ENTIRE STAGE BY NORMAN-BEL GEDDES

10. Several figures appear out of the darkness, approach silently like shadows in quiet suspense and stand listening and watching.
11. In the darkness at the right and left, three crowned visions become visible.
12. They resemble in their fantastic ornate costumes, and their motionless wooden attitudes the Three Holy Kings, as they are portrayed in the Christmas mangers of the Middle Ages.
13. At the right the older and younger king, at the left the black one.
14. They have a group of followers who lose themselves in the dark and carry golden vessels and gifts.
15. The whole reminds one of early paintings by primitive masters.
16. The singing ceases.
17. The Nun opens her eyes and stares first to the right.
18. The old king has the features of the Emperor, the younger one those of the young Prince.
19. The Nun frightened, turns her face to the left.
20. There she recognizes the Shadow as the black king.
21. He wears a sparkling crown and carries a long flashing sword in his right hand.
22. The Nun stares horrified at this threatening apparition.
23. The shadow takes off his mask slowly. His death's head becomes visible.
24. The face of the Nun becomes distorted in speechless horror. She stands up suddenly with shaking knees in order to protect her child with pleading gestures.
25. The figures remain immovable.
26. In wild terror, the Nun lifts the child wrapped in rags out of the crib, presses it passionately to her and flees as if pursued by the furies.
27. A nuns' choir sings fervently.
28. At the same time a procession seems to pass through the church; headed by cross and church standard-bearers,

altar boys, choir boys with incense containers, many priests and higher church dignitaries with burning candles.

29. Out of the incense vessels a heavy mist rises, which, as in the first forest pictures, envelops the scene.

30. In the mist various soldiers seem suddenly to march by in a long procession. They also carry flags and lances.

31. A soldier's march with drums and fifes approaches, increasing in loudness. It competes in the storm with the Nuns' choir and finally drowns it out.

32. The vague skeleton of a forest in winter garb is recognisable; concealing the high altar stand with snow-covered pines.

33. In front, in the footsteps of the ecclesiastical procession, soldiers move from left to right in the darkness.

34. A gray light, as from the moon. A few stars.

35. The particular character of this picture is the ceaselessness of the procession.

36. It is as if the action flows, the whole world is under way.

37. Ghostly shadows dance wierd fantasies on the falling snow against a dark sky.

38. Many women muffled in winter clothing march in the procession of soldiers who carry with them furled banners, lances, baggage carts.

39. Between a larger and a smaller division of the procession of soldiers, a small group comes which from the distance reminds one of the biblical Flight into Egypt. A donkey is fairly heavily laden. The Piper, as a soldier, is seated on it, cracking his whip.

40. The Nun drags herself painfully beside the donkey. She carries in her arms a child wrapped in rags.

41. She suddenly breaks down, exhausted.

42. The Piper takes no notice of it and the wagon rolls over her.

43. The soldiers' procession continues. Soldiers come. One of them raises the semi-conscious woman, looks at her,

and laughingly throws her to the next advancing soldier, who does the same. The next one lets her sink into the snow heedlessly, just where she encamped with the Knight on that spring night.

44. Half fainting, dull and desperate, she lies there, without even being able to give expression to her pain.

45. A ghostly procession, led by the shadow with the uncovered death's head, now crosses the road. With visible bones he strikes an invisible drum.

46. In this procession, for which a death dance is played, come: the Emperor, the Prince, the Count, the Knight.

47. Among these figures: the executioner, soldiers, judges, hangman's assistants and black-clad shadows acting like Revolutionists.

48. The four main figures are particularly illuminated, and are constantly accompanied by the shadowy apparition of the death's head.

49. He drums solemnly and pompously back of the Emperor, at the same time striking his forehead; lightly and impertinently back of the Prince; heavily and rudely back of the Count; and on his heart back of the Knight.

50. He dances to his drumming, now lightly and elegantly, then heavily and grotesquely, finally earnestly and dejectedly—always in the rhythm of the Passacaglia.

51. Each of the apparitions turns his head in passing slowly towards the Nun; looks at her long and sadly.

52. The Piper suddenly stands next to her. He plays on his flute.

53. She stares horrified at the long procession. When the Knight has passed, she stretches out her arms feebly toward him, in pain and yearning.

54. The Piper stops. Even he seems for a moment to be exhausted and overcome by the spectacle of all this misery.

55. He casts his looks upward as if questioning whether the frightful test were not yet at an end.

[317]

56. But, as if at a higher command, he places the flute again to his mouth and plays alluringly, pressing himself upon her. He wishes to take her along.

57. She defends herself with passionate despair, summoning the remainder of her strength. He tempts her for the last time.

58. She is finished with life, finished with him. Life has no longer anything alluring for her, only menaces.

59. In her great distress she folds her hands, numb with frost, and begins to pray.

60. The Lord's Prayer.

61. These are the only audible words in the play, except the Latin chants and the singing. All other human sounds, cries and words, belong like the choirs and songs, like thunder and wind to the musical instrumentation of this work. Only in this lyrical moment, which is also the turning point of the action, can the spoken and generally understood word be permitted as a last heightening.

62. Slowly and with difficult articulation the once so familiar words are wrung from her pale lips. She begins very simply, jerkingly, haltingly, shyly, becomes gradually more fervent, louder—finally screaming with despairing force, but always without pathos, calling for help, a direct appeal to the Highest Being; uttering each word with new feeling.

63. Flowing tears release her, give wings to the words, overwhelm her and finally choke her.

64. Her voice refuses; she can proceed no further; she raises her arms and lets them sink helplessly.

65. She kneels, released, with tears streaming down her face. Her lips move silently, her hands are passionately clasped together.

"THE MIRACLE"

Scene IX—The Cathedral

CHARACTERS

The Nun

The Abbess

The Old Sacristan

The Lame Piper

The Knight

The Madonna

Nuns and Novices. Peasants, Townsfolk and Children. Bishops, Priests, Monks and Pilgrims. Cripples, Blind, Lame and Lepers. Patricians of the Two.

1. After a silence, bells ring from a celestial height.
2. A choir of voices is heard high up in the distance.
3. Her prayer has been heard.
4. The Piper, who had lingered in visible suspense, abandons her.
5. The bells and song come nearer and clearer.
6. The snow fall ceases.
7. Stars seem to be slowly falling from their place in the sky.
8. A shadow darkens the moon.
9. A warm light, streaming out of an opening portal of a brightly lit church, strikes her.
10. She rises with difficulty, sinks in rapture on her knees and crawls toward the light.
11. In the mist, soldiers seem to march again.
12. Grill work is visible between columns which only a moment before had been trees.
13. The stars have become candles on the grilled altars, and Christmas trees appear before the altar.
14. Colored reflections as from church windows play on the floor.
15. Sunlight comes through windows, filling the space high up between the columns.

16. The interior of the church gradually becomes recognisable.
17. What appeared to be soldiers are darkly clad nuns, who walk through the church and swing incense burners.
18. The mist seems now to evolve out of the incense vessels and sinks the whole church once more into darkness.
19. The black figures in the background become the nuns. The nuns come downstage and light the Christmas tree on the altar, which now becomes visible once more.
20. The Madonna has taken the Nun's place.
21. As the light comes on, the Madonna is alone. She opens the door of the left lodge and lets in the children, one of whom she takes in her arms.
22. Children wear winter wraps.
23. One child falls down on its knees, thinking she is the Madonna.
24. Three kings appear as in the Manger Scene and give the children presents.
25. A little girl with primitive angelic wings appears carrying a dancing star on a pole, walking in front of the kings.
26. The children leave, the nuns depart also and the Madonna is left alone.
27. She takes off the Nun's clothes, crucifix, etc., and puts them on the steps. She then takes the crown, puts it on, and starts up the steps to her pedestal. When in position, she picks up the robe from the pedestal and puts it on, and becomes statue again.
28. There is a tremendous storm outside, which makes the candles flicker whenever a door is opened and whirls in the snow.
29. Suddenly a gust of wind blows the door open and the Nun comes in, clutching her child, which is wrapt in swaddling clothes. This, of course, is the same door through which she departed.
30. She sinks to the floor and the door bangs shut. She is

NUN AND MADONNA IN "THE MIRACLE"

Scene from the Berlin Production at the Zirkus Busch, April, 1914

(Left to right) Rosamond Botsford, as the Nun; Asta Fleming, as the Madonna

Maria Carmi (Principessa Matchabelli)

Goldberg, N. Y.

Lady Diana Manners (Duff-Cooper)

THE RIVAL MADONNAS

In the New York Production of "The Miracle," January, 1924

petrified at the sound, looks shyly around, fears the demon, but suddenly sees the Madonna who seems to smile as ever. She has recognized the church.

31. She moves on her knees toward the Madonna and prays. She takes the hem of her garment.

32. A voice high up in the air (in ventilation shaft of auditorium).

33. She finds her dress there, thinks it is a miracle, radiantly and in haste puts it on; she is alone with the Madonna.

34. She suddenly sees her child lying on the pavement where she had left it, shows it to the Madonna, confesses. A shock, a scream, the child is dead.

35. She falls in a faint.

36. The warm light of life shines down from the canopy over the statue. The statue moves, leans over, lifts the child. The rags fall off, the child glows.

37. The original cold light returns. The Madonna becomes a statue again.

38. The bells begin to toll.

39. Nuns enter with the Abbess, who sees the Nun lying in a faint and thinks she is praying. They are about to continue, when they are seized with a terrific fright; the statue has appeared again. At first they are stupefied, then they all run, shout with joy. All the bells ring; the Madonna has returned.

40. The Nun wakes from her faint. She is lifted by the same nuns to look at the miracle. And the other nuns fall down on their knees before her as the savior of the miracle statue. The Nun feels guilty, hides her face in deep shame and wishes to run away. They think she is merely suffering from ecstasy and lift their arms in adoration.

41. Far away a laugh is heard.

42. The doors are thrown open, the populace pours in, called by the bells.

43. The Bishop also enters and now the Nun, although she

understands nothing at all this, lets everything happen to her, completely overcome.

44. While the Nun is being cheered, others lift the Madonna down from her pedestal on a stand to show it to the populace.

45. The Nun falls at the feet of the Madonna; all sing Salve Regina, standing in a long row on the steps; angels sing in the air.

46. The statue is lifted up on high.

47. Stars appear through the roof of the church, above the altar and the audience.

48. They begin to float downward like flashes of illuminated snow.

APPENDIX II

I

VIGNETTES FROM REINHARDT'S PRODUCTIONS

BY SIEGFRIED JACOBSOHN

REINHARDT'S aim was the same as that of the Meiningen Company: to assure every dramatic action its full poetic rights by giving it an appropriate scenic frame, with the result that the performance of every drama is an individual and harmonious work of art. His means, however, were different. The assistance of other arts was sought by the Meiningers to create a "natural" atmosphere through faithful representation of the outside world. Reinhardt on the other hand, claimed their aid, not to create "reality," but to assist him in endowing the inner spirit of a play with life and visible form, by transforming the outer aspects, by giving them a deeper expressiveness than that of their indifferent surface, by use of the simplest elementary forms of color and line, by revealing perspectives and distant views, as alluring as melodies. From the post of mere assistant to the stage manager, the painter had become an artist of equal standing with the dramatist whom he served. Historic accuracy had been replaced by the reawakening of the genuine atmosphere of an historic period.

While most performances of "The Merchant of Venice" before Reinhardt had made of that play the tragedy of Shylock, Reinhardt centers his attention on the Venetian joy of living. Everyone sings and dances with joy, and it is Shylock, with his suffering who forms a disturbing dissonance in the atmosphere of light-hearted Venetian cheer.

[323]

APPENDIX II

The opening performance of Ibsen's "Ghosts" at the Kammerspiele made an overwhelming impression. Criticism which measures achievements by what is achievable, has nothing to measure here. All it can do is to try to understand the secret cause of such unparalleled effects. Brahm, as an interpreter of Ibsen's art, remained dull because he was matter-of-fact; the Russians have lost reality by their extreme devotion to color. Reinhardt's interpretation was neither too dull nor too brilliant. It was rich, warm and deep, issuing from the heart and speaking to the heart of the audience. With him, the accent falls not on the spirit of revolt, but on the mother's suffering. To have brought to light the human Ibsen is the achievement and the inexpressible beauty of this new conception of "Ghosts." Every sentence sounds as if it had just been created; every situation has a face of its own, every pause its importance, every figure stands at the right spot. Nothing disturbs, nothing is there for its own sake only. These are no longer the personalities of the actors; they are the persons in the poet's world brought to life.

Reinhardt sees the tragedy of "King Lear" as a wild legend from dark ages.

The magician takes the old tragedy of "Clavigo" into his strong hands, gives it the breath of youth, and it is new.

The problem in performing Schiller is this: to respect the golden mean between pathos and naturalism; to exhaust Schiller's psychology without restraining the flight of his language. This is a problem which personalities like Kainz, Matkowsky and Mitterwurzer have solved in their own way; a problem which was first approached with an ensemble of actors by Brahm, in "Love and Intrigue"—in his attempt at destroying the revolutionary pathos—but which was fully appreciated and solved, by Reinhardt only, in his performance of "Don Carlos."

A GENTLEMAN GUEST
COSTUME PLATE BY NORMAN-BEL GEDDES

38. The guests sway from side to side stiffly as the Piper plays into the ear of the Count.

39. The couples begin to dance stiffly, Gothically, without leaving their places.

40. The Piper leads them on and they begin to dance a csardas, slowly at first and then wilder until the scene becomes an orgy.

41. The Count tries to kiss the Nun, who sits ever motionless and without interest.

42. The Piper plays to her the tune of the Knight and suddenly a vision of the Knight appears in a blood red light, rising out of the ground with a dagger in his heart at exactly the place where the Madonna had floated in the first scene.

43. The vision disappears weirdly.

44. Now the Piper plays in the ear of the horrified Nun the tune of her dance for the Knight.

45. Finally she begins to move, to dance mechanically, remembering in desperation her first love.

46. A bell sounds softly as for midnight-mass.

47. The choir sounds from above.

48. Nuns go toward the stage in two columns and disappear through the stained glass windows.

49. The Sacristan stares and points at the procession.

50. The clock strikes far away.

51. All are rigid.

52. The Piper jumps toward the gypsies and stirs them on to a wild csardas. The Nun dances as if driven by a demon.

53. The Piper dances, with his violin, up an aisle to meet a new arrival who has just appeared at the back of the auditorium.

54. He is a Prince, a degenerate libertine and is accompanied by six friends.

55. The Nun collapses, sinking back into her throne, exhausted. All look at her.

the windows, then from the front. The costumes are lit with a warm light in front and by a cold light behind. On the table are lights in glass pitchers, vessels and fruit in all colors.

23. The Count sits at the private centre table with the Nun on his right and another woman on his left.

24. The Count's seat is higher than the other two chairs.

25. Two women and two men stand at each of the other two centre arch tables.

26. Two men and two women in alternate positions at the tables in each of the side arches.

27. The guests stand between the tables and the window in the side arches.

28. The women are very sensual looking in contrast to the Nun. All sit or stand without moving.

29. Eight gypsies, sitting on the steps, play music. The orchestra consists of a primitive cymbolon played sitting on the floor, two violins, 'cello, contrabass and clarinet.

30. Eight servants pass food and wine.

31. The sermon from the pulpit has become a dinner speech by the Piper.

32. Now a flourish and music by the gypsies.

33. The Count raises his goblet, then all raise theirs to the Count.

34. Every movement is stylized, to preserve the effect of stained glass figures. When there is no action, one position is held by all.

35. The Nun, in all her gorgeousness, sits motionless.

36. The distant choir of nuns above develps into a worldly song of the banqueters. The guests make gestures but do not sing. The singers are invisible, standing behind the windows.

37. The Piper comes in as the leader of the gypsy orchestra and plays to each of the guests in turn.

[269]

SCHILLER'S "THE DEATH OF WALLENSTEIN"

A Design for a Setting by Ernst Stern for the Production at the Deutsches Theater, November, 1914

VIGNETTES FROM REINHARDT'S PRODUCTIONS

Reinhardt has surpassed his predecessors in the production of "Judith," from the standpoint of refined taste and intensity. Here he is systematic without pedantry, simple without meagerness, bright in coloring without garishness, fond of contrasts, yet not too exactly planned. What is lacking—because the actors lack it—is: an untamed wildness, stormy passion, exaggerated proportions.

"Much Ado about Nothing": In Reinhardt's hands, Shakespeare's world is as beautiful as on the day of its creation. You dance rather than walk on leaving this performance. Light as a feather, you keep time with Beatrice's blithe love dance, joyful and grateful to the artist who makes you see life so optimistically. Relying on himself alone, Reinhardt wiped the dust off that comedy and revealed its immortal face.

Reinhardt's ear hears all of Strindberg's music, even its dissonances, without attempting to make harmonies of them. He venerates the Strindberg who is kind beyond measure, just as he does the one who is tortured beyond measure and who tortures the rest of us. He carries the victims of this fanatic lover of the truth into an atmosphere so distorted, so gloomy, so full of fantastic life and motion, that it might be Van Gogh's. Within ten yards of you, a ventilator begins whirling at a given signal, and it seems to you that the elements have broken loose and are sweeping over a shivering, desperate, shrieking humanity.

Some years ago when I saw "Wallenstein" at the Königliches Schauspielhaus, I said: This play has many elements which may have been artistically justified at the time of its creation, but which have since become obsolete. These archaisms will disappear some day when one with youthful eyes looks at this poem, and plays it as if it had been written today. Then there will be an end of the pathetic recitation through which Schiller's irresistible words lose their rhythm, their music, their color. This destined reformer is Reinhardt.

[325]

APPENDIX II

Goethe's "Stella" is Reinhardt's masterpiece. The tangled, torn, and tortured present which is so full of longing for new ideals, gives him the required courage, the essential excess of "Sturm und Drang" enthusiasm. He sees the divine harmony in all the discords of the human soul. "Stella": this star irradiates light even in the darkness of the present hour.

THE KING'S CHAMBER

THE AUDIENCE HALL

TWO DESIGNS BY ERNST STERN FOR SCHILLER'S "DON CARLOS"

DEUTSCHES THEATER, NOVEMBER, 1909

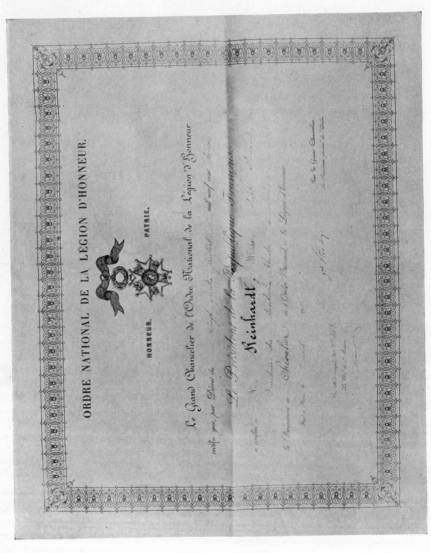

MAX REINHARDT, CHEVALIER IN THE LEGION OF HONOR

II

AN INTERNATIONAL SYMPOSIUM ON REINHARDT

(Austria)

It may be that no definite style will remain which one can call "Reinhardt style," only because every one of his works has a style of its own, its inherent style. In all probability, this will be the style of the future: a style conceived from out of the individuality of the work and its author, a style created by disregard of tradition. Today, Reinhardt is the most powerful creator of the "living theatre." He is not an academic manager, nor the vainglorious tyrant who refuses to acknowledge the independent individuality of an actor. But he yields to that individuality only in the service of the ensemble, to which he gives his own individual stamp and that of the art of the theatre, an art which he elevated from one that serves to one that reigns. We may disagree on details in Reinhardt's performances. The essential point is the struggle upwards, the acquisition of a modern style of dramatic staging, as the result of successful and unsuccessful experiments.

RICHARD SPECHT,
Viennese Critic.

Reinhardt's unique characteristic is that he begins to plan and to build up from single elements. The danger that lies therein is that at any moment a chaotic condition may result. When completely unrestrained the dramatic action may lead to emptiness, to vulgarity or to nothing at all. That was the end of the *commedia dell'arte*. Not for a moment is an enterprise of Reinhardt safe from this danger, but he defies it again and

[327]

APPENDIX II

again, not on principle or through mannerisms, but by a marvelous sensibility, by an imagination which constantly kindles its flame at the inner contacts and harmonies in his work and thus always rises again above the chaotic. There is continual overflow, but he masters it all the time, playing one element against the other, the dramatic action against the picturesque, the poetic element against both, smothering one flame by another. This method of working is immensely fertile, and so individual that it can not be copied. Reinhardt's task, as with every creative personality, lies in more and more accentuating a strict style of his own, after having mastered the elements of his art.

HUGO VON HOFMANNSTHAL.

Reinhardt's internationalism consists in the fact that it is a characteristic of high quality to be international. If he were not that, he would not be of first rank, but would be a national *regisseur*, or of only local fame. Since he is of the first rank, he is international, and the fact that he is international proves that he must be of first rank. Poetry can be of the first rank and still be impossible for another nation, first of all because of having to be translated, or because its nature may be so penetrated with a specific nationalism that another nation remains cold and a stranger to it. Reinhardt's activity consists, first of all, in giving form to things which do not receive their form through words or reveal their life between these words— things, therefore, of a visual, musical, and spiritual nature, things which are not bound by language, such as music, rhythm, appearance, color, tempo of emotion, suggestive power of pose, and, above all, vitality of impression: things of sound, which are not national, but universally human, and which can neither become obsolete nor be misunderstood. Anyone who creates artistically with these means must be international, if he is of first rank.

Reinhardt was born in Baden, near Vienna, and grew up in Vienna in such an atmosphere as can develop only in that city.

AN INTERNATIONAL SYMPOSIUM ON REINHARDT

It would take too long to give a sketch of Austrian history to explain this. But through its geographical situation alone, on a stream which flows down through southern Slavic regions to the Black Sea, and on a commercial highway, Vienna was always a gathering-place of strong, virile people, rejoicing in life, color, and music. The population of Vienna was and still is strongly affected by the elements that have had their trade-colonies there: Greeks, Orientals, and, at the time when Austria had Italian possessions, a strong Italian influence, when the Hapsburgs reigned in Spain, Spanish, so that there is scarcely a southern element which has not been thrown into this melting-pot. The Princes who reigned there, the clerical rulers who had their dioceses there, all these have had a feeling and love for the pomp of show, the decoratively royal manner and attitude of life. And the festivals which have been given there, of an artistic or courtly nature, are ever to be traced back to this sensuous joyousness.

If Reinhardt at any point in his career has laid unusually spirited emphasis on pomp, color, music, and visual proportion, so was he completely within the tradition of the country in which he grew up. I think I may say that he has never forgotten that all these things possess more than passing value only when they are used in the service of the spiritual and transcendental.

Because of their situation, their distance from the Orient and from primitive peoples, the other great cities which have held artistic leadership, could never be favored with this sensuous joyousness which is natural and self-evident to the Austrians.

RICHARD BEER-HOFMANN,
Viennese Poet and Playwright.

(BELGIUM)

All I know about the Deutsches Theater is that the beautiful and noble enterprise of that theatre seems at present to be the most active, the most daring, the most literary and the most artistic of the civilized world. I owe to it, and herewith pro-

APPENDIX II

nounce, my greatest gratitude, because it has been the only theatre which had the courage to bring out two or three of my plays which all the other stages were sure could not be materialized.

MAURICE MAETERLINCK.

(From a letter to Friedrich von Oppeln Bronikowski.)

(DENMARK)

I have seen only five plays—"The Merchant of Venice" and "A Midsummer Night's Dream" among them. Strange to say, but a performance of "A Midsummer Night's Dream" at the Royal Theatre in Copenhagen bores you. Though the greater number of Reinhardt's actors were inferior to the Danish in training, his performance was a festival; everything became play and fun; the wonderful light poetic grace of this play, composed by the young Shakespeare, stood out in full light. In "The Merchant of Venice," the scenes of Italian life not only made you realize the quick pulse of that people, but also the impetuous festive spirit of the early Renaissance. The stage pictures were reminders of paintings by Carpaccio, then by Giovanni Bellini, again by Paris Bordone or Paolo Veronese. The hairdress and costumes, the carriage and gestures of the actors were of the year 1500. At no time, when Shakespeare's humanity and superior wisdom break through the restless activity of the legend, were his words dwarfed by too insistent a stage picture. It is not true that Reinhardt permits the manager to thrust the poet aside, as his critics would like us to believe. He enhances the poet.

Not everything was perfect that evening. But when the play was over, you had been in the fantastic Venice of the Middle Ages. The air was filled with its melodies. And while your ear caught them, colors and forms danced before your eyes, and Portia's humble utterances of love, Lorenzo's learned words on music, and the judge's wise speech on the magnificence of mercy—all these descended like a message from Shakespeare's own heaven.

GEORG BRANDES.

He is a wizard—this strange little man. He always sits there so silently during the first rehearsals—listening to and watching the actors. In his mind he has already worked out, by patient and arduous study, the *mise-en-scène*. He pictures there every gesture and every facial expression of each character as he wishes to see them conjured forth, and he can hear in his imagination every inflection of voice and change in intonation.

He sits there, silent and motionless, contrasting the growing, unfinished creations of his actors with the complete picture of the play which he has worked out in his own mind.

A few days later he returns to the rehearsals. He now knows all about his players: he remembers every little mistake of theirs; he knows in advance every correct inflection or gesture. They begin to act and then he takes a hand in the playing; but always in a subdued tone of voice, and quiet, almost impressionless, in his demeanor. He whispers a suggestion to the actors but does it in a way that will permit of no misunderstanding, in a manner so unmistakable and so clear that it will remain in the actors' mind forever. He proposes a gesture—but so naturally and characteristically that it could never be forgotten. The players become alert, the atmosphere around them becomes alive, they begin to feel they are on the verge of creating something that is not of themselves entirely. They are under the influence of a personal force—and this personal force goes out to them from this curiously silent man who sits there in the first row in the theatre.

He leaves—and he returns. And as soon as the actors are aware of his presence they are again under the spell of his hypnotic magnetism and his magic.

The knowledge of the theatre that he possesses is as broad and complete as any one could ever possibly gain. He is as

[331]

APPENDIX II

much at home where the most exalted emotions are concerned—
or the most ethereal dream-play—as he is in every imaginable
field of creation for the stage, conceived by human imagination: whether it be burlesque, comedy or the most heartrending
tragedy, whether it depicts the homely humor or the dark,
dreamy side of every-day life.

Here we find a scenic world that we never before have seen
—and it is in Berlin that it has been created by Max Reinhardt
during the last twenty years.

SVEN LANGE,
Danish Critic and Playwright, Author of "Samson and
Delilah."

(ENGLAND)

It seems as though Reinhardt has never considered a piece
unplayable. The more difficult the play to be produced, the
more boldly he has emerged. He embodies, in fact, the modern
militant spirit—a spirit marked by audacity and fighting force.
No one in this century has expressed this spirit in the theatre
more persistently and thoroughly, exhibiting a certain kind
of unchained energy that made progress meteoric but certain.
As a dynamic figure, as a revolutionary who has fired all cultural points in a vigorous endeavor to exalt the Will of the
Theatre, where of recent years emotionless intellect has alone
been enshrined, in his effort to bring himself face to face with
a new theatrical world, the elements of which he has eagerly
absorbed so far as it is possible, and to justify the demands of
his emotional nature, as well as to render himself master of
a chaotic domain, by reducing its chaos to order, he probably
has no equal in the contemporary theatre. In purely artistic
endeavor alone, he has been surpassed.

HUNTLY CARTER,
"The Theatre of Max Reinhardt."

Reinhardt is surely neither dreamer nor logician. His
productions are careless of theory or method. Simply, he

AN INTERNATIONAL SYMPOSIUM ON REINHARDT

takes the short simple way to translate his imaginative conception into visible form. He no longer believes in realism for its own sake. He tears violently from its frame the neatly colored photograph we knew so well. He works on a level plain cleared of the old ideas as to his craft and function.

JOHN PALMER,
"The Saturday Review."

(GERMANY)

Every one of Reinhardt's performances that I have seen stands out in my memory. The daring joy with which he masters new problems, manifold in character and always growing in difficulty; the genuine effort he devotes to solving every one of them, from the standpoint of its individual laws and claims—these traits must refresh every spectator. It is not in Reinhardt's nature ever to rest on his laurels or to do anything without giving it full care and attention. He has his own way of assimilating and studying and carefully working out every scene and every line of a play. The great number of new ideas we owe to him has always been elucidating, never confusing. He more than satisfies the claims of the moderns; his art threw a new and surprising light on the classics which filled us with curiosity and admiration; although, in their new form, we could hardly recognize their dear familiar faces.

That the new theatre ventured to establish new relations between culture and the drama was another imposing feature. Not only did its miracle-working magician attract the best painters, actors, musicians; he wished the drama to stand on the stage as the art of arts, and to be the centre whence should radiate all the artistic effects which otherwise reach us separately. Besides, it was meant to penetrate our whole culture in a shorter time and with greater intensity than all the other arts in their isolated circles of light.

Our time, however, is not well adapted to such a wonderful union between culture and drama. Its poets are not, nor

[333]

is its public. The climate in which we are living does not ripen such goodly fruit. Many a time, Reinhardt had to cater to the generation he lives in, to its desire for mere show, for superficial amusement, for authors who are the fad, for loud advertisement.

Neither did Reinhardt's ever-changing dynamic art bring about a reciprocal reaction between poet, actor and public such as emerged from Vienna's old Burg Theater, rejuvenating itself by means of its own traditions, or as a few performances of Gerhart Hauptmann and Ibsen are able to produce—impressions which really do away with the "world of stage illusion" and lift us into a sphere of the most real, most intense and yet most spiritual existence.

I do not like to ask myself where this very latest, this contemporary art will lead, and what connection the stage of the future will have with it, for I adhere to the broad view, that we have lost an old culture and have not yet acquired a new one, and that we lose the very best element in our being, unless we devote all our strength to finding a new home. Whether and when we shall find it, must not be our concern; but all of us must be awake to the necessity that we have to seek and seek again, beyond all success and failure. And that is what I admire in Reinhardt: the gift, the strength, the courage, the cheerful assiduity to seek again and again for the art of which he dreams, the art for which he sacrifices himself again and again, and to whose cause he tries to win the ablest of his contemporaries.

PROFESSOR FRIEDRICH VON DER LEYEN.

(HOLLAND)

Only he who has an idea and a vision of the dramatic art of the future will be able to understand and to estimate the importance of Reinhardt's stage. We can not prove that our idea and vision are the right one. Nor is that necessary. It is sufficient that we stand by our individual view and give every-one full freedom to attack it or to accept it.

Some day, probably during the next generation, an art of the theatre will arise which will unite dramatic poetry, music and staging into one harmonious whole, into an artistic unity of the highest standard. The opera is only a variation of the art of the theatre; Wagner's music drama is merely a subtle, ex-aggerated modification of it. Both, according to Schopenhauer, are "no product of a pure artistic sense, but rather the product of a somewhat barbaric conception of enhancing esthetic en-joyment by accumulating the means of expression." The music drama owes its existence to a temporary tendency in art, which, placed on the stage and supported by a powerful creative tal-ent, will keep us in its spell for one or two generations.

The repute and the value of all such tendencies rest, as Schopenhauer continues, on the fact that those who will con-tradict them and prove where they are wrong, are not yet born. But "those" will come. And when I saw, for the first time, the performances of Reinhardt's stage, it dawned on me how "those" will come. For that consummation, a great dra-matist, a great musician and a Reinhardt will be required.

The dramatic poet will have to stand for his full rights and must not permit his verses to be torn by speech, as the words of the music drama are sung asunder. He will not permit his dramatic motives to be interpreted by music, any more than he will consent to have them used as an opera text.

The great musician, conscious of the spiritual character of his art, will never condescend to depict in tones the dramatic human passions and emotions. He will translate into his purely musical language what is translatable, and that only in its proper place. He will not perpetrate any bad jokes, such as carica-turing Beckmesser, or making the dragon sing.

The theatrical director will delight the eye by an expres-sive, effective stage picture, as beautiful and powerful as the Greek landscape that served Aeschylus. He will create won-ders of staging by combining costumes and gestures, colors and

[335]

light effects, and thus will perfect the great impression without weakening the poetry of the spoken word or the sublimity of the music.

To attain this, we need more than a Reinhardt and good actors. These we have. We need a new Shakespeare, a new Goethe or Lessing, and a new Beethoven or Mozart, and—their collaboration.

Reinhardt has no co-workers of this calibre, and that is why he goes back to the classics again and again. At that, sponsorship of the new art costs money. The public, it is true, repays these costs later—as proof, observe the music drama of today—but the first suggestion entails a vast outlay, and you can not always afford to follow only the purest artistic motives.

Even supposing Reinhardt had the literary taste to select from the throng of modern authors and composers the great artists whom he needs for the full development of his personality, he would hardly be able again and again to perform their works and only their works, in contradiction to the taste of the public. Nevertheless, he has achieved great things. He will be a continuous inspiration to the young generation of artists. May he succeed in finding among the young dramatists a master in the interpretation of whose works he may show what the classics have taught him.

FREDERIK VAN EEDEN.

(POLAND)

There is, somehow, a mysterious sort of union between all the theatres of the civilized world. Inwardly and outwardly, something seems to connect their activities and to lead them towards a new and common growth. There is no city in the world where the outcome of this subtle and mystic force—all the new methods and ideas in playwriting, acting and production—can be so freely displayed and experimented with as in New York. Here these tendencies can all meet and cross and struggle and fuse, sure of a sincere, interested audience. The last few seasons in New York have plainly manifested a real progress in the choice of plays and in the form of their presentation. Eagerness, energy and ultimately discrimination; a demand for a certain standard, and an exciting quality in plays and in their theatrical frame—these qualities predominate today. It is at a most fortunate moment that Reinhardt enters the American theatre. Our audiences and managers are perhaps better able to appreciate his genius now than at any other time in the history of the American theatre; and his influence will be exercised in many ways. If the faculty to absorb the meaning of a play completely, and the power to project this meaning vividly and luminously, is the art of the theatre, Max Reinhardt is the epitome of that art. He grasps all the means at hand. He focuses and fuses all the instruments of the theatre towards an ultimate harmony. He permits no waste of energy or material. Every step of labor advances to a contemplated goal. The theatre of Max Reinhardt is the theatre in all its completeness, with all its colors, all its music, all its movements.

RICHARD ORDYNSKI.

(RUSSIA)

In Reinhardt's productions the spectator is placed in a direct contact with the performers, and this causes him to be drawn into the atmosphere of the play. The union is effected in two forms: first, by leaving the spectator in the position of a mere observer, which is the main form, and second, by bringing him almost to the verge of acting. When merely observing the action of the play, Reinhardt's spectator can be likened to a member of a crowd watching a street accident. As in the latter case, he is clearly conscious of opposition between himself and the actual heroes of the scene observed. But whereas in the street crowd the onlooker is face to face with real life, in a Reinhardt performance the world of the play remains imaginary, whilst the spectator is transformed into a member of a real crowd living in that world and witnessing

[337]

the events there proceeding. The effect of unity in this case is, therefore, based not so much on an illusion of reality of the play enacted, as, if I may say so, on an illusion of "reality of onlooking." This circumstance serves to explain the use of the second means employed by Reinhardt in bridging the actors and the audience. The reality of his being an onlooker in a crowd is brought to the mind of the spectator by the scenic transformation of the auditorium into a part of the general setting. After what had been said before on the significance of various perceptions of space, there will be no difficulty in understanding the suggestive power which both these means bring to bear on the spectator. Thus, the first element in the impression of unity is contributed by the fused masses of spectators in the amphitheatre. The latter element of architectural unity with the Arena, made manifest by the setting, supplies another link. On the other hand, the detached figures of the performers, together with the marked forms of the architectural scenery both in the arena and the auditorium, qualify the elements of unity as those operating within a realistic, i. e., objectively present and inwardly discontinuous world. The latter element, however, is apt to lose much of its restrictive force in the case of those scenes in which the Arena itself becomes crowded with performers. The continuity of the amphitheatre is then extended from end to end of the theatrical building, and the audience, drawn into the whirl of action in the Arena, is lifted, so to speak, to the state of potential actors, which brings the performance almost to the verge of the theatre of action. That this limit is never crossed in Reinhardt's productions, as it was in the early period of the Greek orchestra, and that the potential actor fails to convert his worked up energy into a kinetic action, is entirely due to the inner contradiction of Reinhardt's method, which is hidden in its substitution of make-believe emotionalism for the religious actuality characteristic of the true theatre of action.

ALEXANDER BAKSHY,
"Living Space and the Theatre."

[338]

AN INTERNATIONAL SYMPOSIUM ON REINHARDT

(The United States)

The essence of this man's work is not to be sought in his revolving stages, his tiny or gigantic playhouses, or even in the unexampled wealth of great dramatic literature which he persuaded his public to accept. His secret is his inner and initial conception of his task; his triumph is in the lonely hours of contemplation before his vision was transferred to the theatre.

What was the character of the vision that came to him? It was a vision of the play's soul, of its innermost nature in terms of images and sounds. What came to him was the play's intimate "style," its inner music, its inevitable rhythm of tune and color. The sudden vision revealed to him how, in this special instance, the "intensity of nature" could be equaled—the intensity of the play's own interpretation of nature, be it observed. For Reinhardt's imagination is synthetic, not analytic.

Ludwig Lewisohn,
"The Drama and the Stage."

There is at least one level head in Europe, and it sits on the shoulders of one Max Reinhardt of the Deutsches Theater, Berlin. He has swallowed Craig, but he has digested him. He knows just how far to go with him. He knows where to end with realism and begin with Craig, and where to dismiss Craig and revert to realism. To my mind, Reinhardt does more to assist and less to impede the author than any living producer. If he wants a great scenic effect, he is careful to place it in such a way that it is not going to kill the lines. He makes his effects belong. They are not dragged in. They are not glaringly apparent. A little of Craig goes a long way, and Reinhardt knows how to use him.

Arthur Hopkins.

APPENDIX II

III

MEMORIAL

At its tenth meeting on May 29, 1921, with Ferdinand Gregori as its chairman, the Association of Artistic Stage Directors unanimously nominated Max Reinhardt its honorary president. By this resolution, we fulfil the demand of the hour, in assuring this unique man, who is just about to resign from certain official positions, that the gratitude for his work will always live in the hearts of all those aspiring to similar ideals.

MAX REINHARDT

A landmark visible from afar on the road of theatrical history, at its turn from a one-sided literary management of the stage to one essentially dramatic, from one hemmed in by historic considerations to one which heeds solely the artist's conceptions, unbounded by time; discoverer of innumerable secrets among the apparently exhausted treasures of classical world literature, and patron of many contemporary talents, authors as well as actors; ingenious executor of his visions by the most complete mastery over all stage expedients: of man in ecstasy and in sorrow, of light, of color, of form; finder of lost paths and builder of new ones in the manifold uses of perspective; faithful guardian of former achievements of dramatic art and indefatigable creator of new and fertile possibilities in enabling stagecraft to rely on its own resources; strengthener and expander of the field of "stage-management" and thus enhancer of our professional standing which, through him at last, has been brought home to the mind of the general public.

Composed by FERDINAND GREGORI,
By order of the Association of Artistic Stage Directors.

[340]

IV

A SHEAF OF LETTERS ON REINHARDT'S FIFTIETH BIRTHDAY

50 BARERSTRASSE,
MUNICH, September 6, 1923.

Dear Max Reinhardt:

I am told that, on the day after tomorrow, you too, dear friend, will enter upon the fifties, and thus pass the threshold of the age in which we have to remind ourselves every morning that we are "still" young. This "still" tastes rather bitter, and I who talk from experience desire to express to you my most heartfelt sympathy.

Although the laziest of all letter writers, I do not wish to let this opportunity pass without telling you that my acquaintance with you has been among the most treasured that have fallen to my lot. In this spirit, though only from a distance, I have taken interest in your life, which seemed from the start like a fairy-tale, and appears almost like a myth today. And I have watched your tireless personality push its way upward with the same vital force that made it grow broader. I may even tell you that what Fate brings you is as close to me as if it were a part of my own life.

It is time to stop, else I might become sentimental, which is not my nature, mine still less than yours who also know how to protect yourself against that mistake. I simply wished you to know the emotions with which I think of you on your fiftieth birthday.

My wife shares my heartiest congratulations for you, and we both send you our greeting in old, faithful friendship.

Always yours,

HERMAN BAHR.

[341]

APPENDIX II

To Max Reinhardt:

On your fiftieth birthday, I send you, as the pioneer of the new German drama, my heartiest congratulations.

PRESIDENT EBERT.

AGNETENDORF,
September 11, 1923.

Dear Max Reinhardt:

The very heartiest congratulations on your anniversary from myself and family. You have stirred up the Germany of yesterday by a storm of beauty and a whirl of magic, which will live in the memories of all those who have experienced it. Take many greetings in friendship!

GERHART HAUPTMANN.

THE MINISTER OF ARTS

Office of the Secretary of the Interior

6 KOENIGSPLATZ,
BERLIN, N. W. 40,
September 9, 1923.

Much Esteemed Professor Max Reinhardt:

I desire to tell you that I am taking part in the celebration of your fiftieth birthday with veneration and gratitude. It is to your art that I, with a great number of friends and colleagues, owe the first decisive impressions, when, as young artists and critics, we witnessed Maeterlinck, Shakespeare and "Oedipus" from the top gallery of the Deutsches Theater. Unswervingly and with ever increasing force you made your way, and whenever we ourselves reached out farther in our thoughts and plans, we often found that you gave us the very thing for which we were still striving.

LETTERS ON REINHARDTS FIFTIETH BIRTHDAY

This explains the gratitude, in others perhaps the grudge, with which you meet again and again.

At this present moment, new and vital developments seem to be on foot once more. I must come to this conclusion when I see how many of those who represent the best in our generation, you have won for your work: Poelzig, with his whirlwind-like ingenuity, and many another, down to Pillartz with his cheerful self-reliance, and Hartung with the manly forcefulness of the craftsman.

Though I had only once the pleasure of meeting you, fifteen years ago at a performance of "A Winter's Tale," I feel that I wish to grasp your hand and give expression to my veneration for you.

Yours very truly,
EDWIN REDSLOB.

ASSOCIATION OF ARTISTIC STAGE DIRECTORS

(Editorial Office of the "Scene")

24 Kronprinzenufer,
BERLIN, N. W. 40,
September, 7, 1923.

Dear Professor Reinhardt:

Our organization is happy to have an opportunity again to pay homage to its honorary president. I am sorry to say that, on account of the general unfortunate conditions of our times, the August number of the "Scene," which is dedicated to your anniversary, did not appear and could not reach you on time. For this, I need not stammer a lengthy apology, as irregularity has become the rule of the day. Since you yielded to our request to become the honorary president of our organization, you have not been able to do anything for us directly; but indirectly, quietly, you are, of course, continuously at work for our cause. Every one of your achievements, every one of your successes, is, at the same time, an accomplishment of our profession, a success of the theatre as a whole.

I well remember the first years of our common work in Berlin. It was not vanity and self-glory which urged you to make trial of yourself as a manager. But you realized the inefficiency of the staging and scenic settings of classic plays as they emerged under the hand of Otto Brahm. Unworthy of the great writers, of the excellent ensemble, and of the audience —no milder judgment can be passed on them—were these performances of "Kabale und Liebe" ("Love and Intrigue"), "Don Carlos," "The Robbers," "Faust," "Käthchen," "Weh dem der Lügt" ("Woe to the Liar"), "The Jewess of Toledo," "Romeo," and "Henry the Fourth." From year to year, the whole repertory became narrower, from a literary as well as a dramatic point of view. What did Brahm know of the forceful vitality of the spoken word, what of the creative atmosphere in which a stage manager can and should live? With him, nothing was clear and bright, striking and dashing.

You made an end of all that—you gave the art of the stage many new ambitions, and led it to many victories. It is unnecessary to report on them, one after the other, because we all live within the circle of your achievements. And all the capricious attempts to undermine your work were defeated or disappeared in the sand. Besides giving to the stage manager the first place among the dramatic artists, you have helped the actor, too, to win back rights for which he had fought passionately. And finally, you have wedded the spirit of the drama— of whatever epoch—to your spirit and the spirit of your time. For those who stayed away from performances of classical dramas, or went only because they considered it their duty, you transformed that empty duty into a series of festivals.

As a rule, the technical expedients of which you made use and perfected, have been overvalued. Then, too, your love for the wonderful individuality of the word, the syllable, the sound, the punctuation, has been overrated. We are proud to know what you are, however, and we therefore feel called upon before anyone else to wish you good luck and blessing for the next decades (and quarters of centuries) of your life. That will also mean good luck and a blessing for us.

I, personally, with my wife and daughter, send you cordial greetings, and wish to report a little personal incident, an omen of joy for you and me: the rose plant which was part of the flower arrangement you sent me for my fiftieth birthday, is in full bloom.

As a representative of our organization, and with personal veneration,

FERDINAND GREGORI.

P.S.: The enclosed leaf was meant to be an artistic diploma, which, like so many good intentions, could not be executed.

APPENDIX III

CHRONOLOGY OF REINHARDT PRODUCTIONS

FIRST SEASON 1902–1903

Serenissimus, by Leo Feld, Kleines Theater, Berlin, September 25, 1902

There Are Crimes and Crimes, by August Strindberg, Kleines Theater, Berlin, October 13, 1902

Ackermann, by Felix Hollaender and Lothar Schmidt, Kleines Theater, October 29, 1902

Salome, by Oscar Wilde, and *The Importance of Being Earnest,* by Oscar Wilde, Kleines Theater, Berlin, November 15, 1902

Erdgeist ("The Spirit of the Earth"), by Frank Wedekind, Kleines Theater, Berlin, December 17, 1902

The Lower Depths, by Maxim Gorky, Kleines Theater, Berlin, January 23, 1903

Die Lokalbahn ("The County Railroad"), by Ludwig Thoma, Neues Theater, Berlin, February 25, 1903

Die Kreuzelschreiber ("Those Who Sign with a Cross"), by Ludwig Anzengruber, Neues Theater, Berlin, March 19, 1903

Pelléas et Mélisande, by Maurice Maeterlinck, Neues Theater, Berlin, April 3, 1903

SECOND SEASON 1903–1904

Doppelselbstmord ("Double Suicide"), by Ludwig Anzengruber, Neues Theater, Berlin, August 25, 1903

A Woman of No Importance, by Oscar Wilde, Neues Theater, Berlin, September 4, 1903

[346]

CHRONOLOGY OF REINHARDT PRODUCTIONS

Der Kammersänger ("The Tenor"), by Frank Wedekind, Neues Theater, Berlin, September 30, 1903

Les Corbeaux ("The Vultures"), by Henri Becque, Kleines Theater, Berlin, October 16, 1903

Elektra, by Hugo von Hofmannsthal, Kleines Theater, Berlin, October 30, 1903

Le Cœur a ses Raisons ("The Logic of the Heart"), by Robert de Flers and G. A. de Caillavet, Neues Theater, Berlin, November 24, 1903

So ist das Leben ("Such is Life"), by Frank Wedekind, Neues Theater, Berlin, November 27, 1903

The Fruits of Enlightenment, by Lyoff Tolstoy, Neues Theater, Berlin, December 9, 1903

Der Strom ("The Stream"), by Max Halbe, Neues Theater, Berlin, December 19, 1903

Unter sich ("Among Themselves"), by Hermann Bahr, Kleines Theater, Berlin, December 31, 1903

Minna von Barnhelm, by Gotthold Ephraim Lessing, Neues Theater, Berlin, January 14, 1904

Die Doppelgänger-Komödie ("The Comedy of the Double"), by Adolf Paul, Kleines Theater, Berlin, January 16, 1904

The Man of Destiny, by George Bernard Shaw, Kleines Theater, Berlin, February 10, 1904

Sœur Béatrice ("Sister Beatrice"), by Maurice Maeterlinck, Neues Theater, Berlin, February 10, 1904

Medea, by Euripides, Neues Theater, Berlin, February 19, 1904

Mutter Landstrasse ("Mother Highroad"), by Wilhelm Schmidt-bonn, Kleines Theater, Berlin, February 27, 1904

Candida, by George Bernard Shaw, Neues Theater, Berlin, March 3, 1904

Des Pastor's Rieke ("The Pastor's Rieke"), by Erich Schlaikjer, Kleines Theater, Berlin, March 12, 1904

Königsrecht ("A King's Right"), by W. A. Paap, Neues Theater, Berlin, March 19, 1904

APPENDIX III

Martyrer ("Martyrs"), by Georg Reicke, Kleines Theater, Berlin, April 6, 1904

Koketterie ("Flirtation"), by Raoul Auernheimer, Neues Theater, Berlin, April 12, 1904

Kabale und Liebe ("Love and Intrigue"), by Friedrich von Schiller, Neues Theater, Berlin, April 22, 1904

Miss Julia, by August Strindberg, Kleines Theater, Berlin, May 10, 1904

Einen Jux will er sich machen ("He Wants to Play a Joke"), by Johann Nestroy, Neues Theater, Berlin, May 18, 1904

THIRD SEASON 1904–1905

The Pretenders, by Henrik Ibsen, Neues Theater, Berlin, October 7, 1904

The Merry Wives of Windsor, by Shakespeare, Neues Theater, Berlin, October 21, 1904

Die Morgenröte ("The Dawn"), by Josef Ruederer, Neues Theater, November 15, 1904

Der grüne Kakadu ("The Green Cockatoo"), by Arthur Schnitzler, Kleines Theater, November 22, 1904

Der tapfere Cassian ("Gallant Cassian"), by Arthur Schnitzler, Neues Theater, Berlin, November 22, 1904

The Quiet Rooms, by Sven Lange, Kleines Theater, Berlin, December 8, 1904

Der Graf von Charolais ("The Count of Charolais"), by Richard Beer-Hofmann, Neues Theater, December 23, 1904

The Newly Married Couple, by Björnsterne Björnson, Kleines Theater, December 30, 1904

Abschiedssouper ("A Farewell Supper"), by Arthur Schnitzler, Kleines Theater, Berlin, December 31, 1904

A Midsummer Night's Dream, by Shakespeare, Neues Theater, Berlin, January 31, 1905

[348]

CHRONOLOGY OF REINHARDT PRODUCTIONS

Angele, by Otto Erich Hartleben, and *Abschied vom Regiment* ("Leaving the Regiment"), by Otto Erich Hartleben, Kleines Theater, Berlin, February 4, 1905

A Bear, by Anton Tchehoff, Kleines Theater, Berlin, February 12, 1905

Sanna, by Hermann Bahr, Kleines Theater, Berlin, March 10, 1905

Meta Konegen, by Hermann Stehr, Neues Theater, Berlin, March 31, 1905

Vater Riekemann ("Father Riekemann"), by Karl Strecker, Kleines Theater, Berlin, April 7, 1905

Rosmersholm, by Henrik Ibsen, Kleines Theater, Berlin, April 28, 1905

FOURTH SEASON 1905–1906

Das Käthchen von Heilbronn ("Käthchen of Heilbronn"), by Heinrich von Kleist, Deutsches Theater, Berlin, October 19, 1905

The Merchant of Venice, by Shakespeare, Deutsches Theater, Berlin, November 9, 1905

Amants ("Lovers"), by Maurice Donnay, Neues Theater, Berlin, December 30, 1905

A Florentine Tragedy, by Oscar Wilde, *The Well of the Saints,* by John Millington Synge, and *Le Commissaire est Bon Enfant* ("The Commissioner"), by Georges Courteline, Deutsches Theater, Berlin, January 12, 1906

Oedipus und die Sphinx ("Oedipus and the Sphinx"), by Hugo von Hofmannsthal, Deutsches Theater, Berlin, February 2, 1906

Boubouroche, by Georges Courteline, Neues Theater, Berlin, March 16, 1906

Cæsar and Cleopatra, by George Bernard Shaw, Neues Theater, Berlin, March 31, 1906

[349]

APPENDIX III

Tartuffe, by Molière, and *Die Mitschuldigen* ("The Accomplices"), by Johann Wolfgang von Goethe, Deutsches Theater, Berlin, April 25, 1906

Orphée aux Enfer ("Orpheus in the Underworld"), by Jacques Offenbach, Neues Theater, Berlin, May 11, 1906

FIFTH SEASON 1906–1907

A Winter's Tale, by Shakespeare, Deutsches Theater, Berlin, September 15, 1906

Der Liebeskönig ("The Love King"), by Leo Greiner, Deutsches Theater, Berlin, October 17, 1906

Ghosts, by Henrik Ibsen, Kammerspiele, Berlin, November 8, 1906

Frühlingserwachen ("The Awakening of Spring"), by Frank Wedekind, Kammerspiele, Berlin, November 20, 1906

Man and Superman, by George Bernard Shaw, Kammerspiele, Berlin, December 6, 1906

Ringelspiel ("The Merry-go-round"), by Hermann Bahr, Deutsches Theater, Berlin, December 20, 1906

Die Geschwister ("Brothers and Sisters"), by Goethe, Deutsches Theater, Berlin, January 4, 1907

Das Friedensfest ("The Coming of Peace"), by Gerhart Hauptmann, Kammerspiele, Berlin, January 7, 1907

Romeo and Juliet, by Shakespeare, Deutsches Theater, Berlin, January 29, 1907

The Inspector General, by Nikolai Gogol, Deutsches Theater, Berlin, March 8, 1907

Hedda Gabler, by Henrik Ibsen, Kammerspiele, Berlin, March 11, 1907

The God of Vengeance, by Sholom Ash, Deutsches Theater, Berlin, March 19, 1907

Love's Comedy, by Henrik Ibsen, Kammerspiele, Berlin, March 25, 1907

CHRONOLOGY OF REINHARDT PRODUCTIONS

Aglavaine et Sélysette, by Maurice Maeterlinck, Kammerspiele, Berlin, April 15, 1907

Robert und Bertram, by Gustav Raeder, Deutsches Theater, Berlin, April 25, 1907

Gyges und sein Ring ("Gyges and His Ring"), by Friedrich Hebbel, Kammerspiele, Berlin, May 2, 1907

Sixth Season 1907–1908

Prinz Friedrich von Homburg ("The Prince of Homburg"), by Heinrich von Kleist, Deutsches Theater, Berlin, September 14, 1907

Liebelei ("Light o' Love"), by Arthur Schnitzler, Kammerspiele, Berlin, September 19, 1907

Twelfth Night, by Shakespeare, Deutsches Theater, Berlin, October 17, 1907

Esther, by Franz Grillparzer, and *The Servant of Two Masters,* by Carlo Goldoni, Kammerspiele, Berlin, October 26, 1907

Marquis von Keith ("The Marquis of Keith"), by Frank Wedekind, Kammerspiele, Berlin, November 9, 1907

Der Arzt seiner Ehre ("The Physician of His Honor"), by Calderon-Presber, Deutsches Theater, Berlin, December 2, 1907

Catharina Gräfin von Armagnac und ihre beiden Liebhaber ("Catherine, Countess of Armagnac and her two Lovers"), by Karl Vollmoeller, Kammerspiele, Berlin, December 9, 1907

Die Räuber ("The Robbers"), by Schiller, Deutsches Theater, Berlin, January 10, 1908

Hochzeit ("Wedding"), by Emil Strauss, Kammerspiele, Berlin, January 23, 1908

Lysistrata, by Aristophanes-Greiner, Kammerspiele, Berlin, February 27, 1908

[351]

APPENDIX III

Der Kompagnon ("The Partner"), by Adolph L'Arronge, Deutsches Theater, Berlin, March 7, 1908

Der Tor und der Tod ("Death and the Fool"), by Hugo von Hofsmannthal, and *Nju*, by Ossip Dymow, Kammerspiele, Berlin, March 30, 1908

Ulrich, Fürst von Waldeck ("Ulrich, Prince of Waldeck"), by Herbert Eulenberg, Deutsches Theater, Berlin, May 16, 1908

SEVENTH SEASON 1908–1909

Des Meeres und der Liebe Wellen ("The Waves of the Ocean and of Love"), by Franz Grillparzer, Deutsches Theater, Berlin, August 8, 1908

Medea, by Franz Grillparzer, Deutsches Theater, Berlin, August 28, 1908

Sozialaristokraten ("Social Aristocrats"), by Arno Holz, Kammerspiele, Berlin, September 4, 1908

Links of a Chain, by Herman Heijermans, Deutsches Theater, Berlin, September 9, 1908

Terakoya, by Takeda Izumo, and *Kimiko*, by Wolfgang von Gersdorf, Kammerspiele, Berlin, September 14, 1908

King Lear, by Shakespeare, Deutsches Theater, Berlin, September 16, 1908

Clavigo, by Goethe, Kammerspiele, Berlin, October 16, 1908

Die Verschwörung des Fiesco zu Genua ("Fiesco or The Genoese Conspiracy"), by Schiller, Deutsches Theater, Berlin, October 21, 1908

The Wedding, by Nikolai Gogol, Kammerspiele, Berlin, October 30, 1908

Revolution in Krähwinkel, by Johann Nestroy, Deutsches Theater, Berlin, November 14, 1908

The Doctor's Dilemma, by George Bernard Shaw, Kammerspiele, Berlin, November 21, 1908

Niemand weiss es ("No One Knows"), by Theodor Wolff, Kammerspiele, Berlin, December 5, 1908

ORFEUS

OFFENBACH'S "ORPHEUS IN THE UNDERWORLD"

COPENHAGEN, FEBRUARY, 1921

A Costume Plate for Orpheus by Max Rée

OFFENBACH'S "ORPHEUS IN THE UNDERWORLD"

COPENHAGEN, FEBRUARY, 1921

A Costume Plate for Diana by Max Rée

CHRONOLOGY OF REINHARDT PRODUCTIONS

Der Graf von Gleichen ("The Count of Gleichen"), by Wilhelm Schmidtbonn, Kammerspiele, Berlin, December 22, 1908

Die Lehrerin ("The Teacher"), by Alexander Brody, Deutsches Theater, Berlin, January 29, 1909

Faust I, by Goethe, Deutsches Theater, Berlin, March 25, 1909

Wolkenkuckucksheim, by Josef Ruederer, Kammerspiele, Berlin, April 25, 1909

Der unverstandene Mann ("The Man who Found no Sympathy"), by E. von Wolzogen, Kammerspiele, Berlin, May 4, 1909

Hamlet, by Shakespeare, Budapest, May, 1909

Twelfth Night, by Shakespeare, Budapest, May, 1909

The Doctor's Dilemma, by George Bernard Shaw, Budapest, May, 1909

Revolution in Krähwinkel, by Johann Nestroy, Budapest, May, 1909

Lysistrata, by Aristophanes, Breslau, May, 1909

Revolution in Krähwinkel, by Johann Nestroy, Breslau, May, 1909

Hamlet, by Shakespeare, Künstler Theater, Munich, June-July, 1909

A Midsummer Night's Dream, by Shakespeare, Künstler Theater, Munich, June-July, 1909

Faust I, by Goethe, Künstler Theater, Munich, June-July, 1909

Twelfth Night, by Shakespeare, Künstler Theater, Munich, June-July, 1909

Die Räuber ("The Robbers"), by Schiller, Künstler Theater, Munich, June-July, 1909

Die Räuber ("The Robbers"), by Schiller, Frankfort-on-Main, July, 1909

Lysistrata, by Aristophanes, Frankfort-on-Main, July, 1909

Twelfth Night, by Shakespeare, Frankfort-on-Main, July, 1909

[353]

APPENDIX III

Le Refuge ("The Refuge"), by Dario Nicodémi, Kammerspiele, Berlin, October 8, 1909

Hamlet, by Shakespeare, Deutsches Theater, Berlin, October 16, 1909

Major Barbara, by George Bernard Shaw, Kammerspiele, Berlin, November 5, 1909

Don Carlos, by Schiller, Deutsches Theater, Berlin, November 10, 1909

The Home, by Octave Mirbeau and Thadé Natanson, Kammerspiele, Berlin, December 9, 1909

The Taming of the Shrew, by Shakespeare, Deutsches Theater, Berlin, December 15, 1909

Le bon Roi Dagobert ("Good King Dagobert"), by André Rivoire and Felix Salten, Deutsches Theater, Berlin, January 19, 1910

Der natürliche Vater ("The Natural Father"), by Herbert Eulenberg, Kammerspiele, Berlin, January 21, 1910

Cristinas Heimreise ("Cristina's Homecoming"), by Hugo von Hofmannsthal, Deutsches Theater, Berlin, February 11, 1910

Judith, by Friedrich Hebbel, Deutsches Theater, Berlin, February 25, 1910

Hilfe ein Kind ist vom Himmel gefallen ("Help, a Child has Fallen from Heaven"), by Wilhelm Schmidtbonn, Kammerspiele, Berlin, February 28, 1910

Gawân, by Eduard Stucken, Kammerspiele, Berlin, March 30, 1910

Die Braut von Messina ("The Bride of Messina"), by Schiller, Deutsches Theater, Berlin, April 12, 1910

Sumurûn, by Friedrich Freksa and Victor Hollaender, Kammerspiele, Berlin, April 22, 1910

The Taming of the Shrew, by Shakespeare, Budapest, May, 1910

CHRONOLOGY OF REINHARDT PRODUCTIONS

Le bon Roi Dagobert ("Good King Dagobert"), by André Rivoire and Felix Salten, Budapest, May, 1910

Judith, by Friedrich Hebbel, Budapest, May, 1910

Ghosts, by Henrik Ibsen, Budapest, May, 1910

A Winter's Tale, by Shakespeare, Budapest, May, 1910

Cristinas Heimreise ("Cristina's Homecoming"), by Hugo von Hofmannsthal, Budapest, May, 1910

A Midsummer Night's Dream, by Shakespeare, Vienna, May, 1910

Minna von Barnhelm, by Lessing, Vienna, May, 1910

Sanna, by Hermann Bahr, Vienna, May, 1910

Der Graf von Charolais ("The Count of Charolais"), by Richard Beer-Hofmann, Vienna, May, 1910

Cristinas Heimreise ("Cristina's Homecoming"), by Hugo von Hofmannsthal, Vienna, May, 1910

The Merchant of Venice, by Shakespeare, Vienna, May, 1910

Sumurûn, by Friedrich Freksa and Victor Hoellander, Vienna, May, 1910

Hamlet, by Shakespeare, Vienna, May, 1910

Twelfth Night, by Shakespeare, Vienna, May, 1910

Lysistrata, by Aristophanes, Vienna, May, 1910

Die Räuber ("The Robbers"), by Schiller, Vienna, May, 1910

Judith, by Friedrich Hebbel, Vienna, May, 1910

The Merchant of Venice, by Shakespeare, Munich, June-August, 1910

A Midsummer Night's Dream, by Shakespeare, Munich, June-August, 1910

A Winter's Tale, by Shakespeare, Munich, June-August, 1910

Twelfth Night, by Shakespeare, Munich, June-August, 1910

Lysistrata, by Aristophanes, Munich, June-August, 1910

Minna von Barnhelm, by Lessing, Munich, June-August, 1910

NINTH SEASON 1910–1911

Samson and Delilah, by Sven Lange, Deutsches Theater, Berlin, August 19, 1910

APPENDIX III

Amphitryon, by Heinrich von Kleist, Deutsches Theater, Berlin, September 5, 1910

The Last, by Maxim Gorky, Kammerspiele, Berlin, September 6, 1910

Les Romanesques, by Edmond Rostand, Deutsches Theater, Berlin, September 21, 1910

Le Cloître ("The Cloister"), by Emile Verhaeren, Kammerspiele, Berlin, September 23, 1910

Le Mariage Forcé ("The Forced Marriage"), by Molière, and *The Comedy of Errors,* by Shakespeare, Kammerspiele, Berlin, October 7, 1910

Herr und Diener ("Master and Servant"), by Ludwig Fulda, Deutsches Theater, Berlin, October 29, 1910

Œdipus Rex, by Sophocles, Vienna, October, 1910

Œdipus Rex, by Sophocles, Budapest, with Hungarian players, October, 1910

Œdipus Rex, by Sophocles, Zirkus Schumann, Berlin, November 7, 1910

L 'Oiseau Blessé ("The Wounded Bird"), by Maurice Donnay, Kammerspiele, Berlin, November 18, 1910

Un Ange ("An Angel"), by Alfred Capus, Kammerspiele, Berlin, December 8, 1910

Othello, by Shakespeare, Deutsches Theater, Berlin, December 10, 1910

Lumpacivagabundus ("The Jolly Vagabonds"), by Johann Nestroy, Deutsches Theater, Berlin, December 31, 1910

Lanzelot, by Eduard Stucken, Kammerspiele, Berlin, January 3, 1911

Der Rosenkavalier, by Richard Strauss and Hugo von Hofmannsthal, World Premiere, Dresden, January, 1911

Sumurûn, by Friedrich Freksa and Victor Hollaender, Coliseum, London, January 30, 1911

Der Schatz ("The Treasure"), by David Pinski, Deutsches Theater, Berlin, February 2, 1911

Faust, II, by Goethe, Deutsches Theater, Berlin, February 7, 1911

CHRONOLOGY OF REINHARDT PRODUCTIONS

Der Riese ("The Giant"), by Carl Sternheim, Kammerspiele, Berlin, February 15, 1911

Die Königin ("The Queen"), by Theodor Wolff, Kammerspiele, Berlin, March 29, 1911

Bankban, by Josef Katona, Deutsches Theater, May 24, 1911

La Belle Helene, by Jacques Offenbach, Künstler Theatre, Munich, July, 1911

TENTH SEASON 1911–1912

Der fette Cæsar ("The Fat Cæsar"), by Friedrich Freksa, Deutsches Theater, Berlin, August 26, 1911

Lanvâl, by Eduard Stucken, Kammerspiele, Berlin, September 9, 1911

Penthesilea, by Heinrich von Kleist, Deutsches Theater, Berlin, September 23, 1911

Vertauschte Seelen ("Souls Exchanged"), by Wilhelm Scholz, Kammerspiele, Berlin, October 5, 1911

Nathan der Weise ("Nathan the Wise"), by Lessing, Kammerspiele, Berlin, October 9, 1911

The Oresteia, by Aeschylus, Zirkus Schumann, Berlin, October 13, 1911

Turandot, by Carlo Gozzi and Karl Vollmoeller, Deutsches Theater, Berlin, October 27, 1911

Die Kassette ("The Small Box"), by Carl Sternheim, Deutsches Theater, Berlin, November 24, 1911

Everyman, adapted by Hugo von Hofmannsthal, Zirkus Schumann, Berlin, December 1, 1911

Offiziere ("Officers"), by Fritz von Unruh, Deutsches Theater, Berlin, December 15, 1911

Das Mirakel ("The Miracle"), by Karl Vollmoeller and Engelbert Humperdinck, London, December 23, 1911

Der Zorn des Achilles ("The Wrath of Achilles"), by Wilhelm Schmidtbonn, Deutsches Theater, Berlin, January 13, 1912

[357]

APPENDIX III

Œdipus Rex, by Sophocles, Covent Garden, London, with Martin Harvey and English players, January 15, 1912

Sumurûn, by Friedrich Freksa and Victor Hollaender, Casino Theatre, New York, with American and German players, January 16, 1912

A Happy Marriage, by Peter Nansen, Kammerspiele, Berlin, January 20, 1912

Much Ado About Nothing, by Shakespeare, Deutsches Theater, Berlin, January 23, 1912

Œdipus Rex, by Sophocles, Petrograd, Moscow, Riga, Warsaw, Kieff, Odessa, and Stockholm, Winter, 1912

J'en ai Plein le dos de Margot ("I'm Fed Up with Margot"), by Georges Courteline and Pierre Wolff, and *Pierrots letztes Abenteuer* ("Pierrot's Last Adventure"), by Victor Arnold, Kammerspiele, Berlin, March 19, 1912

Der Feind und der Bruder ("Enemy and Brother"), by Moritz Heimann, Kammerspiele, Berlin, March 26, 1912

George Dandin, by Molière, Deutsches Theater, Berlin, April 13, 1912

Mon Ami Teddy ("My Friend Teddy"), by André Rivoire and L. Besnard, Kammerspiele, Berlin, May 7, 1912

Everyman, adapted by Hugo von Hofmannsthal, Frankfort-on-Main, May, 1912

Hidalla, by Frank Wedekind, Deutsches Theater, Berlin, June 4, 1912

Musik ("Music"), by Frank Wedekind, Deutsches Theater, Berlin, June 7, 1912

Oaha, by Frank Wedekind, Deutsches Theater, Berlin, June 12, 1912

Marquis von Keith ("The Marquis of Keith"), by Frank Wedekind, Deutsches Theater, Berlin, June 15, 1912

The Oresteia, by Aeschylus, Austellungs Halle, Munich, August, 1912

Orphée aux Enfer ("Orpheus in the Underworld"), by Jacques Offenbach, Austellungs Halle, Munich, August, 1912

CHRONOLOGY OF REINHARDT PRODUCTIONS

Don Juan, by Carl Sternheim, Deutsches Theater, Berlin, September 13, 1912

The Dance of Death, by August Strindberg, Deutsches Theater, Berlin, September 27, 1912

Das Mirakel ("The Miracle"), by Karl Vollmoeller and Engelbert Humperdinck, Vienna, September, 1912

King Henry IV (Part 1), by Shakespeare, Deutsches Theater, Berlin, October 12, 1912

King Henry IV (Part 2), by Shakespeare, Deutsches Theater, Berlin, October 18, 1912

Ariadne auf Naxos, by Richard Strauss and Hugo von Hofmannsthal, Stuttgart, October, 1912

Venetianische Nacht ("Venetian Night"), by Karl Vollmoeller, Palace Theatre, London, November 11, 1912

Maria Magdalena, by Friedrich Hebbel, Kammerspiele, Berlin, November 12, 1912

L'Oiseau Bleu ("The Blue Bird"), by Maurice Maeterlinck, Deutsches Theater, Berlin, November 23, 1912

Sumurûn, by Friedrich Freksa and Victor Hollaender, revived in London, Winter, 1912

Everyman, adapted by Hugo von Hofmannsthal, Budapest, Winter, 1912

Turandot, by Carlo Gozzi and Karl Vollmoeller, Budapest, Winter, 1912

Gyges und sein Ring ("Gyges and his Ring"), by Friedrich Hebbel, Budapest, Winter, 1912

Fiorenza, by Thomas Mann, Kammerspiele, Berlin, January 3, 1913

Les Belles Femmes ("Beautiful Women"), by Etienne Rey, Kammerspiele, Berlin, January 17, 1913

Astrid, by Eduard Stucken, Deutsches Theater, Berlin, January 24, 1913

The Living Corpse, by Lyoff Tolstoy, Deutsches Theater, Berlin, February 7, 1913

[359]

APPENDIX III

Bürger Schippel ("Citizen Schippel"), by Carl Sternheim, Kammerspiele, Berlin, March 5, 1913

La Prise de Berg-op-Zoom ("The Conquest of Berg-op-Zoom"), by Sacha Guitry, Kammerspiele, Berlin, April 4, 1913

The League of the Weak, by Sholom Ash, Kammerspiele, Berlin, May 8, 1913

The Living Corpse, by Lyoff Tolstoy, Prague, May, 1913

Kaiserliche Hoheit ("His Imperial Highness"), by Simon Mees, Kammerspiele, Berlin, June 4, 1913

Sumurûn, by Friedrich Freksa and Victor Hollaender, revived in London, May-June, 1913

Jahrhundertfestspiel 1813 ("The Centenary Festival 1813"), by Gerhart Hauptmann, Breslau, Summer, 1913

Twelfth Season 1913–1914

Venetianische Nacht ("Venetian Night"), by Karl Vollmoeller, and *The Stronger,* by August Strindberg, Kammerspiele, Berlin, August 29, 1913

Franziska, by Frank Wedekind, Kammerspiele, Berlin, September 5, 1913

Das Mirakel ("The Miracle"), by Karl Vollmoeller and Engelbert Humperdinck, Leipzig and Dresden, September, 1913

Musik ("Music"), by Frank Wedekind, Dresden, September, 1913

Ghosts, by Henrik Ibsen, Dresden, September, 1913

L 'Habit Vert ("The Green Coat"), by R. de Flers and G. A. de Caillavet, Kammerspiele, Berlin, October 1, 1913

Der Verlorene Sohn ("The Prodigal Son"), by Wilhelm Schmidtbonn, Kammerspiele, Berlin, October 24, 1913

Emilia Galotti, by Lessing, Kammerspiele, Berlin, October 31, 1913

Das Mirakel ("The Miracle"), by Karl Vollmoeller and Engelbert Humperdinck, Elberfeld, Breslau and Cologne, October, 1913

OFFENBACH'S "ORPHEUS IN THE UNDERWORLD"

COPENHAGEN, FEBRUARY, 1921

A Costume Plate for Jupiter in Flight (Max Pallenberg) by Max Rée

JUPITER

OFFENBACH'S "ORPHEUS IN THE UNDERWORLD"

COPENHAGEN, FEBRUARY, 1921

A Costume Plate for Jupiter by Max Rée

CHRONOLOGY OF REINHARDT PRODUCTIONS

Sumurûn, by Friedrich Freksa and Victor Hollaender, Paris, Fall, 1913

Das Mirakel ("The Miracle"), by Karl Vollmoeller and Engelbert Humperdinck, Prague, Fall, 1913

Androcles and the Lion, by George Bernard Shaw, Kammerspiele, Berlin, November 25, 1913

The Thunderstorm, by August Strindberg, Kammerspiele, Berlin, December 11, 1913

La Parisienne, by Henri Becque, Kammerspiele, Berlin, December 29, 1913

Das Mirakel ("The Miracle"), by Karl Vollmoeller and Engelbert Humperdinck, Frankfort-on-Main, December, 1913

Das Mirakel ("The Miracle"), by Karl Vollmoeller and Engelbert Humperdinck, Hamburg and Karlsruhe, January, 1914

Der Snob ("The Snob"), by Carl Sternheim, Kammerspiele, Berlin, February 2, 1914

In the Claws of Life, by Knut Hamsun, Kammerspiele, Berlin, March 6, 1914.

The Yellow Jacket, by George Hazelton and J. Harry Benrimo, Kammerspiele, Berlin, March 30, 1914

Der Verlorene Sohn ("The Prodigal Son"), by Wilhelm Schmidtbonn, Hamburg, March, 1914

The Pelican, by August Strindberg, Deutsches Theater, Berlin, April 9, 1914

Freiheit ("Freedom"), by Max Halbe, Kammerspiele, Berlin, April 28, 1914

Das Mirakel ("The Miracle"), by Karl Vollmoeller and Engelbert Humperdinck, Zirkus Busch, Berlin, April 30, 1914

Der Snob ("The Snob"), by Carl Sternheim, Frankfort-on-Main, April, 1914

The Pelican, by August Strindberg, Vienna, April, 1914

Der Verlorene Sohn ("The Prodigal Son"), by Wilhelm Schmidtbonn, Vienna, May, 1914

The Pelican, by August Strindberg, Budapest and Bremen, May, 1914

[361]

APPENDIX III

The Thunderstorm, by August Strindberg, Budapest, May, 1914

Ghosts, by Henrik Ibsen, Budapest, May, 1914

Bürger Schippel ("Citizen Schippel"), by Carl Sternheim, Budapest, May, 1914

Der Verlorene Sohn ("The Prodigal Son"), by Wilhelm Schmidtbonn, Budapest and Prague, May, 1914

Der Snob ("The Snob"), by Carl Sternheim, Budapest, May, 1914

Der Stein der Weisen ("The Stone of Wisdom"), by Frank Wedekind, Kammerspiele, Berlin, June 9, 1914

THIRTEENTH SEASON 1914–1915

Zopf und Schwert ("Queue and Sword"), by Karl Gutzkoff, Deutsches Theater, Berlin, September 12, 1914

1914, by Wilhelm Schmidtbonn, Deutsches Theater, Berlin, September 25, 1914

Wallensteins Lager ("Wallenstein's Camp"), by Schiller, Deutsches Theater, Berlin, September 25, 1914

Die Piccolomini ("The Piccolomini"), by Schiller, Deutsches Theater, Berlin, October 9, 1914

Die Deutschen Kleinstädter ("The German Provincials"), by Kotzebue, Kammerspiele, Berlin, October 30, 1914

Wallensteins Tod ("The Death of Wallenstein"), by Schiller, Deutsches Theater, Berlin, November 13, 1914

Genoveva ("Genevieve"), by Friedrich Hebbel, Deutsches Theater, Berlin, December 8, 1914

Rappelkopf ("Firehead"), by Ferdinand Raimund, Deutsches Theater, Berlin, January 18, 1915

Der Charmante ("The Charming Fellow"), by Carl Sternheim, Kammerspiele, Berlin, February 26, 1915

Der Weibsteufel ("The Demon in Woman"), by Karl Schönherr, Kammerspiele, Berlin, April 6, 1915

Das Jahrmarktsfest zu Plundersweilern ("The Fair at Plundersweiler"), by Goethe, Deutsches Theater, Berlin, May 21, 1915

CHRONOLOGY OF REINHARDT PRODUCTIONS

Die Räuber ("The Robbers"), by Schiller, ⎫
Twelfth Night, by Shakespeare,   Stockholm and
Faust, by Goethe,   ⎬ Christiania,
A Midsummer Night's Dream, by Shakespeare,   1915
Minna von Barnhelm, by Lessing, ⎪
The Dance of Death, by August Strindberg, ⎭

FOURTEENTH SEASON 1915–1916

College Crampton ("Colleague Crampton"), by Gerhart Hauptmann, Deutsches Theater, Berlin, September 29, 1915

The Tempest, by Shakespeare, Volksbühne, Berlin, October 8,
1915

The Father, by August Strindberg, Kammerspiele, October 27,
1915

Maria Stuart, by Schiller, Deutsches Theater, Berlin, September
29, 1915

Das Nürnbergisch Ei ("The Egg of Nuremberg"), by Walter
Harlan, Deutsches Theater, Berlin, October 27, 1915

Der Liebestrank ("The Love Potion"), by Frank Wedekind,
Kammerspiele, Berlin, November 5, 1915

Traumulus, by Arno Holz and Oscar Jerschke, Volksbühne,
Berlin, November 29, 1915

Der Stern von Bethlehem ("The Star of Bethlehem"), by Otto
Falkenberg, Deutsches Theater, Berlin, December 27,
1915

Der Biberpelz ("The Beaver Coat"), by Gerhart Hauptmann,
Deutsches Theater, Berlin, January 12, 1916

Fuhrmann Henschel ("Drayman Henschel"), by Gerhart Hauptmann, Volksbühne, Berlin, February 18, 1916

Macbeth, by Shakespeare, Deutsches Theater, Berlin, February
29, 1916

Le Malade Imaginaire ("The Imaginary Invalid"), by Molière,
Kammerspiele, March 10, 1916

Die Schäferinnen ("The Shepherdesses"), a ballet, by Hugo

[363]

APPENDIX III

von Hofmannsthal, Kammerspiele, Berlin, March 16, 1916

Doppelselbstmord ("Double Suicide"), by Ludwig Anzengruber, Volksbühne, Berlin, March 21, 1916

Die Mottenburger ("The People of Mottenburg"), by Kalisch and Weirauch, Volksbühne, Berlin, April 18, 1916

Die Lästigen ("The Bores"), by Hugo von Hofmannsthal, and *Die Grüne Flöte* ("The Green Flute"), ballet, by Hugo von Hofmannsthal, Mozart and Nilson, Deutsches Theater, Berlin, April 26, 1916

Macbeth, by Shakespeare,
The Dance of Death, by August Strindberg,
Twelfth Night, by Shakespeare,　　　　　　Rotterdam,
Minna von Barnhelm, by Lessing,　　　　　The Hague,
Ghosts, by Henrik Ibsen,　　　　　　　　Amsterdam,
Der Biberpelz ("The Beaver Coat"), by　　April-May, 1916
　　Gerhart Hauptmann,

FIFTEENTH SEASON 1916–1917

Der Schnellmaler ("The Rapid Painter"), by Frank Wedekind, Kammerspiele, Berlin, September 2, 1916

Rose Bernd, by Gerhart Hauptmann, Deutsches Theater, Berlin, September 11, 1916

Master Olaf, by August Strindberg, Volksbühne, Berlin, September 22, 1916

The New York Idea, by Langdon Mitchell, Kammerspiele, Berlin, September 30, 1916

Soldaten ("Soldiers"), by Lenz, Deutsches Theater, Berlin, October 13, 1916

The Spook Sonata, by August Strindberg, Kammerspiele, October 20, 1916

Das Leidende Weib ("Suffering Woman"), by Klinger-Sternheim, Deutsches Theater, Berlin, October 30, 1916

Armut und Liebe ("Poverty and Love"), by Anton Wildgans, Kammerspiele, Berlin, November 29, 1916

[364]

CHRONOLOGY OF REINHARDT PRODUCTIONS

Die Grüne Flöte ("The Green Flute"), ballet, by Hugo von Hofmannsthal, Mozart and Nilson, Hamburg, Düsseldorf, Duisburg, and Mannheim, November, 1916

Dantons Tod ("Danton's Death"), by Georg Büchner, Deutsches Theater, Berlin, December 15, 1916

Die Ratten ("The Rats"), by Gerhart Hauptmann, Volksbühne, Berlin, December 23, 1916

Le Mariage de Figaro ("The Marriage of Figaro"), by Pierre Augustin Caron de Beaumarchais, Deutsches Theater, Berlin, December 31, 1916

Das Konzert ("The Concert"), by Hermann Bahr, Kammerspiele, Berlin, January 30, 1917

The Oresteia, by Aeschylus,
A Midsummer Night's Dream, by Shakespeare,
Kabale und Liebe ("Love and Intrigue"), by Schiller,
The Dance of Death, by August Strindberg,
Twelfth Night, by Shakespeare,
Dantons Tod ("Danton's Death"), by Georg Büchner,
} Zürich, Berne, Basle, St. Gallen, Davos, Lucerne, January, 1917

Weh Dem, der Lügt ("Woe to the Liar"), by Franz Grillparzer, Volksbühne, Berlin, February 10, 1917

John Gabriel Borkman, by Henrik Ibsen, Deutsches Theater, Berlin, March 14, 1917

Der G'wissenswurm ("The Gnawing Conscience"), by Ludwig Anzengruber, Volksbühne, Berlin, March 16, 1917

Tobias Buntschuh, by Carl Hauptmann, Deutsches Theater, Berlin, March 26, 1917

Fasching ("Carnival"), by Franz Molnar, Kammerspiele, Berlin, April 2, 1917

L'Avare ("The Miser"), by Molière, Deutsches Theater, Berlin, April 16, 1917

Volk in Not ("A People in Trouble"), by Karl Schönherr, Volksbühne, Berlin, April 20, 1917

Elga, by Gerhart Hauptmann, Volksbühne, Berlin, May 11, 1917

[365]

APPENDIX III

Othello, by Shakespeare,
The Spook Sonata, by August Strindberg,
The Lower Depths, by Maxim Gorky,
Rose Bernd, by Gerhart Hauptmann,
Die Deutschen Kleinstädter ("The German
   Provincials"), by Kotzebue,
Minna von Barnhelm, by Lessing,
Das Mirakel ("The Miracle"), by Karl Voll-
   moeller and Engelbert Humperdinck,

Stockholm,
Göteborg,
Malmö and
Helsingburg,
May, 1917

Rose Bernd, by Gerhart Hauptmann,
The Spook Sonata, by August
   Strindberg,
Dantons Tod ("Danton's Death"),
   by Georg Büchner,
Die Deutschen Kleinstädter ("The
   German Provincials"), by
   Kotzebue,

Basle, Berne,
Zürich, St. Gallen,
Schaffhausen, Lucerne,
and Davos,
June, 1917

Minna von Barnhelm, by Lessing,
Kabale und Liebe ("Love and Intrigue"), by
   Friedrich Schiller,
Twelfth Night, by Shakespeare,
Das Mirakel ("The Miracle"), by Karl Voll-
   moeller, and Engelbert Humperdinck,
The Merchant of Venice, by Shakespeare,

Bucharest,
June, 1917

Sixteenth Season 1917–1918

Das Lumpengesindel ("The Mob"), by Ernst von Wolzogen,
   Volksbühne, Berlin, September 3, 1917
Madame d'Ora, by Jensen-Vollmoeller, Kammerspiele, Berlin,
   September 13, 1917
Winterballade ("Winter Ballad"), by Gerhart Hauptmann,
   Deutsches Theater, Berlin, October 17, 1917
Kinder der Freude ("The Children of Joy"), by Felix Salten,
   Kammerspiele, Berlin, October 26, 1917

[366]

CHRONOLOGY OF REINHARDT PRODUCTIONS

Edelwild ("The Deer"), by Emil Gött, Volksbühne, Berlin, November 19, 1917

A Doll's House, by Henrik Ibsen, Kammerspiele, Berlin, November 23, 1917

Blutopfer ("Blood Sacrifice"), by Georg Reicke, Volksbühne, Berlin, December 14, 1917

Der Bettler ("The Beggar"), by Reinhard Sorge, Das Junge Deutschland, Berlin, December 23, 1917

Die Koralle ("The Coral"), by Georg Kaiser, Kammerspiele, Berlin, January 17, 1918

Die Hermannsschlacht ("Hermann's Battle"), by Heinrich von Kleist, Volksbühne, January 25, 1918

The Power of Darkness, by Lyoff Tolstoy, Deutsches Theater, Berlin, February 9, 1918

Hanneles Himmelfahrt ("The Assumption of Hannele"), by Gerhart Hauptmann, Volksbühne, Berlin, February 23, 1918

The Black Glove, by August Strindberg, Kammerspiele, Berlin, February 26, 1918

Seeschlacht ("A Sea Battle"), by Reinhard Goering, Das Junge Deutschland, Berlin, March 3, 1918

Der Sohn ("The Son"), by Walter Hasenclever, Das Junge Deutschland, Berlin, March 24, 1918

Le Bourgeois Gentilhomme ("The Citizen Who Apes the Nobleman"), by Molière, Deutsches Theater, Berlin, April 9, 1918

Die Richtige ("The Right One"), by Ludwig Fulda, Volksbühne, Berlin, April 13, 1918

Der Besuch aus dem Elysium ("The Visitor from Elysium"), by Franz Werfel, and *Kain* ("Cain"), by Friedrich Koffka, Das Junge Deutschland, Berlin, June 9, 1918

SEVENTEENTH SEASON 1918–1919

Arbeit ("Labor"), by Siegfried Giedion, Kleines Schauspielhaus, Berlin, September 21, 1918

[367]

APPENDIX III

Der Erste ("The First One"), by Reinhard Goering, Kammer spiele, Berlin, October 25, 1918

Phèdre, by Racine, Kleines Schauspielhaus, Berlin, October 31 1918

Der Brand im Opernhaus ("The Fire at the Opera House"), b Georg Kaiser, Kleines Schauspielhaus, Berlin, Novem ber 26, 1918

Michael Kramer, by Gerhart Hauptmann, Kleines Schauspiel haus, Berlin, December 3, 1918

The Light that Shines in Darkness, by Lyoff Tolstoy, Deutsche Theater, Berlin, December 13, 1918

Die Büchse der Pandora ("The Box of Pandora"), by Franl Wedekind, Kleines Schauspielhaus, December 21, 1918

Ein Geschlecht ("One Family"), by Fritz von Unruh, Das Junge Deutschland, Berlin, December 29, 1918

Der Sturz des Apostels Paulus ("The Fall of the Apostl Paul"), by Rolf Lauckner, Das Junge Deutschland Berlin, January 26, 1919

Von Morgens bis Mitternachts ("From Morn to Midnight") by Georg Kaiser, Deutsches Theater, Berlin, January 31, 1919

Narrenspiel des Lebens ("The Farce of Life"), by Karl Schön herr, Kammerspiele, Berlin, February 4, 1919

As You Like It, by Shakespeare, Deutsches Theater, Berlin February 27, 1919

Unterwegs ("On the Way"), by Thaddaeus Rittner, Kammer spiele, Berlin, March 19, 1919

Der Arme Heinrich ("Henry of Aue"), by Gerhart Hauptmann, Deutsches Theater, Berlin, April 4, 1919

Der Star ("The Star"), by Hermann Bahr, Kammerspiele, Ber lin, April 10, 1919

Die Wupper ("The Wuppers"), by Elsa Lasker-Schüler, Das Junge Deutschland, Berlin, April 26, 1919

Der Kinderfreund ("The Children's Friend"), by Mechthild Lichnowsky, Kammerspiele, Berlin, May 10, 1919

[368]

· C Y B E L E ·

OFFENBACH'S "ORPHEUS IN THE UNDERWORLD"

COPENHAGEN, FEBRUARY, 1921

A Costume Plate for Cybele by Max Rée

S K Y. II.

OFFENBACH'S "ORPHEUS IN THE UNDERWORLD"

Copenhagen, February, 1921

A Costume Plate for a Cloud by Max Rée

CHRONOLOGY OF REINHARDT PRODUCTIONS

Der Brennende Dornbusch ("The Burning Briar Bush"), by Oscar Kokoschka, Das Junge Deutschland, Berlin, May 25, 1919

EIGHTEENTH SEASON 1919–1920

Cymbeline, by Shakespeare, Deutsches Theater, Berlin, October 10, 1919

Ivanoff, by Anton Tchehoff, Kammerspiele, Berlin, October 17, 1919

Jaákobs Traum ("Jacob's Dream"), by Richard Beer-Hofmann, Deutsches Theater, Berlin, November 7, 1919

The Oresteia, by Aeschylus, Grosses Schauspielhaus, Berlin, November, 1919

Advent, by August Strindberg, Kammerspiele, December 9, 1919

Und Pippa tanzt ("And Pippa Dances"), by Gerhart Hauptmann, Deutsches Theater, Berlin, December 16, 1919

Die Sendung Semaels ("Semael's Mission"), by Arnold Zweig, Das Junge Deutschland, Berlin, January 25, 1920

Der Unmensch ("The Monster"), by Hermann Bahr, Kammerspiele, Berlin, February 10, 1920

Danton, by Romain Rolland, Grosses Schauspielhaus, Berlin, February 14, 1920

Gabriel Schillings Flucht ("Gabriel Schilling's Flight"), by Gerhart Hauptmann, Kammerspiele, Berlin, March 4, 1920

Helios, by Gerhart Hauptmann, Grosses Schauspielhaus, Berlin, March 28, 1920

Dame Kobold, by Calderon, Deutsches Theater, Berlin, April 3, 1920

Stella, by Goethe, Kammerspiele, Berlin, April 13, 1920

Antigone, by Walter Hasenclever, Grosses Schauspielhaus, Berlin, April 18, 1920

Himmel und Hölle ("Heaven and Hell"), by Paul Kornfeld, Deutsches Theater, Berlin, April 21, 1920

[369]

APPENDIX III

Julius Cæsar, by Shakespeare, Grosses Schauspielhaus, Berlin,
May 25, 1920

Everyman, adapted by Hugo von Hofmannsthal, Salzburg, August, 1920

NINETEENTH SEASON 1920–1921

After the Fire, by August Strindberg, Kammerspiele, Berlin,
September 17, 1920

Einsame Menschen ("Lonely Lives"), by Gerhart Hauptmann,
Deutsches Theater, Berlin, September 29, 1920

The First Distiller, by Lyoff Tolstoy, and *The Gamblers,* by
Nikolai Gogol, Kammerspiele, Berlin, October 19, 1920

Urfaust, by Goethe, Deutsches Theater, Berlin, October 22,
1920

Europa, by Georg Kaiser, Grosses Schauspielhaus, Berlin, November 5, 1920

Chauffaur Martin ("Chauffeur Martin"), by Hans Rehfisch,
Deutsches Theater, Berlin, November 20, 1920

Cæsar and Cleopatra, by George Bernard Shaw, Deutsches Theater, Berlin, December 22, 1920

Urfaust, by Goethe,
Stella, by Goethe,
The Pelican, by August Strindberg,
The Dance of Death, by August Strindberg,
The Merchant of Venice, by Shakespeare,
Kabale und Liebe ("Love and Intrigue"), by Schiller,
The First Distiller, by Lyoff Tolstoy,
Grosse Szene ("The Big Scene"), by Arthur Schnitzler,
The Thunderstorm, by August Strindberg,

} Copenhagen, Göteborg, Stockholm, Aarhus, with Danish and Swedish players, November-December, 1920

Florian Geyer, by Gerhart Hauptmann, and *Florindo,* by Gerhart Hauptmann, Grosses Schauspielhaus, Berlin, January 5, 1921

CHRONOLOGY OF REINHARDT PRODUCTIONS

Der *Abenteurer und die Sängerin* ("The Adventurer and the Singer"), by Hugo von Hofmannsthal, Kammerspiele, Berlin, January 7, 1921

Der *Pathetische Hut* ("The Pompous Hat"), by Karl Roessler, Kammerspiele, Berlin, January 21, 1921

La *Passion* ("The Hobby"), by Raoul and Simon Greban, Grosses Schauspielhaus, Berlin, February 5, 1921

Die *Jungfrau von Orleans* ("The Maid of Orleans"), by Schiller, Deutsches Theater, Berlin, February 19, 1921

Jenseits ("Beyond"), by Walter Hasenclever, Kammerspiele, Berlin, February 24, 1921

Orphée aux Enfer ("Orpheus in the Underworld"), by Jacques Offenbach, Copenhagen, with Danish Players and Singers, February, 1921

The King of the Dark Chamber, by Rabindranath Tagore, Kammerspiele, Berlin, March 4, 1921

The Merchant of Venice, by Shakespeare, Grosses Schauspielhaus, Berlin, March 12, 1921

Woyzeck, by Georg Büchner, Deutsches Theater, Berlin, April 5, 1921

Kräfte ("Powers"), by August Stramm, Kammerspiele, Berlin, April 12, 1921

A Midsummer Night's Dream, by Shakespeare, Grosses Schauspielhaus, Berlin, April 19, 1921

Misalliance, by Bernard Shaw, Kammerspiele, Berlin, May 2, 1921

Everyman, adapted by Hugo von Hofmannsthal, Domplatz, Salzburg, August, 1921

TWENTIETH SEASON 1921–1922

The Dream Play, by August Strindberg, Stockholm, with Swedish players, October, 1921

Die Räuber ("The Robbers"), by Schiller, Grosses Schauspielhaus, Berlin, September 26, 1921

[371]

APPENDIX III

The Dream Play, by August Strindberg, Deutsches Theater, Berlin, December 13, 1921

Dantons Tod ("Danton's Death"), by Georg Büchner, Grosses Schauspielhaus, Berlin, December, 1921

Orphée aux Enfer ("Orpheus in the Underworld"), by Jacques Offenbach, Grosses Schauspielhaus, Berlin, December 30, 1921

Orphée aux Enfer ("Orpheus in the Underworld"), by Jacques Offenbach, Stockholm, with Swedish players and singers, January, 1922

Das Grosse Salzburger Welttheater ("The Great World-Theatre"), by Hugo von Hofmannsthal, Kollegienkirche, Salzburg, August, 1922

Twenty-first Season 1922–1923

Clavigo, by Goethe, Theater in dem Redoutensaal, Vienna, September, 1922

Stella, by Goethe, Theater in dem Redoutensaal, Vienna, October, 1922

Dame Kobold, by Calderon, Theater in dem Redoutensaal, Vienna, November, 1922

Les Belles Femmes ("Beautiful Women"), by Etienne Rey, Theater in dem Redoutensaal, Vienna, December, 1922

Les Ratés ("The Failures"), by H. R. Lenormand, Deutsches Volks Theater, Vienna, January, 1923

Le Malade Imaginaire ("The Imaginary Invalid"), by Molière, Schloss Leopoldskron, Salzburg, August 20, 1923, and Municipal Theatre, Salzburg, August 21, 1923

INDEX

[373]

INDEX

Berlin, Zirkus Busch, 144.
—, Zirkus Schumann, 91, 144.
Berlioz, Louis Hector, 17.
Bernard, Tristan, 70.
Bertens, Rosa, 12.
"Bettler, Der," 241, 244.
Bie, Oskar, 55.
Biensfeld, Paul, 110.
"Birth of Christ, The," 30.
Bismarck, Prince Otto von, 36-37.
"Blaubart," 235.
Blech, Leo, 126.
"Blue Bird, The," 90-91.
"Bluebeard." *See* "BLAUBART."
"Blumenboot, Das," 232.
Blumenthal, Oskar, 220.
Bonaparte, Napoleon, 174, 216, 236.
Bonn, Ferdinand, 245.
Borchardt, Rudolf, 144, 153.
Bordone, Paris, 330.
Brahm, Otto, 2, 34-35, 41, 46-48, 60,
    76, 145, 220, 222, 228, 230-233, 235-
    237, 324, 344.
"Brand," 231.
Brandes, Georg, 229.
"Braut von Messina, Die," 130, 200.
Breuer, Robert, 144, 151.
"Bride of Messina, The." *See* "BRAUT
    VON MESSINA, DIE."
Bronikowski, Friedrich von Oppeln,
    330.
Browning, Robert, 174.
Büchner, Georg, 77.
Burckhard, 39.
"Bürger Schippel," 244.

C SHARP MINOR IMPROMPTU, 126.
"Cæsar and Cleopatra," 135, 168.
Calderon de la Barca, Pedro, 14, 17,
    70, 77, 155, 159, 165, 191, 201-202,
    219, 231.
Callot, Jacques, 142.
Carl August, Duke of Weimar, 239.
Carl VI, Emperor, 31.
Carmi, Maria, 22, 90.
Carpaccio, Vittore, 330.
Carter, Huntly, 332.
Chaplin, Charles Spencer, 62.

"Charlemagne's Hostage." *See* "KAI-
    SER KARL'S GEISEL."
"Charley's Aunt," 9.
"Cherry Orchard, The," 167.
Chopin, Frederick, 126.
Church Plays, 30.
Church Theatre, 59.
"Clarissa Harlowe," 70.
Classical Style, 46.
"Clavigo," 83, 165, 324.
Cochran, Charles, 13.
Cohan, George M., 94.
"Comedy of Errors, The," 126.
"Coming of Peace, The." *See* "FRIED-
    ENSFEST, DAS."
Commedia dell'arte, 186-187, 327.
Comstock, F. Ray, 249.
"Concert, The," 28.
Coogan, Jackie, 62.
Copeau, Jacques, 92, 164.
Copenhagen, Royal Theatre, 330.
Corinth, Lovis, 135.
Corneille, Pierre, 14, 167.
"Count of Charolais, The." *See* "GRAF
    VON CHAROLAIS, DER."
Craig, Edward Gordon, 19, 22, 45-46,
    53, 72, 90, 93, 136, 139, 170, 232,
    339.
Craven, Hawes, 141.
Cunard, Lady, 19.
"Cymbeline," 17.

DALY, AUGUSTIN, 90.
"Dame Kobold," 165.
"Danton," 56, 142, 144.
"David Copperfield," 70.
"Dawn." *See* "MORGENRÖTE."
"Demon in Woman, The." *See*
    "WEIBSTEUFEL, DER."
Dent, E. J., 131, 137.
Dernburg, Hermann, 144.
Deutsch, Ernst, 107.
Dick, Joseph, 67.
Diderot, Denis, 69.
Diegelmann, Wilhelm, 110.
Dietz, Wilhelm, 55.
Dingelstedt, Friedrich von, 39, 218.
"Don Carlos," 83, 231, 324, 344.

[374]

INDEX

"Don Giovanni," 139.
"Don Juan," 200-201.
"Don Quixote," 70-71.
"Drama and the Stage, The," 339.
"Dream a Life." *See* "TRAUM EIN LEBEN, DER."
Dreyer, Maximilian, 67.
Durable Theatre, 91, 93.
Durieux, Tilla, 12, 90, 110.
Duse, Eleonora, 19.
Dvorsky, 119.
Dymow, Ossip, 14.

EBERT, PRESIDENT FRIEDRICH, 342.
Eckhof, 228.
Edwards, Norman, 169.
Eeden, Frederik van, 336.
Eibenschütz, Camilla, 110.
"Einen Jux will er sich machen," 135.
"Elektra," 16, 83, 135, 190.
Elizabeth, Queen, 59.
Elizabethan Drama, 6, 199.
"Emperor and Galilean," 231.
English Theatre, 19, 59, 139, 154.
Erlach, Fischer von, 177, 191.
Erler, Fritz, 55.
Eulenberg, Herbert, 8, 231, 235.
Euripides, 14, 167.
"Europa," 142, 202.
"Everyman," 25, 49, 84, 124, 126, 128, 155, 177, 184, 186, 190-191, 196, 202-203.
Expressionism, 64.
Eysoldt, Gertrud, 12, 90, 98, 109.

"FAITH AND HOME." *See* "GLAUBE UND HEIMAT."
"Faust," 84, 91, 137, 139, 201-202, 344.
Fehling, Richard, 171.
Fein, Maria, 90.
Ferdinand III, Emperor, 31.
Film. *See* MOTION PICTURES.
Firmian, Archbishop Leopold, 15, 177-178, 184.
Fleming, Asta, 12.
"Flower Boat, The." *See* "BLUMEN-BOOT, DAS."
Fontane, Theodor, 228.

Forbes-Robertson, Sir Johnston, 248.
Förster, 222.
Francis Joseph I, Emperor, 39, 189.
Frederick the Great, 135, 174, 239.
"Freischütz, Der," 201.
French Theatre, 19, 154.
"Friedensfest, Das," 83.
"Frühlingserwachen," 83, 150.
Fulda, Ludwig, 220, 231.

GALSWORTHY, JOHN, 19.
Garrick, David, 19, 223.
Geddes, Norman-Bel, 169, 183, 249.
Gémier, Firmin, 248.
George, Duke of Meiningen, 46, 222.
"George Dandin," 124.
Georgian Theatre, 169.
"Gerettete Venedig, Das," 235.
German Shakespeare Society, 17.
German Theatre, 18, 42, 76, 92, 137, 155, 227.
Gest, Morris, 183, 249.
"Getting Married," 168.
"Ghosts," 26, 52, 67, 149, 324.
Giotto di Bondone, 141, 153.
"Glaube und Heimat," 237.
Gluck, Christoph Willibald, 17, 200-201.
Göchhausen, Luise von, 238-239.
"God of Vengeance, The," 14.
Goethe, Johann Wolfgang von, 6-7, 14, 17-18, 25, 39, 48, 70, 77, 140, 155, 158-159, 165, 199-200, 215, 220, 230, 234, 239, 246, 326, 336.
Goldoni, Carlo, 14, 70.
Goldsmith, Oliver, 168.
Gorky, Maxim, 14, 22, 67, 70, 76, 166, 217.
Gozzi, Carlo, 70, 77.
"Graf von Charolais, Der," 67.
"Great World-Theatre, The," 16, 49, 83, 124, 184, 186, 191, 202, 206-208.
Greek Theatre, 58, 77, 142, 168.
Gregori, Ferdinand, 340, 344.
Grieg, Edvard, 199.
Griffith, David Wark, 62.

[375]

INDEX

INDEX

INDEX

Mozart, Wolfgang Amadeus, 5, 17, 131, 176, 178-179, 184-185, 188, 190, 192-193, 195, 197, 199-201, 245, 336.

"Much Ado About Nothing," 124-125, 325.

Müller, Hans, 10.

Munch, Edvard, 26, 52.

Munich, Künstler Theater, 54, 136, 139, 168.

—, Residenz Theater, 139.

Music under Reinhardt, 52, 86, 124-130.

"Nachtasyl." *See* "Lower Depths, The."

"Nathan the Wise," 150.

Naturalism, 6, 40-41, 46, 79.

Neo-romanticism, 5.

Nestroy, Johann, 125, 135.

New York, Booth Theatre, 168.

—, Casino Theatre, 89.

—, Century Theatre, 249.

—, Henry Miller's Theatre, 168.

—, Little Theatre, 168.

—, Plymouth Theatre, 168.

—, Selwyn Theatre, 168.

Nietzsche, Friedrich Wilhelm, 216.

Nikisch, Arthur, 69.

Nilson, Einar, 124.

"Nju," 14.

"Oberon," 201.

"Odyssey," 71.

"Œdipus and the Sphinx," 114, 130.

"Œdipus Rex," 23, 27, 56, 80, 128, 130, 136, 342.

Offenbach, Jacques, 14, 91.

"On the Art of the Theatre," 45.

O'Neill, Eugene, 14.

Ordynski, Richard, 12, 337.

"Oresteia, The," 70, 124, 128, 130, 149.

Orlik, Emil, 54-55, 136.

"Orpheus in the Underworld," 12, 91.

Osborne, Max, 131.

"Othello," 80, 84, 226.

Pallenberg, Max, 11, 90, 102, 184.

Palmer, John, 382.

Pantomime, 126.

"Papa," 14.

"Paradoxe du Comédien," 69.

Paris, Comédie des Champs-Elysées, 168.

—, Comédie Française, 37, 59.

—, Théâtre du Vieux-Colombier, 164.

—, Théâtre Libre, 48.

Passarge, 229.

"Peer Gynt," 231.

"Pelican, The," 126.

"Pelléas and Mélisande," 83, 134, 244.

Perishable Theatre, 91, 93.

Pfitzner, Hans, 215.

"Pillars of Society," 229.

Pillartz, 343.

Piloty, Karl Theodor von, 133, 153.

Pinchot, Rosamond, 22.

Pinski, David, 14.

Poelzig, Hans, 50, 192-193, 197-198, 342.

"Potash and Perlmutter," 96.

"Power of Darkness, The," 67.

Pre-Raphaelites, 135.

"Pretenders, The," 231.

Prince of Wales, 51.

"Princess Brambilla," 224.

"Princesse de Clèves," 71.

"Prometheus Bound," 202.

"Prunella," 167.

Rabelais, François, 198.

Racine, Jean Baptiste, 14, 167, 201.

Raimund, Ferdinand, 125, 201.

Rainer, Luis, 165.

Rameau, Jean Philippe, 126.

"Rappelkopf," 124.

"Räuber, Die," 34, 114, 155, 344.

Realism, 47, 79.

"Redemption," 244.

Redslob, Edwin, 343.

Rée, Max, 12.

Regie Book, 85, 117-118, 125-126, 182, 249.

Reinhardt and the Actor, 11, 23, 55-56, 61-62, 76, 86, 98-115, 113, 223, 247.

Reinhardt and the Chorus, 113, 130-131.

[378]

INDEX

INDEX

INDEX

"Weh dem der Lügt," 344.
"Weibsteufel, Der," 237.
Westheim, Paul, 197.
Whitman, Walt, 68.
"Wild Duck, The," 231.
Wilde, Oscar, 25, 76-77, 107, 134, 167, 217, 220, 226, 231.
Wildenbruch, Ernst von, 10.
Wilhelm II, 8-9, 237.
Wilson, Woodrow, 3.
"Winter's Tale, A," 53-54, 114, 136, 343.
Winterstein, Eduard von, 110.
Winterstein, Wilhelm, 90.

"Woe to the Liar." *See* "WEH DEM DER LÜGT."
Wright, Frank Lloyd, 169.

"YELLOW JACKET, THE," 14.
"Young Medardus, The." *See* "JUNGE MEDARDUS, DER."

"ZACHES," 224.
"Zalamea," 238.
"Zauberflöte," 195, 200-201.
Zola, Emile, 234.
Zukunft, Die, 209.
"Zwillingschwester, Die," 232.